B1 Preliminary
for Schools
Trainer

Six Practice Tests with answers
and Teacher's Notes

with digital pack

2

Shaftesbury Road, Cambridge CB2 8EA, United Kingdom

One Liberty Plaza, 20th Floor, New York, NY 10006, USA

477 Williamstown Road, Port Melbourne, VIC 3207, Australia

314–321, 3rd Floor, Plot 3, Splendor Forum, Jasola District Centre, New Delhi – 110025, India

103 Penang Road, #05–06/07, Visioncrest Commercial, Singapore 238467

Cambridge University Press & Assessment is a department of the University of Cambridge.

We share the University's mission to contribute to society through the pursuit of education, learning and research at the highest international levels of excellence.

www.cambridge.org
Information on this title: www.cambridge.org/9781108902564

First published 2024

20 19 18 17 16 15 14 13 12 11 10 9 8 7 6 5 4 3 2 1

Printed in Malaysia by Vivar Printing

A catalogue record for this publication is available from the British Library

ISBN 978-1-108-90256-4 Student's Book with answers with audio and digital pack
ISBN 978-1-108-90257-1 Student's Book without answers with audio and digital pack

Contents

Introduction

Who is this book for?

If you are aged between 11 and 15 and want to take **B1 Preliminary for Schools**, this book is for you!

Why is this book called 'Trainer'?

This book is called '**Trainer**' because it is full of exercises to help you get better and better at doing each part of **B1 Preliminary for Schools**. So, complete all the exercises, then do all the Practice Tests. If you train and work hard, you will soon be ready to take **B1 Preliminary for Schools**!

How do I use this book?

First do the exercises on each **Training** page. Then do the task on the **Exam Practice** pages and check your answers.

Tests 1–2: Training

On Training pages (Tests 1 and 2 only), you will find:

 Cambridge Learner Corpus

This shows information about mistakes that some **B1 Preliminary for Schools** candidates make. If you do these useful exercises, you will learn <u>not</u> to make these mistakes when <u>you</u> do the exam.

This provides ideas to help you do well in the exam. For example: *Make a list of useful phrases and remember them by making your own example sentences with them.*

Remember

This gives a quick reminder about grammar points or vocabulary that you should learn. For example: *Understanding narrative tenses helps understand the order of events in an article or a story.*

Advice

This gives you help when completing a Practice Test, and guides you to getting the correct answer or a better score. For example, *After you finish writing your email, always read through your answer to make sure it's clear and you have covered all four content points.*

Tests 1–2: Exam Practice

On Exam Practice pages in Tests 1 and 2, you will find:

- a **B1 Preliminary for Schools** exam task for you to try and complete.
- further tips and advice to help you with different parts of the task.

Tests 3–6

When you finish Tests 1 and 2 you will be ready to do some complete **B1 Preliminary for Schools** Practice Tests.

Tests 3, 4, 5 and 6 are just like real **B1 Preliminary for Schools** Reading, Writing, Listening and Speaking papers. Doing these tests will give you extra help to prepare for the exam.

Keep a record of your scores as you do the tests. You may find that your scores are good in some parts of the test, but you may need to practise other parts more. Make simple tables like this to record your scores.

Reading	Part 1	Part 2	Part 3	Part 4	Part 5	Part 6
Test 3	4	5				
Test 4						
Test 5						
Test 6						

Other features of the *B1 Preliminary for Schools* Trainer

- **Visual material**

In the Speaking test the examiner will give you a booklet with photographs and pictures in it. The visual material in the colour section from pages C1–C16 will help you practise and become familiar with the type of pictures and photographs you will see in the test and help you increase your confidence.

- **Sample Answer Sheets**

Look at these to see what the *B1 Preliminary for Schools* Answer Sheets in the test look like and learn how to complete them. Ask your teacher to photocopy them so that you can use them when you do your Practice Tests.

- **Downloadable audio online**

Listen to these to practise the Listening paper. You will also need to listen to these to complete some of the Training exercises and to hear a demonstration of each part of the Speaking test.

The structure of the *B1 Preliminary for Schools* exam

The *B1 Preliminary for Schools* exam has four papers:

Reading: 45 minutes

There are six parts to the Reading test, and you will need to be able to read and understand a range of texts from short notices and messages to longer articles from brochures, magazines and newspapers. For two of the parts you will also have to choose the correct words to complete a text – in one, you choose from the words provided and in the other you use your own words.

Writing: 45 minutes

In the two parts of the Writing test you will write an email and then an article or a story, each about 100 words long.

Listening: 30 minutes (approximately)

In the four parts of the Listening test you will need to be able to listen and understand people who are talking together and people who are giving information about something. You will have to choose or write the answers to the questions which are about what these people say. Don't worry! The people talk about everyday topics, speak clearly and don't talk fast.

Speaking: 12 minutes (pairs) 17 minutes (groups of three)

You will need to be able to listen and understand what the examiner is saying. You will have to answer some questions about yourself, and you will need to speak on your own about a photograph. You will then be given some pictures to look at and you will use the pictures to do a speaking task with another candidate. In the final part you and the other candidate will answer questions based on the topic in the pictures. Usually candidates take the Speaking test with just one other candidate, but sometimes they do it in groups of three. For this reason there are additional pictures for Candidate C in this book.

Frequently asked questions

> Is my English good enough for
> B1 Preliminary for Schools?

The level of the exam is Council of Europe Level B1. At B1 level, students can:

- understand the main points of straightforward instructions or public announcements
- understand instructions in classes and on homework given by a teacher
- understand factual articles in magazines and letters from friends expressing personal opinions
- understand most information of a factual nature in their school subjects
- ask simple questions and take part in factual conversations in school
- talk about things such as films and music and describe their reactions to them
- write letters or make notes on familiar or predictable matters
- take basic notes in a lesson
- write a description of an event, for example a school trip.

Note that different students have different strengths and weaknesses. Some may be good at speaking but not so good at writing; others may be good at reading but not so good at listening. The B1 level 'Can Do' statements above simply help teachers understand what **B1 Preliminary for Schools** candidates should generally be able to do at this level.

> What grade do I need to pass
> B1 Preliminary for Schools?

There are four possible grades given to candidates – Grade A, B, C or Level A2. Candidates who score between 120–139 will not receive a Preliminary English certificate, but the scores will be reported on your Statement of Results.

Basic		Independent		Proficient	
A1	**A2**	**B1**	**B2**	**C1**	**C2**
	A2 Key for Schools	B1 Preliminary for Schools	B2 First for Schools		

What marks do I need to pass each paper, and to pass the exam?

Candidates do not have to get a certain mark to pass each paper in the exam. The overall score is the average of the individual scores that you receive for the four skills: Reading, Writing, Listening and Speaking. There are an equal number of possible marks for each paper in **B1 Preliminary for Schools**.

How can I find out about my performance in each paper of B1 Preliminary for Schools?

Before you get a certificate you will get a Statement of Results telling you how well you did in **B1 Preliminary for Schools**. As well as your result and your score, it also gives you your 'Candidate Profile'. This is an easy-to-read graph that shows how you performed in all the papers of the exam. If you do not get the score that you wanted, the Candidate Profile will show you which of the skills (Reading, Writing, Listening and Speaking) you did well in and which you need to improve.

Is B1 Preliminary for Schools suitable for candidates of any age?

B1 Preliminary for Schools is more suitable for students who are at school and aged from 11–15. To make sure that the material is interesting for this age group and not too difficult or too easy for the B1 level, all the parts of the Reading, Writing, Listening and Speaking papers are pre-tested. This means that different groups of students try the materials for each part of the tests first. The material will then only be used in real exams if the results of the pre-tests show that they are suitable for candidates who want to take **B1 Preliminary for Schools**.

Can I use pens and pencils
in the exam?

In **B1 Preliminary for Schools** candidates must use **pencil** in the Reading and Listening papers. It's useful for you if you want to change one of your answers on the answer sheet. However, you must use a **pen** for the Writing paper.

What happens if I don't have enough
time to finish writing?

You can only be given marks for what you write on the answer sheet, so if you do not complete this then you will miss the chance to show the examiner what you can do and how good your English is. Watch the clock and plan your time carefully. Do not waste time writing your answers on other pieces of paper in Reading and Writing; however, in the Listening test it is a good idea to write your answers on the question paper first. You will have time at the end to move your answers from the question paper to your answer sheet.

If I write in capital letters, will
it affect my mark?

No. You do not lose marks for writing in capital letters in **B1 Preliminary for Schools**. Whether you choose to use capital letters or not, you should always make sure that your handwriting is clear and easy to read. Remember that the examiners can't mark a piece of writing that they can't read!

In this part you:

- **read**　five different short texts, e.g. advertisements, emails, messages, notices, signs
- **choose**　the option (A, B or C) which means the same as the short text

FOCUS: IDENTIFYING WHO HAS WRITTEN A SHORT TEXT

1　In pairs, look at the five short texts. Who do you think has written each one? What helps you to decide?

① Please don't forget to bring your outdoor boots tomorrow. The game starts at 12 pm, so tell your parents you need to be at the stadium by 11.30 at the latest.

② Hi,
How about going to the park later? I've bought a new skateboard and you can have a go!

③ New items in store weekly – always something new to buy!

④ **Exhibition on ancient Egypt. Tickets available from the office. Booking essential.**

⑤ Tom,
Don't forget you've got the dentist later, so don't be late getting home. We'll go straight out to eat afterwards. We can have pizza if you like!

Remember

Informal language uses contracted forms (*I've*, *it's*, etc.). More formal language uses full forms (*I have*, *it is*, etc.).

VOCABULARY: INFORMAL AND FORMAL LANGUAGE

2　Decide which extracts from short texts use informal language (I) and which use formal (F).

1　It is important to make sure you …
2　Dear Sarah
3　How about doing …?
4　Please ask if you require any help.
5　I really love …
6　Hi, really sorry, but …
7　Let me know what's happening, OK?
8　What about going to …?
9　Please make sure you remember to …
10　Can't wait to see you!
11　Hi there!
12　Is that OK?
13　You should remember to bring …
14　What about you?
15　I'm going to the shops a bit later on.
16　I am extremely interested in …

GRAMMAR: LEAVING WORDS OUT

3　Look at these extracts from signs. Some words are left out. What types of words? Why?

1　Keep gate closed.
2　Return books to shelf when finished.
3　No bags in front of door. Access required at all times.
4　Students only past this door.
5　Library staff currently in meeting.
6　Area for quiet study only.

4　Look at the signs in Exercise 3 again. Write out the sentences in full.

Example　*1 You must keep this gate closed.*

VOCABULARY: USEFUL PHRASES TO DESCRIBE AMOUNTS

5 Match these number phrases with phrases 1–5. There are five that do not match.

| four novels | 46% | €14.50 | 2.50 pm | 13 apples | 3.10 pm |
| five dictionaries | 55% | eight cans of tuna | €16.40 | | |

1 nearly 50% off ....

2 just under €15 ....

3 a little before 3 o'clock ....

4 a minimum of three books ....

5 a maximum of ten food items ....

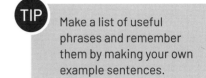

TIP Make a list of useful phrases and remember them by making your own example sentences.

6 In pairs, choose one of these phrases and think of an example sentence for it.

- no more than
- as much as
- not quite
- only just
- almost
- quite a bit
- a little
- at least

FOCUS: IDENTIFYING IMPORTANT INFORMATION

7 Look at messages 1–4. For each one, decide:

- who has written the message
- the reason they are writing
- whether the message is formal or informal

TIP Look at the layout of each short text to quickly decide what type of text it is.

① Hockey players!
Tonight's practice session is cancelled as your coach is ill. You still have a match on Tuesday, so there's an extra session at Monday lunchtime instead.

② Jen
That game you wanted is on offer today – 5% off, or if you buy two games, the discount's 20%. You have to get them before tomorrow though, so make your mind up fast!

③ New Message

For homework, choose a favourite photo, for example, one of a person or a place you know well. Then, write at least 150 words about it. I can't wait to see your work!

④ Pool closed until 12.45 today for the rest of the week. Afternoon lessons start at 1.00 rather than 12.30.

8 Underline the parts of the messages in Exercise 7 that help you find the answers to these questions.

1 When will the hockey players have their next practice?

2 How much is the discount for buying more than one game?

3 What will students write a description of for their homework?

4 What time do swimming lessons begin?

Questions 1–5

For each question, choose the correct answer.

1

Susie

Your swimming coach called about your first competition on Saturday. The race now starts at 4 pm, not 3 pm. She's bringing a team sweatshirt for you, so don't worry about not having one yet.

Dad

Susie's swimming coach rang to

A tell Susie what to bring to the competition.

B help Susie feel confident about her first race.

C update Susie with some important information.

2

Kelly

There's that new thriller at the cinema this weekend if you still want to see it. I've just remembered there's a sci-fi one on, too. I'm happy with either – it's up to you!

Matthew

What is Matthew doing in his text message?

A telling Kelly which film would be his first choice

B letting Kelly make the decision about which film to see

C reminding Kelly about an arrangement for a cinema trip

Advice

Read options A–C carefully. Sometimes they look similar, so it's important to know exactly what you're looking for in the text. For example, three options might be:

A *The music* club will be on a different day *this week.*

B *The music* students will have a different teacher *this week.*

C *The music* practice will start at a different time *this week.*

3

Sale

We're making room for our new
season's clothes (coming soon).
Many items half price.
One week only, so hurry!

A Some clothes are on special offer for a limited time.

B Everything in the shop now costs less than a week ago.

C The shop has reduced the price of the new season's clothes.

4

New Message

📖 **From:** Mrs Fallon

Subject: Art Club project

Make sure your picture
for your 'Friends' project
shows a group of two or
more people. I'll be in the
art room on Wednesday if
you require help.

Mrs Fallon's email gives students information about

A how many pictures to put in their final project.

B what to include in their final project.

C when to hand in their final project.

5

Sorry – my bus is
delayed! I can't meet
you at the ice cream
shop. Why not
go straight to the
skateboard park?
We'll still get ice
cream afterwards –
the place stays open
late.
Sam

A Sam's bus problems mean they will have to change
their plans.

B Sam wants to go to the skateboard park first because
it isn't open later.

C Sam is travelling on a route which doesn't stop near
the ice cream shop.

In this part you:

- **read**   five descriptions of people and eight short texts on a range of subjects
- **match**   what each person requires with information in one of the eight texts

FOCUS: IDENTIFYING TEXT TYPES

1   In pairs, read these short texts. Which is an advert and which are reviews? How do you know?

A This website has something for everyone. There's a useful section on the history of the local area, and while the information might not be particularly easy for younger children to follow, there are plenty of excellent pictures to support what you're reading.

B Here you'll find up-to-date information on a wide range of topics. Most of the articles are written by people who are experts in their subject. This explains why we recently won a prize and are often recommended by teachers.

C For a simple-to-use site that describes what happens on a journey into space, this is a great choice. Those hoping to find out lots of details about future space plans may find the information rather basic, but there's still plenty here to keep most people interested.

VOCABULARY: PARAPHRASING USING THE OPPOSITE KIND OF LANGUAGE

2   Match the things people want (1–5) with sentences from short texts (a–e).

1 Anna doesn't want to spend too much money on presents.

2 Carlos likes watching films with surprising endings.

3 Helen doesn't want to wait ages to buy what she needs.

4 Chen prefers places that aren't too noisy.

5 Keiko needs some public transport options nearby.

a What's great about the area is that it is very peaceful.

b The staff are fantastic and you'll be served quickly.

c There are plenty of items that have a very reasonable price.

d The entrance is not far from bus and tram stops.

e You'll certainly never guess what happens.

 TIP In Reading Part 1, you will read about things that five people want (e.g. *Lisa likes short films.*). The matching short text may contain the opposite kind of language (e.g. *This isn't a particularly long film* uses a negative structure and the opposite of *short*).

FOCUS: IDENTIFYING WHAT PEOPLE REQUIRE

3   Read the descriptions. Underline what each person wants from a writing course.

1 Ali hopes to do a writing course with other young people. He needs tips on writing funny stories and wants to read some of his stories to the group to see what they think.

2 Jane would love to learn from a successful writer and to find out about how to add pictures to her stories. She's interested in learning how to put her stories online.

VOCABULARY: PARAPHRASING WHAT PEOPLE REQUIRE

4   Work in pairs. For each person in Exercise 3, choose the words and phrases you might expect to see in a matching advertisement or a review.

advice   comedy   drawings and cartoons   for children and teenagers   get opinions
publish on a website   share your stories   well-known author

Questions 6–10

For each question, choose the correct answer.

....

Advice

Underline each person's requirements and then quickly read through all the eight texts. Find the review that matches all the person's requirements – not just one of them.

The young people below all want to visit a transport museum.
On the next page there are eight reviews of transport museums.
Decide which museum would be the most suitable for the young people below.

6 Amal and her family want to have a day out at a museum. Amal hopes to see inside an old ship, and the family need somewhere for Amal's small brother to play.

7 Niall hopes to watch a film about transport methods around the world and learn how transport might change in the future. He'd like to buy something to remind him of his trip.

8 Kazue wants to learn about the history of trains and to know more about the people who work on important transport projects. Her family hope to have a picnic during the visit.

9 Dariusz wants to know about early space travel and to find out about working in the airline industry. His family don't have a car, so need to visit a city centre museum.

10 Esme and her dad want to do a museum tour with a guide and to see some old racing cars. Esme wants to experience what it's like to drive a train.

Reviews of transport museums

A   **Central Transport Museum**

If you're concerned about the planet, don't miss the *Next Steps* exhibition, all about how we could be travelling in the years ahead. The exhibition includes videos about transport used in other countries, from bikes to high-speed trains, and the cards in the shop make fantastic souvenirs.

B   **The Talbot**

This place has loads to entertain for the whole day, including a garden where little ones can run around safely. The latest exhibit is a large 18th-century boat in incredible condition – find out what life on board was like as you walk around. It transported goods world-wide, and you can imagine it racing across the seas!

C   **Transport Hub**

The great thing about this museum is that its displays change frequently. Currently, visitors discover the work involved in planning city transport systems, and a future exhibition will be 'space travel', concentrating on technology in modern rockets. The gift shop has interesting things to buy too.

D   **All about Transport**

This museum's perfect for the whole family, with guided tours aimed at younger visitors. You can watch a film about the world's most beautiful train rides and learn how engineers build the bridges and tunnels that keep traffic moving!

E   **Garston Place**

Just inside the entrance, don't miss displays about those who design, build and run international city transport centres, like airports or ports. The hall has an exhibition about the start of the rail industry, with videos of early passenger trains. There are tables outside if you're bringing food – there's lots of space for active kids!

F   **Explore!**

This museum has something for everyone, and it's worth booking to go round with an expert. We've got a section on motor-racing history, with early record-breaking vehicles on display and the chance to operate the controls of a real train, travelling along a track! It's not suitable for young children, but you'll remember the experience for years.

G   **Marley's Museum**

With a convenient location not far from the heart of the city, it's easy to spend several hours in this small museum. Listen to interviews with people talking about transport-related jobs: everything from pilots to cruise ship captains! You'll also see plans for the first space rockets and learn about problems engineers faced.

H   **Herston Museum of Transport**

If you're interested in how transport could change the future of the world, then you'll love this place. Everyone, young or old, will enjoy the interactive video games. Race a super-car, or be in charge of a spaceship! Don't miss the café – buy a cake to eat in the museum garden.

In this part you:

- **read** a long text that includes opinions and feelings
- **choose** the correct answer (A, B, C or D) from five multiple-choice questions

GRAMMAR: ORDERING EVENTS USING NARRATIVE TENSES

👁 *B1 Preliminary* candidates often make mistakes with the past continuous and past perfect.

1   **Match the tenses (1–4) with how they are used (a–d).**

   1   past simple

   2   present perfect

   3   past perfect

   4   past continuous

   a   used to describe unfinished actions in the past

   b   used to describe completed actions in the past

   c   used to describe an action that took place before another past action

   d   used to describe an action that happens from some time in the past up until now

2   **Look at these extracts from an article. In pairs, explain the order in which the events happened.**

   1   Sally took climbing lessons. By the time she had her fifteenth birthday, she had climbed three mountains.

      Example   Sally took climbing lessons. Sally climbed three mountains. Sally had her fifteenth birthday.

   2   Juan decided he wanted to sail around the world after watching a sailing documentary that a friend had recommended to him.

   3   Just before Emilie started her final year at university, she applied to go on an amazing trip to Antarctica.
       She got on a plane to South America as soon as she had finished her degree, eventually arriving in Antarctica after catching a flight from Chile.

   4   Gavin was walking along the beach when he stopped and picked something up. It was a necklace!
       He had noticed it because it was so shiny. Someone had dropped it in the sand.

3   **Write complete sentences using these ideas and narrative tenses.**

   1   I – never be close to – elephant – before – do a safari

   2   I – know – do enough training – still worried – complete long bike race

   3   Shelly – cycle in mountains – get a flat tyre – luckily, mum – pack a repair kit

VOCABULARY: ADJECTIVES TO DESCRIBE OPINIONS AND FEELINGS

4 **Match these adjectives with extracts 1–8. There might be more than one option.**

| afraid | amusing | anxious | confusing | efficient | enjoyable |
| exhausted | nervous | rude | surprised | unexpected | |

TIP Some questions in Reading Part 3 focus on a person's opinions or feelings.

1 I couldn't believe …

2 I didn't stop laughing the whole way through …

3 I really didn't think it would happen …

4 We didn't waste any time at all …

5 We could hardly move when we finally got off our bikes …

6 There were so many fun activities to do …

7 He didn't even say thanks …

8 We told each other to be brave before opening the door …

FOCUS: DEALING WITH QUESTION 15

TIP For Question 15, you need to look at the whole text in order to find the right answer, and to check the other options are wrong.

5 **Read extracts 1–4 from an article about Sam, a tennis player, and choose the correct answer for Question 15 below.**

1 Now I'm doing so well, I have to practise most of the time. Luckily, my coach believes it's important to have a social life too. So, when I do get to see my friends, I make sure I plan really special activities.

2 It's funny, but my friends are always asking for a game, as they like it when they manage to hit a ball back! They'll never beat me, of course, but it's fun for them to try.

3 My mum and dad were excellent tennis players when they were younger, and no matter how busy they were with work, they've always made time for tennis matches. They particularly enjoy playing together against other couples. My mum has a better technique, but my dad is faster, so they make a good team!

4 When I went to my first big competition, I remember walking out onto the court and there was music playing for the crowd. I just thought – this is so cool! And that feeling of excitement has stayed with me ever since.

5 What would Sam's friends say about him?

A
> Sam's a great tennis player. He's so good that we've given up playing against him because he wins so easily. It's a real shame!

B
> Sam spends so long practising. It's not surprising that he has hardly any time to come out with us, but when he does, we always do something exciting!

C
> Sam always gets nervous before important matches. He says the only thing that keeps him calm is listening to music.

D
> Sam was always going to be a tennis player. After all, his parents were professional players, so everyone expected he would become one too!

Questions 11–15

For each question, choose the correct answer.

Toby Harris, actor

17-year-old Toby Harris has already appeared in a number of films

Acting is something that I've been interested in for ages. My aunt belonged to a drama group, and I used to watch her shows when I was a child. But it was only when I was 11 that I joined a theatre club and started acting regularly. I had accompanied a school friend, who was nervous about going alone, and I signed up that same evening! My drama teacher was happy because she'd always said I was talented.

A while later, a film director saw me in one of the club's plays and asked me to be in her film. I said yes, and for me, that was the start of everything. I thought the film would be scary to do, as I was the youngest person at the film studio. I was really calm during the whole thing though, which I hadn't expected. Everyone was so friendly! I didn't have that much to do, not like the main star. He's become very well-known since we worked together. All his films are extremely successful.

I've done a few films now. The last was a comedy, which I was glad to finish – it's not something I find easy! I often get asked for tips about getting into films. Everyone thinks that who you know is important. Maybe that used to be true. Nowadays, it's about experience. There are lots of directors looking for new actors for different film projects, so accept as much work as you can! Even two minutes on camera is useful. Also, ignore reviews. Positive comments are lovely to get, but people can also be unkind!

Recently, I finished a big film, and now I'm planning for the future. I tried for a part in a television series; they chose someone else in the end unfortunately – I'm fine with it, though. It's part of being an actor! I'm taking advantage of a break to do some horse riding. I was taught how to do it on an advanced acting course last year and I need to make sure I still remember everything – it's good for my CV, to show I'd be good in action films, for example!

11 Toby decided to join a theatre club after

    A his teacher recommended it to him.

    B his aunt was involved in running it.

    C he saw other children acting in one of its plays.

    D he enjoyed a session he'd gone to with a friend.

12 How did Toby feel about the first film he acted in?

    A excited about working with the famous people in it

    B surprised at how relaxed he felt when making it

    C pleased to have such a big part in it

    D amazed at how popular it was

13 Toby advises young people interested in being in films to

    A ask for people's opinions about their performance.

    B watch a range of films by different directors.

    C get to know other people in the industry.

    D take any roles that are offered.

14 What is Toby going to do next?

    A practise a useful skill

    B star in a TV programme

    C play a part in an exciting film

    D teach on a course for advanced actors

15 What would Toby write in his blog about acting?

A

> I'm still trying to find a good way to deal with being told I'm not the right person for a role – it just doesn't get any easier, I'm afraid!

B

> I'm so pleased I've been in such a variety of films. My favourites are the funny ones – they're always fun, as you'd expect!

C

> All my success has come because of someone who was in the audience at a show I did. I'm very lucky!

D

> I regret wasting time deciding whether to get involved in my first drama group. If you think you'll enjoy something, try it!

Advice

The answer to Question 15 can be found anywhere in the text, so you may need to read the whole text again.

Remember

We often use reference words like *it* or *they* to avoid repeating a word or phrase. We can use these reference words as clues in this part of the test.

In this part you:

- **read**   a text from which five sentences have been removed
- **choose**   the correct sentence from eight options to fill each gap

FOCUS: GIVING EXTRA DETAILS ACROSS SENTENCES

1   **In pairs, match the sentences 1–6 with the sentences a–f. Which words helped you to decide? Underline them.**

1   This creature is incredibly clever.
2   But they're not only fantastic swimmers.
3   Students have different ways to find out.
4   Butterflies have some amazing abilities.
5   It was much harder than I realised.
6   There are all sorts of challenges to come.

a   The route is very steep and takes ten hours.
b   Getting to the top is just the first.
c   It can make a safe home from just leaves and sticks.
d   They can also run incredibly fast.
e   They can look online or go to the library.
f   For example, they can fly over 1,000 km.

FOCUS: PARAPHRASING ACROSS SENTENCES

2   **Look at the extracts from a text and find examples of how the same idea is expressed using different words.**

1   The building is designed to allow as much light as possible into each room. The kitchen has a huge window which lets in the sun. It also gives amazing views over the countryside around the home.

Example   *The building = the home*

2   For some holidaymakers, an activity holiday might be a problem, as things can get very busy! There's no time for lying around the pool. Another thing is that there's no internet, which might be an issue for some tourists.

3   Scientists did experiments and looked at how fish were changing in different conditions. In warmer water, the creatures were seen to move faster. The experts agree that this is something that needs further study.

FOCUS: LINKERS OF ADDITION

3   **Look back at extracts 1 and 2 in Exercise 2. Find linking words or expressions which show that the writer wants to add extra information or details.**

4   **Choose a linking word or expression from the box to add to the second sentence in examples 1–4. Add any other words necessary.**

also	apart from	as well	besides	in addition	too

1   There is a football pitch on the campsite. There is a swimming pool.
2   We saw a huge range of animals on our trip. We saw lots of interesting buildings.
3   The musicians played all their hit songs. They played songs from their new album.
4   There are ski lessons available. There is a place where you can hire equipment.

Questions 16–20

Five sentences have been removed from the text below. For each question, choose the correct answer. There are three extra sentences which you do not need to use.

Bees play games too!

We know that some animals love playing games. Dogs, for example, spend hours running after sticks. But recently, scientists have carried out experiments using bees and small wooden balls. [16] And the idea that the insects do so is making experts ask questions about insect intelligence.

In one experiment, bees were put in a box with separate spaces, rather like rooms. The bees could move around the box into the different 'rooms'. One contained pollen, bees' favourite food. The bees had to get from their starting point at one side of the box to the area with the food. They could choose one of two routes through spaces containing small wooden balls. One area had balls which were stuck to the floor. [17] The scientists discovered that as the experiment was repeated, the bees chose the route through this second room much more frequently, stopping to 'play' with the balls as they passed. Some bees were seen moving the balls over 100 times. This again made scientists believe that the insects were doing it just for fun. [18] Therefore, there had to be a particular reason for the bees' decision.

In another experiment, two rooms were used, one painted blue and the other yellow. The scientists put the small wooden balls in just one of these rooms. In this experiment, the balls were not stuck to the floor. The bees were then allowed in to explore the areas. [19] When the bees were then put back in again, scientists could clearly see a difference in which room they entered. For example, if the balls had been in the yellow room, more bees chose that room, even though the balls were no longer there.

Scientists also found that results varied depending on individual bees, with younger ones pushing the balls more often than older ones. [20] Adult males spent longer on the activity than females, for example.

A   Despite this, the scientists knew their ideas were correct.

B   In the other, however, they could be moved.

C   That wasn't the only difference seen.

D   The method therefore produced an unusual result.

E   They say the results show bees also have the ability to enjoy an activity.

F   After a while, the bees and the balls were removed.

G   Such changes were challenging for smaller bees.

H   After all, both ways led to a reward.

Advice

When you are choosing the gapped sentence, check that it fits grammatically and any reference words match the sentences around it.

In this part, you:

- **read**   a text with six gaps in it
- **choose**   the correct word for each gap from four options

TIP When you read a sentence with a gap, think of possible words that can fill the gap. Think about the type of word you need (e.g. a verb, a noun, an adjective, an adverb).

FOCUS: PREDICTING WORDS

1   Read the sentences and decide what type of word is needed in each gap. Then decide what might be a suitable word in each gap.

   1   The explorer .... a new species of plant.

   2   Because it is a .... challenging task, a lot of people make mistakes.

   3   The designer used a .... range of colours in her designs.

   4   The man .... over to where the animal had disappeared.

   5   There are lots of reasons why the research was said to be .... to scientists.

VOCABULARY: VERB–NOUN COLLOCATIONS

2   Work in pairs. Look at these verbs and nouns. How many collocations can you make (e.g. *accept an offer*)?

verbs

accept	begin	enter	give	have
make	regret	offer	tell	

nouns

a break	a competition	a decision	a journey	a mistake
an offer	a reason	some help	the truth	

VOCABULARY: WORD BEGINNINGS AND ENDINGS

3   Read the text quickly. Think about the kinds of words that are missing in each gap. Then choose the correct options (A–D) to complete the text.

Remember

Prefixes (word beginnings) can give you more information about a word. For example, words beginning with *un-* usually have a negative meaning. Suffixes (word endings) often tell you what type of word it is (a noun, an adjective, etc.).

It has always been my (1) .... to travel around the world. I knew it was quite (2) .... that I would be able to get enough money to buy a ticket for a trip like that. So when I read about a company who organise jobs for people to do as they travel from country to country, I knew it was a wonderful (3) .... that I didn't want to miss! Immediately, I looked them up.

  1   **A** imagination   **B** situation   **C** invention   **D** ambition

  2   **A** unlikely   **B** unlucky   **C** unusual   **D** unimportant

  3   **A** ability   **B** opportunity   **C** reality   **D** quality

Advice

Read the text and think about the type of words that might go in each gap. Remember that you might need to choose words that are part of a collocation.

Questions 21–26

For each question, choose the correct answer.

All about octopuses

There are many different types of octopuses. These sea creatures are found in many **(21)** .... around the world, and actually live in every ocean on the planet. They live quite near the coast and use their eight 'arms' to build homes among the rocks on the sea floor. They **(22)** .... live alone, and they will defend their homes from attack from other sea creatures. They can move quickly through the water, **(23)** .... speeds of up to 40 kilometres per hour. Octopuses can produce ink which they use to make the water around them go black if they are in danger. They hide in this ink as they swim away, which **(24)** .... other animals from seeing where they have gone. Octopuses also have very high **(25)** .... of intelligence. For example, they have been filmed taking the tops off jars in **(26)** .... to get to the food inside!

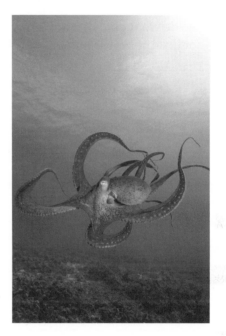

| 21 | A positions | B situations | C locations | D directions |

| 22 | A nearly | B exactly | C typically | D regularly |

| 23 | A completing | B succeeding | C aiming | D achieving |

| 24 | A prevents | B avoids | C escapes | D protects |

| 25 | A values | B numbers | C levels | D quantities |

| 26 | A order | B case | C fact | D full |

In this part, you:

- **read**   a text with six gaps in it
- **write**   one word in each gap

TIP

In Reading Part 6, it is important to read the words before and after each gap. What comes later in a sentence can affect the type of word you need to write in the gap.

FOCUS: READING FURTHER IN THE TEXT

1 **Decide what kind of word is missing in each sentence. Make sure you read the whole sentence, not just the words immediately before and after the gap.**

   1   I .... never been on a boat ride in my city until my cousins came to stay.

   2   Because he doesn't pay attention, he often .... off the train at the wrong station.

   3   Before I .... able to take the bus on my own, my mum made me practise a few times with my older sister.

   4   .... are you getting to the party? If it's by car, can I come too?

GRAMMAR: PRONOUNS AND POSSESSIVE ADJECTIVES

 B1 Preliminary candidates often make mistakes with reference words like *it* and *them*.

2 **Decide what kind of word is missing in each gap. Complete the sentences.**

TIP

If you decide you need a pronoun or a possessive adjective in the gap, make sure that you have read enough of the text to be sure which one you need.

My mum and I went to a new restaurant in town. The waiter took **(1)** .... coats and showed **(2)** ....

to a really nice table by the window. **(3)** .... both liked being able to look out at the people walking past.

(4) .... were all hurrying because **(5)** .... was such a cold day. All of **(6)** .... were wearing

warm coats and hats and scarves.

VOCABULARY: IDENTIFYING SHORT PHRASES

3 **Decide which word goes in each gap. Underline the phrases that the missing words are part of.**

   1   Thanks for offering to lend me a bag for my holiday, but I really need to get one of .... own! I can't keep borrowing yours.

   2   This cake is .... of the best I have ever eaten!

   3   When I went to the cinema, I had to go by .... because my friend was too busy to come with me.

   4   I will go for a bike ride as soon .... I've finished my homework.

Remember

Look forward and backwards in the text around the gap to help you find the right word.

Questions 27–32

For each question, write the correct word.
Write **one** word for each gap.

Review of our school trip to City Theatre

Last week, my class and I went to the City Theatre to see a play called *Surprise Party*. Our teacher wanted us to see it because it is **(27)** .... of the plays that we are studying at school this year. I **(28)** .... never been to the City Theatre before the class trip, so I was really excited about it. I am pleased to say that I certainly wasn't disappointed! There

was a great view **(29)** .... the stage from our seats, and my friends and I were able **(30)** .... hear everything the actors said very clearly. On the coach on the way home after the performance, **(31)** .... all agreed that the actor in the lead role was particularly good. If you want a good night out, and a change from the cinema, I would definitely recommend going to the theatre to watch **(32)** .... live performance.

Advice

Make sure you check your answers when you have finished. Reading the whole text and making sure everything makes sense will help you spot any mistakes.

Training Test 1 — Writing Part 1

TIP In Writing Part 1, the instructions will tell you if you need to write to an English-speaking friend or someone else like a teacher. You need to make sure you use the appropriate style (formal or informal) in your email.

In this part, you:

- **read**   an email with four notes attached
- **write**   a reply to the email, using all the notes

FOCUS: UNDERSTANDING THE TASK

1 Look at the Part 1 exam task on page 30. Are sentences 1–6 true or false?

1	You must write no more than 100 words.	T / F
2	You need to write an informal email to Jessie.	T / F
3	You can choose which of the four notes to write about.	T / F
4	Jessie has decided how to get to the Beach Clean event.	T / F
5	Jessie hasn't decided about posting photos on social media.	T / F
6	Jessie would like to make some plans after the Beach Clean.	T / F

2 Match each of the notes (1–4) in Jessie's email with two possible responses (a–h).

1 Me too!

2 Tell Jessie.

3 Yes, because …

4 Suggest …

a Why don't we bring sandwiches instead?
b It'll encourage others to get involved.
c I think the bus might be faster.
d I'm really looking forward to it.
e Perhaps we should cycle there.
f I know a café near the beach that's good.
g I'm excited about taking part as well.
h Then people can see how much litter we collect.

3 In pairs, talk about how you would reply to each of the notes for the Part 1 exam task on page 30.

TIP Always study the notes to identify what you need to write about for each of them. For example, 'Me, too!' is asking you to share the same opinion as Jessie about the Beach Clean. You need to demonstrate that you can handle various language functions such as agreeing, disagreeing, giving an opinion, offering, recommending and explaining.

VOCABULARY: THE ENVIRONMENT

4 Match the vocabulary in the box with the correct photo A–E.

litter   pollution   recycling   the coast   wildlife

A

B

C

D

E

Remember

In the Writing exam, try to use a range of vocabulary to show how much you know. If possible, use your own words instead of repeating words from the email.

VOCABULARY: WORD BUILDING

5 Complete the table.

noun	adjective	verb
the environment	(1)	–
(2)	polluted	(3) ....
the coast	(4)	–
recycling	(5)	(6) ....
(7)	(8)	to damage

VOCABULARY: MAKING SUGGESTIONS

👁 *B1 Preliminary* candidates often make mistakes with *should* and *shouldn't*.

6 Use *should* or *shouldn't* to say whether something is a good or bad idea in the following sentences.

1 We definitely .... leave litter all over the beach.
2 Everyone .... recycle as much as possible.
3 Most people agree that we .... harm the environment.
4 Everybody .... prevent waste from going in the sea.
5 More young people .... volunteer at Beach Clean events.
6 We .... damage our forests or our wildlife will suffer.

TIP In Part 1, you sometimes have to recommend something such as an activity or a location. When you do this, you can use *should* or *shouldn't* + infinitive.

You **must** answer this question.

Write your answer in about **100 words** on the answer sheet.

Question 1

Read this email from your English-speaking friend Jessie and the notes you have made.

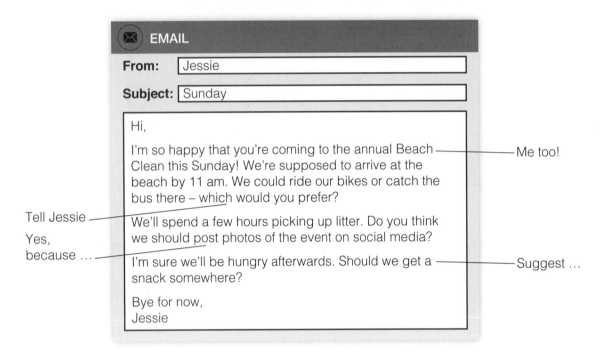

EMAIL

From: Jessie

Subject: Sunday

Hi,

I'm so happy that you're coming to the annual Beach — Me too!
Clean this Sunday! We're supposed to arrive at the
beach by 11 am. We could ride our bikes or catch the
bus there – which would you prefer? — Tell Jessie

We'll spend a few hours picking up litter. Do you think
we should post photos of the event on social media? — Yes, because …

I'm sure we'll be hungry afterwards. Should we get a — Suggest …
snack somewhere?

Bye for now,
Jessie

Write your **email** to Jessie using **all the notes**.

 TIP After you finish writing your email, always read through your answer to make sure it's clear and you have covered all four content points.

Advice

When you write in the exam, it is very important to make sure your writing is clear so the examiners can read your answer easily.

Advice

Your email needs to be well organised so it is easy to follow and it also needs to be an appropriate length. If you write too little, you may not include enough information about each content point.

In this part, you:

- **choose** to write either an article or a story
- **write** a text of about 100 words

FOCUS: UNDERSTANDING THE TASK

1 In pairs, look at the example of a Part 2 exam task below. Are sentences 1–5 true or false?

1	You should give your personal opinion of fashion.	T / F
2	Your article might appear on an English-language website.	T / F
3	You need to decide which question you want to write about.	T / F
4	Your article needs to be approximately 100 words.	T / F
5	Your article should include information about what you do with old clothes.	T / F

Write your answer in about **100 words** on the answer sheet.
You see this notice on an English-language website for young people.

Articles wanted!

STAYING IN FASHION

- Is wearing the latest fashion trends important to you? Why?
- What do you do with clothes that you no longer wear?

The best articles answering these questions will appear on our website.

Write your **article**.

TIP The article is asking for your opinion about a particular topic. In tasks like this, make sure you always fully answer all the questions and provide reasons for your views.

FOCUS: STUDYING AN EXAMPLE ANSWER

2 Complete the sample answer for the question in Exercise 1 with these expressions. You do not need to use them all.

above all	another thing	especially	finally	firstly
for example	for instance	in particular	such as	

(1) .... , I'm not interested in wearing the latest trends, but that doesn't mean I'm not into fashion.
(2) .... , I love learning how to sew some of the things I wear. (3) .... , I really don't want to dress like everyone else, so I wear stuff that suits me. (4) .... , I recently made a long black dress that I (5) .... love wearing. (6) .... is that I always give my old clothes to charity shops. I would never throw anything away as this creates unnecessary waste. (7) .... , I like knowing that other people will still enjoy the things I once wore by giving them to second-hand shops.

3 Read the sample answer in Exercise 2 again and answer questions 1–4.

    1 Has the writer answered all parts of the question correctly?

    2 How does the writer give examples?

    3 How does the writer give opinions?

    4 Is the sample answer long enough?

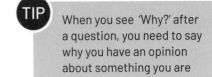

TIP When you see 'Why?' after a question, you need to say why you have an opinion about something you are being asked to write about.

FOCUS: LINKING IDEAS TOGETHER

4 Complete the table using these expressions from Exercise 2.

> above all   another thing   especially   finally   firstly
> for example   for instance   in particular   such as

ordering information	stressing a point	giving an example
....	....	....
....	....	....
....	....	....

Remember

You should try to use linking expressions in your article to connect your ideas and make them easy for the reader to follow.

TIP In an article, try to share your personal experiences. You can do this by giving examples to help support some of your ideas.

GRAMMAR: *DURING, FOR, SINCE*

B1 Preliminary candidates often make mistakes with the present perfect with *for* and *since*.

5 Choose the correct words.

    1 I've made my own clothes *during / since* I was 12.

    2 I haven't visited any charity shops *for / since* two months.

    3 A documentary about fast fashion will be on TV at some point *since / during* the weekend.

    4 My family isn't going to buy any new clothes *for / during* a year.

    5 It's been a long time *since / for* I last went shopping.

    6 My phone kept ringing *since / during* the film.

6 Complete the rules using *during*, *for* or *since*.

    1 We use .... when we mention a specific point in the past.

    2 We use .... when we mention a length of time.

    3 We use .... when something happens in the middle of something else.

Choose **one** of these questions.
Write your answer in about **100 words** on the answer sheet.

Advice

Before you decide which question you want to do, study each task carefully and think about the vocabulary you will need to use. Choose the task that you find the most interesting and would be able to write most confidently about.

Question 2

You see this notice on an English-language website.

Articles wanted!

SOCIAL MEDIA

Millions of young people use social media every day.

Does it matter how much time you spend on social media? Why?

What do you like and dislike about social media?

The best article will be published on our website!

Write your **article**.

Question 3

Your English teacher has asked you to write a story. Your story must begin with this sentence.

They jumped up and down with excitement when they heard the news.

Write your **story**.

Advice

Always put the first line at the beginning of your story and include this as part of the word count. Your story must follow on from this line. If there are any pronouns (e.g. he, she, they), make sure you use them consistently in your story.

Advice

Be ambitious when you write your story by showing a range of tenses and vocabulary. Make sure it has a clear beginning, middle and end.

In this part, you:

- **listen**   to one or two people talking in seven short situations
- **choose**   the picture that answers the question

> **TIP**   In Part 1, think about the words that each picture shows before you listen.

VOCABULARY: PLACES AND ACTIVITIES

1   Complete the table with the words in the box.

> band   café   cottage   coat   cupboard   diving   DJ   fishing
> football   glove   keyboard   railway station   recording   scarf
> shelf   shopping centre   sink   surfing   tie   wardrobe

furniture	clothes	sport	music	buildings

2   Choose the correct options to complete the sentences.

1. We had a lovely day at the *museum / farm / beach*. There were great waves for surfing.
2. There was a *tower / fountain / statue* in the middle of the square. The sound of the water was relaxing.
3. I bought my sister *earrings / a necklace / tights* for her birthday. They're made of silver.
4. I *record music / play chess / do puzzles* on my phone. I sometimes sing with a friend and sometimes by myself.

3   Listen to what the six people say. Match each person (1–6) with a picture.

01

☐ A

☐ B

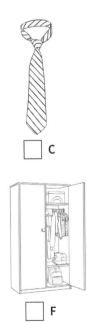
☐ C

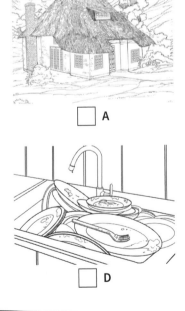
☐ D

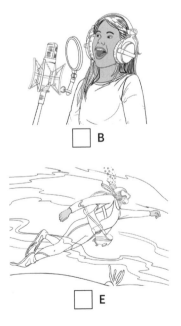
☐ E

☐ F

GRAMMAR: TIME EXPRESSIONS AND VERB FORMS

4 **Write *past*, *present* or *future* after each sentence.**

1 Let's play football after class. ....

2 He's in the middle of an important meeting. ....

3 I'll do that when I have time. ....

4 He's lost his camera. ....

5 We're going on the trip in a couple of days. ....

6 He used to play a lot of tennis. ....

7 The bus goes at six, so hurry up. ....

8 I'm taking the exam the week after next. ....

 In Part 1, read each question carefully and think about whether the answer is going to be something that happened in the past, the present or the future.

Remember

He's / She's can be either *he/she is* or *he/she has*. Listen for the main verb afterwards to help you know which one it is.

5 **Look at the pictures and listen to six conversations. Decide if the speakers did the activity in the picture in the past, are doing it in the present or will do it in the future.**

02

1 ....

2 ....

3 ....

4 ....

5 ....

6 ....

6 **What expressions and verb tenses do the speakers use to show the time of the activity? Listen again and complete the sentences.**

02

1 I'll have to do it ....

2 We .... though, and I .... a lot of points!

3 He hasn't stopped practising .... !

4 She's out at sea ....

5 I .... doing the experiment in the exhibition at school
   ....

6 I .... the bus.

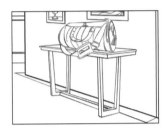

TIP You don't always hear the information in the same order as the pictures.

Questions 1–7

03 For each question, choose the correct answer.

1 Where does Danny usually keep his sports bag?

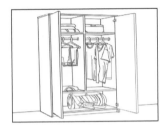

A

B

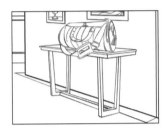

C

2 Which T-shirt did Tammy wear?

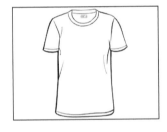

A

B

C

3 What's the girl's brother's new hobby?

A

B

C

Advice

(1) Can the boy find his bag? Which word tells you where he usually keeps his bag?

4   Who gave the girl her purse back?

A

B

C

5   Why does the boy like the café?

A

B

C

6   What does the boy have to wear for the school play?

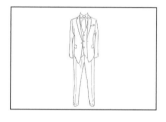

A

B

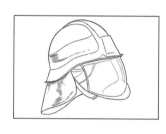

C

7   Why is the train late?

A

B

C

Advice

(6) When is the school play? Which character is the boy going to play? What does he need to wear for this character?

In this part, you:

- **listen**   to two speakers talking about a topic
- **answer**   six multiple-choice questions

VOCABULARY: ADJECTIVES

1   **Listen to the speakers. Choose the correct option.**

04

   1   The boy is *embarrassed / anxious*.

   2   The girl thinks the animal was *cute / frightening*.

   3   The children have to be *patient / quick*.

   4   The building was *tall / modern*.

   5   Their friend is *reliable / amusing*.

   6   The park is *enormous / boring*.

2   **Listen again and write the words you hear that have a similar meaning to the answers in Exercise 1.**

04

> **TIP**   Keep a record of vocabulary with synonyms and antonyms, e.g. *anxious*: synonyms – *nervous, worried*; antonyms – *relaxed, calm*.

FOCUS: EXPLAINING WHY

3   **Match the sentence halves.**

   1   I didn't like the camera   **a**   so that everyone could share it.

   2   We stopped at the café   **b**   because the weather was excellent.

   3   They bought a large pizza   **c**   to have something to drink.

   4   I paid a lot of money,   **d**   because the pictures weren't clear.

   5   My computer was broken,   **e**   to use in the presentation.

   6   The family went to the coast   **f**   so I expected a better room.

   7   She looked for some good images   **g**   so I asked my uncle to help me fix it.

4   **Listen and choose the correct option.**

05

You hear a boy talking about his holiday. Why did he go home early?

   A   because he was ill

   B   to study for a test

   C   so that he could play in a match

> **TIP**   Speakers often explain why they do or feel something. They use words like *because, so that, to*, or *so* before giving the reason.

Questions 8–13

06 For each question, choose the correct answer.

8 You will hear two friends talking about their school website. The friends agree that

A the information is confusing.

B the photos are attractive.

C the articles seem interesting.

9 You will hear a girl telling her friend about a documentary on space travel. What surprised her about it?

A Nobody has been to the Moon in recent years.

B It has taken a long time to prepare for the trip.

C Space travel for tourists is expensive.

10 You will hear a boy telling his friend about a cookery course. Why did he enjoy most about it?

A something his classmate did

B something his teacher taught them

C something he made

11 You will hear two friends talking about singing in a concert. The girl is worried because she thinks that

A her clothes are wrong.

B she'll make a mistake.

C the other singers need to prepare more.

12 You will hear a boy telling his friend about a maths test. The boy recommends

A working with the class book.

B working with a friend.

C working with an app.

13 You will hear a girl talking about a new snowboard. How does she feel about it?

A satisfied with the colour

B pleased she bought it

C confident it'll help her win

In this part, you:

- **listen** to one speaker talking about a topic
- **complete** six gaps with one or two words

FOCUS: PREDICTING ANSWERS

1 Work in pairs. What information do you think completes these sentences?

1 She needed a .... for the exam.
2 They finally went to a .... for lunch.
3 In the end, he came .... in the race.
4 He saw the advertisement in a ....
5 She gave a .... during the interview.
6 He didn't go to the party because he was feeling ....
7 She learned about the expedition from a ....
8 The train journey lasted ....

2 Listen and complete each gap in Exercise 1 with one or two words or a number. Did you predict the correct answers?

07

TIP In Listening Part 3, think about the type of information needed in a gap before you listen.

Remember

How do you say different numbers in English, e.g. £10.30, the telephone number 01345 26647, the date 22/5 or the year 2023? It's important to practise saying and listening to different numbers.

FOCUS: UNDERSTANDING CONTRASTING INFORMATION

3 Complete the sentences with these words.

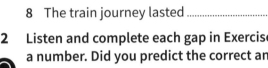

| actually | although | despite | however | instead | otherwise |

1 I wanted to give Dad a surprise. ...., my sister told him the day before the party.
2 I took a raincoat, but ...., I didn't need it in the end.
3 You should go to bed early .... you'll feel tired in the morning.
4 I enjoyed the film .... my friend didn't.
5 There was no bus for an hour, so I walked into town ....
6 We decided to go to the beach .... the bad weather forecast.

TIP Pay attention to linking words and expressions as they can affect the meaning.

4 Listen and choose the correct options.

1 They went to the *cinema / theatre*.
2 She didn't buy a *suitcase / backpack*.
3 They decided to *play tennis / go running*.
4 He's going to *clean his bike / make a cake*.
5 The ticket cost *£10 / £15*.

08

Questions 14–19

09   For each question, write the correct answer in the gap.
Write **one** or **two words** or a **number** or a **date** or a **time**.

You will hear a boy called Aidan talking on his podcast about a kayaking trip.

Aidan's kayaking trip

Aidan convinced his **(14)** .... to go on the trip.

He especially enjoyed visiting the **(15)** ....

Aidan was relieved he had taken a **(16)** .... to wear.

He was surprised the weather was **(17)** .... all the time.

Aidan suggests that going as a group is better because it costs
£ **(18)** .... per person.

When the day finished, Aidan's **(19)** .... were hurting.

Advice

(16) What types of clothes might someone wear for kayaking?

Advice

(19) What parts of the body might hurt after kayaking?

In this part, you:

- **listen** to an interview
- **choose** from six multiple-choice questions

VOCABULARY: IDENTIFYING A SPEAKER'S INTENTION, OPINION OR ATTITUDE

1 Choose the correct verbs.

1 He *explained* / *warned* to us how to access the website.
2 I tried to *persuade* / *advise* my parents to let me go to the party.
3 My friend's positive comments *encouraged* / *promoted* me to keep trying.
4 What do you *think* / *persuade* about the problem of climate change?
5 The government is *promoting* / *suggesting* public transport with adverts about cheap bus passes.
6 He *suggested* / *encouraged* I should take up swimming for my bad back.
7 Our teacher *advised* / *explained* us to take notes during the talk.
8 She *warned* / *thought* us that walking along that road was dangerous.

TIP A speaker's intention, opinion or attitude is sometimes summarised using words like *suggest*, *explain* and *persuade*.

FOCUS: IDENTIFYING HOW INFORMATION IS PARAPHRASED

2 Match the sentences that have the same meaning.

1 They said they couldn't come to my party.
2 They were anxious about the result.
3 They were confident it would get warmer.
4 They couldn't think of anything else.
5 They weren't allowed to ask more than a few people to come.
6 They set up a company that made toys.

a They were sure the weather was going to improve.
b They could only invite a small number of friends.
c They ran out of ideas.
d They started a business selling children's products.
e They were worried about what would happen.
f They refused my invitation.

3 Listen to the conversation and choose the correct option.

10

The girl's main reason for her decision to go to India was

A to keep her friend company.
B to learn something about the animals there.
C to have a break from studying.

TIP The speaker may express the same idea that appears in one of the options, but in different words.

Questions 20–25

11 For each question, choose the correct answer.

You will hear an interview with a young woman called Jessica Shore, who makes robots.

20 Where did Jessica get the idea for her robot cat?

    A She saw one on a school trip.

    B A relative made something similar.

    C She found information online.

> **Advice**
>
> *(20) What did she use to do with her brother? Where did her teacher say they could get ideas for class?*

21 Jessica feels most proud about

    A making a useful robot.

    B getting first prize.

    C trying something more difficult.

22 What does Jessica do in her free time?

    A She spends time in the countryside.

    B She helps people in the area.

    C She goes on trips with friends.

23 What new project is Jessica working on now?

    A teaching others about technology

    B studying computer programming

    C setting up a business

> **Advice**
>
> *(23) What does she want to do in the future? What is she doing now?*

24 Jessica thinks all teenagers should learn

    A how to mend things.

    B information about things they use every day.

    C about the importance of technology.

25 How does Jessica feel about the future of robots?

    A anxious they'll be bad for us

    B excited about new possibilities for communication

    C confident they'll make our lives better

In this part, you will:

- **talk** to an interlocutor for 2–3 minutes
- **answer** some general questions about you and your family

FOCUS: ANSWERING PERSONAL QUESTIONS

1 Answer these questions about yourself.

    1 What's your name? ....

    2 How old are you? ....

    3 Where do you live? ....

2 Match these things that an interlocutor might ask (1–6) with the responses (a–f).

    1 Tell us about a good friend.

    2 What did you do yesterday?

    3 Which do you like best: mornings or evenings?

    4 What kind of food do you like best?

    5 How do you usually get to school?

    6 What plans do you have for this weekend?

    a Pasta's my favourite. My grandad makes the best spaghetti sauce!

    b I get on well with Alex. He's a classmate from school and we've got similar hobbies.

    c I went to school during the day and played video games with my friends in the evening.

    d It depends. Sometimes Mum gives me a lift and sometimes I walk. It only takes 20 minutes.

    e I'm going swimming with my cousins at the new pool in our town.

    f I like getting up early because it's quiet and I can do my homework before I go to school.

3 Now ask and answer the questions in Exercise 2 with a partner.

FOCUS: UNDERSTANDING THE INTERLOCUTOR

 B1 Preliminary candidates often forget to use the *-ing* form after *like, enjoy, don't mind,* etc.

4 Listen and write what the interlocutor says.

    1 What ....?

    2 How ....?

    3 Tell ....

    4 Which do you prefer, ...?

    5 How ....?

    6 When ....?

12

5 Now ask and answer the questions in Exercise 4 with your partner.

 TIP Listen carefully for the question words *What/ Where/When/Who/How* and make sure you answer correctly.

(2–3 minutes)

Phase 1
Interlocutor

To A/B	Good morning / afternoon / evening. Can I have your mark sheets, please? *(Hand over the mark sheets to the assessor.)*
To A/B	I'm .... and this is ....
To A	What's your name? How old are you? Thank you.
To B	And what's your name? How old are you? Thank you.
To B	**B**, where do you live? Thank you.
To A	And **A**, where do you live? Thank you.

> **Advice**
>
> You can ask the interlocutor to repeat questions or explain something you don't understand, so don't be afraid to do this.

Phase 2
Interlocutor

(The interlocutor may ask you one or more questions similar to the following.)

How long do you spend on a mobile phone every day?

Tell us about your best friend.

Where would you most like to visit in the world? (Why?)

Do you like playing team sports? (Why? / Why not?)

What did you do in your last school holidays?

Tell us about the town where you live.

What do you enjoy learning about at school? (Why?)

How often do you listen to music?

> **Advice**
>
> You may need to answer questions about the present, past or future.

> **Advice**
>
> It's a good idea to practise asking and answering questions with a friend before the exam. This will help you feel more confident.

 Listen to two students answering some of the questions above.

13

In this part, you will:

- **talk** to the interlocutor about a colour photograph
- **describe** what you can see in the photograph

VOCBULARY: DESCRIBING PEOPLE, THINGS AND PLACES

 B1 Preliminary candidates often make mistakes when using the present continuous.

1 Work in pairs. Look at the photograph below (see colour version on page C10). What can you see? Discuss these things.

- Who the people are?
- What they are doing?
- Where they are?
- What else is in the picture?

> ### Remember
> Use the present simple or present continuous tense to describe what you can see in the photo. For example, *The people are sitting around a table. They're having lunch.*

2 Match the adjectives in box A with the items in box B. You can use some adjectives with more than one item.

| A | amusing | close | comfortable | interesting | small | tasty | tidy |

| B | conversation | clothes | joke | kitchen | meal | relationship | space |

3 Listen to a student describing the photo. What does the student say that is different from your own description?

🎧 14

> ### Remember
> It doesn't matter if you don't know the word for something. Try to describe it using different words.

(3–5 minutes)

Interlocutor	Now I'd like each of you to talk on your own about something. I'm going to give each of you a photograph and I'd like you to talk about it. **A**, here is your photograph. It shows some people **working in their garden**.

The interlocutor will place Exam Practice Test 1 Speaking Part 2 picture (see page C1), in front of Candidate A.

	B, you just listen. **A**, please tell us what you can see in the photograph.

Candidate A	*(Approximately 1 minute)*
Interlocutor	Thank you.

Back-up prompts (for **A** and **B**)
- Talk about the person/people.
- Talk about the place.
- Talk about other things in the photograph.

Interlocutor	**B**, here is your photograph. It shows some people **cleaning their home**.

The interlocutor will place Exam Practice Test 1 Speaking Part 2 picture (see page C2), in front of Candidate B.

Interlocutor	**A**, you just listen. **B**, please tell us what you can see in the photograph.
Candidate B	*(Approximately 1 minute)*
Interlocutor	Thank you.

   Listen to students talking about Photos A, B and C. (See pages C1, C2 and C7.)

In this part, you will:

- **look at** information the interlocutor gives you
- **discuss** your views and opinions with your partner

FOCUS: MAKING SUGGESTIONS, AGREEING AND DISAGREEING

1 Look at the pictures below. Who do you think these gifts are for?

2 Listen to two students talking about the items in Exercise 1. Which gift do they agree would be best for a friend who's in hospital and why?

18

> **TIP** Listen to your partner's opinions, but don't worry if you disagree. If you don't agree with what your partner says, try to give a reason why.

3 Look at the phrases from the conversation. Are they used for making a suggestion (S), agreeing (A), or disagreeing (D)?

1 I'm not sure about that. / I don't know about that.
2 I think …
3 I agree.
4 I You're right.
5 I don't agree.
6 Maybe … would be better.
7 What about …? / How about …?
8 I think … would be best.
9 That's a good idea!
10 Why don't we …?

4 Work in pairs. Which gift do you think would be best?

> **TIP** It doesn't matter if you don't have time to reach an agreement, but together with your partner, you should try not to leave any silences or pauses in the conversation.

5 A brother and a sister want to buy a gift for their aunt who has just had a baby. Discuss these ideas for gifts with a partner.

Exam Practice Test 1 Speaking Part 3

Advice

Try to respond to what your partner says so that the conversation is natural. If your partner is quiet, try asking a question, such as What do you think? or offer your opinions, e.g. I think … would be best.

(4–5 minutes)

Interlocutor	Now, in this part of the test you're going to talk about something together for about two minutes. I'm going to describe a situation to you.
	The interlocutor will place Exam Practice Test 1 Speaking Part 3 set of pictures (see page C11), in front of both candidates.
Interlocutor	**A group of friends want to visit an interesting place together this weekend. Here are some places they could visit.** **Talk together about the different places the friends could visit and say which would be best.** All right? Now talk together.
	(Approximately 2–3 minutes)
Interlocutor	Thank you.

 Listen to two students doing the task above.

19

TIP

In Speaking Part 4, the interlocutor will ask individual questions to you and your partner and may also ask you to discuss a question together.

In this part, you will:

- **answer**   questions on a similar topic to Part 3
- **give**   your views and opinions to your partner and the interlocutor

FOCUS: TALKING ABOUT LIKES, DISLIKES AND PREFERENCES

1   **Listen to Olivia and Tomasz giving their opinions about gifts they like to receive. Complete the text with words from the recording.**

20

Olivia: So, I think it's **(1)** .... to receive gifts that people have obviously put a lot of thought into. Like, I collect old records. If someone buys me one they know I'll like, I think that's **(2)** ....

Tomasz: Yes, that **(3)** .... be good.

Olivia: I like food as a gift, **(4)** ...., for example nice chocolates or snacks. You can enjoy them, but you don't need to find somewhere to put them in your house. **(5)** ....? What do you **(6)** .... like?

Tomasz: I **(7)** .... lots of different things. My brother always gets me an interesting book for my birthday and I **(8)** .... that. But I think my **(9)** .... kind of gift is something that someone's made. A friend gave me a wooden box that he made for me to keep all my cables and things in. That's the kind of thing that I **(10)** .... to receive.

TIP

The interlocutor will let you know when you need to talk together. Talk directly to your partner, as this will help the conversation be more natural.

2   **Now look at the second part of Olivia and Tomasz's conversation about giving gifts, and underline the phrases which show likes, dislikes and preferences.**

Olivia: Do you give different kinds of gifts depending on the occasion? For example, if I go to a wedding, I'd give something different to what I'd give someone for their birthday.

Tomasz: Me too. I think I'd probably spend more money on a wedding gift because it's such a special celebration.

Olivia: Exactly. It's difficult to decide what to get for gifts sometimes. I think it's good to give something environmentally friendly, like a gift made from natural materials, such as glass or paper.

Tomasz: Right! That's so important now. I'd rather not buy anything plastic. But it can be hard to avoid.

Olivia: I'm not so sure. I think it depends where you go shopping.

Tomasz: I guess so. Lots of cheap gifts are made from plastic.

Olivia: Right, but you don't have to spend too much money on a gift that's nice and good for the environment.

Remember

Use words and phrases to show that you are listening to your partner and to keep the conversation going, for example, *Really? Me neither, Right*.

3 Work with a partner. Take it in turns to read out sentences 1–6 and use the expressions in the speech bubbles to respond. Keep the conversation going by asking and answering other questions about the topic.

Exactly! | I am! | I don't! | So do I! | I wouldn't! | Is that true? | Me neither! | Me too! | Really?

1 I'm not into extreme sports like climbing or snowboarding.
2 I think travelling is really exciting because you learn about other cultures.
3 I love swimming outdoors.
4 I'd rather go to the cinema than the theatre.
5 I don't really like fast food.
6 I think it's really important for people to be kind to each other.

Exam Practice Test 1   Speaking Part 4

(3–4 minutes)

Interlocutor
(to both candidates)

- Do you prefer to visit places that are indoors or outdoors? (Why?)
- What's an interesting place that you've been to? (Why was it interesting?)
- How do you prefer travelling to new places? (Why?)
- What do you think people can learn from visiting new places?
- Do you think younger people and older people like visiting different kinds of places? (Why?)

Thank you. That is the end of the test.

 Listen to two students doing the task above.

Advice

Think about the kinds of places that you like to visit. Why do you like them? Why might other people like them? Why do people find it interesting to go to new places?

Training Test 2 — Reading Part 1

- What does Reading Part 1 test?
- What kind of texts do you have to read in Part 1?

FOCUS: UNDERSTANDING WHAT YOU HAVE TO FIND

1   In pairs, look at these short texts and the questions that go with them. Underline the words in the questions which tell you what information you need to find.

1

Shop closing early this afternoon at 2.30 due to staff illness. Usual closing time of 5 from tomorrow.

When will the shop shut today?

2

New Message

Hi Nate,
I'm sorry, my bus was cancelled! I'll get the next one, but I'll be really late.
I'll get there as soon as I can, but it won't be before 3 at the earliest.

What transport problem has Nate had?

3

Bring your coats as it will be cold on the river. You'll also need a pen and notebook, but don't worry about snacks.

What are students not required to bring?

4

Don't forget to bring the book to school tomorrow! I can't wait to read it!
Sandra

Why is Sandra writing this message?

2   Look again at the questions in Exercise 1 and find words in the texts which will help you find the correct information. These could be paraphrases or words with a similar meaning.

Example   *1 When … shut today? – closing … this afternoon at 2.30*

3   In pairs, answer the questions in Exercise 1.

4   Match these verbs with sentences 1–10.

| admitting | apologising | choosing | confirming | explaining |
| promising | requesting | ~~reminding~~ | suggesting | warning |

1   Don't forget to be at the cinema at 8.30. *reminding*
2   I'm sorry I'm late.
3   I made a mistake, it's true.
4   You'd better hurry. A storm is coming.
5   It was because I needed a new one.
6   How about having pizza tonight?
7   Would you mind helping me tomorrow?
8   I'll be there at six, as we agreed.
9   I'd prefer to have Indian food tonight.
10 I won't forget, don't worry!

GRAMMAR: THE PASSIVE IN NOTICES AND SIGNS

🔘 *B1 Preliminary* candidates often make mistakes with passive forms.

5 More formal messages often use passive structures. Look at signs 1–5 and decide which use ones use a passive structure.

1

Leave your books on the shelf.

2

Cups must be returned to the kitchen.

3

Visitors must buy their tickets from reception.

4

Access is required at all times.

5

You will be taken to your seat.

TIP

In Reading Part 1, the short texts might use the passive form, while options A–C use active forms. Because of this, it is important to know how to use both.

6 Change the active sentences in Exercise 5 into passive ones.

VOCABULARY: IDENTIFYING EXAMPLES

7 Complete the second sentence so that it has the same meaning as the first. Use words from the box.

| flowers | ice cream | ingredients | mountains |
| rain | racket | trainers | weather |

TIP

Reading Part 1 questions may ask you to find an example of something. In the example below, *a hat* is an example of *what they have to wear.*
Students are told what they have to wear.
All students need a hat because it will be a hot day.

1 While we were walking, there was a big storm.
   There was heavy wind and .... during our walk.
2 We had a choice of different desserts.
   The menu included various flavours of ....
3 All players must wear appropriate shoes.
   Anyone using the tennis courts must have the right ....
4 I really loved the scenery on our holiday.
   There were beautiful .... and lakes where we were on holiday.

Advice

Think about the type of text you are reading and why someone has written it. Is it one that is making facts and details public? Or is it a personal message from one person to another?

Questions 1–5

For each question, choose the correct answer.

1

> Marta
> We've tried booking tickets for tomorrow's theatre trip, but the website isn't working. I'll go to the theatre today and get them. It's probably quicker than waiting for the website to be fixed!
> Kim

What is Kim doing in this message?

A telling Marta why the day of a trip needs to change

B explaining to Marta why she hasn't bought tickets for the theatre yet

C warning Marta not to buy tickets from the theatre website

2

> Hall to be kept clear.
> Use hall lockers provided.
> Any items which are left out will be taken to reception by staff.

A Students have to leave their things at reception.

B Students are able to leave their things in the hall.

C Anything remaining in this area will be put into the lockers by staff.

3

> Nick,
> Don't forget the dentist today. I've just thought, I'd better collect you after school – if you wait for the bus like we agreed, we'll be late getting there. We'll have pizza afterwards, OK?
> Mum

A Nick's mum is asking him not to take too long coming out of school.

B Nick's mum is reminding him about where they are going to eat later.

C Nick's mum is suggesting a new travel arrangement.

4

New Message

 To: students

Subject: concert

To take part, sign up on the noticeboard by this Friday. All welcome, from singers to poets! Volunteers also required to run the event. Email me if that's you!

Mr Roberts

A The teacher is requesting help in organising the concert.

B The teacher is inviting students to watch people perform in Friday's concert.

C The teacher is asking students to email details of their planned performances.

5

Sports Event

Remember: team games in the park tomorrow! All refreshments are provided, plus everything needed for games like badminton and football. Please come to school in sports kit – no uniforms!

The notice tells students that tomorrow they must

A remember some useful equipment.

B bring plenty of food and drink.

C wear clothes that are suitable.

Advice

Look at the options carefully and think about the information you need to find in the texts.

TIP
When you read the information about people and their requirements (what they want), you can start thinking about the language you might expect to see in the options.

- What does Reading Part 2 ask you to read?
- How many texts do you match each person with?

FOCUS: PREDICTING

1 **In pairs, look at these examples of people and their requirements. Give examples of vocabulary you might expect to see about what each person wants.**

1 Tommy wants to do a course for people who haven't sailed before. He and his family only have time to do a short course and they'd like to receive a certificate at the end.

Example   level of course (beginners/advanced)

2 Hannah wants to go to a photography club at least once a month and get advice about taking better photos of animals. She'd like information about photo exhibitions in her local area.

3 James wants to join a writing group with other people his age. He'd like to talk to a famous author and get advice about writing funny stories.

4 Katia wants to go on a walk that's not too challenging, as her grandmother is coming. They want to stop at a café during the walk and Katia wants to have a swim somewhere, too.

FOCUS: UNDERSTANDING REQUIREMENTS

2 **Complete the descriptions with suitable examples that match what Frank and Simone want. Try to use different words from the ones that are underlined.**

Frank wants to visit a museum <u>early in the morning</u>, and he hopes to learn <u>about space travel</u>. He'd like to have a <u>hot meal</u> at the museum.

> This month we have a fantastic exhibition of the **(1)** *technology* that people used to get to the moon! There'll be plenty of time to explore as we **(2)** .... and don't close until evening. Our café serves **(3)** ....

Simone wants to cycle on <u>quiet roads</u>. She wants to see some <u>animals</u>, and cycle with a <u>small group</u>.

> On our cycling holidays, we only use **(4)** .... so you'll always feel safe and all our groups are limited to **(5)** .... As we cycle through some beautiful places, you'll have the chance of seeing **(6)** ....

GRAMMAR: CONDITIONAL STRUCTURES

B1 Preliminary candidates often make mistakes with conditional forms.

3 **Work in pairs. Complete the conditional sentences with your own ideas.**

1 If you love watching films, then ....

2 If you're the sort of person who likes exercise, ...

3 This restaurant is perfect if ....

4 The campsite is a good choice if ....

Advice

Each person has three requirements (things that they want or need). Remember that for each of descriptions 6–10 only one of A–H is correct, so there are three texts you will not use.

Questions 6–10

For each question, choose the correct answer.

The young people below all want to visit a history festival.
On the next page there are eight descriptions of history festivals.
Decide which history festival would be the most suitable for the young people below.

6 Eleanor wants to learn about important historical people from the local area. She'd love to discover how people entertained themselves in the past and buy a history book.

7 Arjun wants information for a school project on old houses, and tips on making sure the information he uses from websites for history homework is accurate. He'd like to learn about clothes people wore long ago.

8 Cassie is interested in food people ate hundreds of years ago and wants to take part in a history quiz. During her visit, she'd love information about joining a local history group for young people.

9 Zander thinks hearing some traditional music would be fun, and he hopes to learn about jobs people used to have. He'd also like to attend a history talk on a battle.

10 Cindy loves art and hopes to see important old paintings. She'd like to make something to take home, and she thinks watching a show about a historical period is a good way to learn about history.

History festivals

A   History world

Have fun working in groups to design an 18th-century costume – better than looking at pictures! You'll also discover fascinating details about the past, including how the places people called home, from simple huts to important castles, have changed over time. Guides also explain how using the internet helps check facts for your research.

B   Days gone by

Discover why being an artist was an important job in previous centuries and create your own painting to put on your wall! Then enjoy a 15th-century lunch, consisting of pies using only vegetables available at the time, and take some home to share with your family!

C   History in focus

Start with a lecture on a decades-long fight between two important 14th-century families. After that, try some of the things people did for work at the time, like making clothes and baking, and finish with a concert in an ancient palace where you'll join in singing traditional songs!

D   All about history

Come and see how ordinary people's lives provide fascinating historical detail; we can easily imagine them having fun after school or work, or relaxing at home! You'll learn about how a history group discovered an ancient theatre, providing us with information about shows people enjoyed.

E   The past comes to life

Explore the life of ordinary people – what they ate, and games and puzzles they enjoyed. The region around the festival also produced people who changed the world, including politicians and musicians. Find out why! If you want something to read at home, there's a selection from various history experts on sale.

F   See the past

If you want to know about the history of this area, the talk by local author Mia Jones is perfect. She examined ruins of an ancient village close to the town and wrote about them for her history show. Although you can watch this online from home, at the event, you'll visit them with her!

G   History all around

Spend the day in a castle, examining special objects, like drums used in ancient battles, and preparing centuries-old recipes. Pay attention – there will be questions, with books and posters for getting all the answers correct! The castle holds regular meetings for a club aimed at history-loving teens, so see staff for details.

H   A day in the past

Our location in a 600-year-old hall offers learning opportunities: answer questions by examining valuable and rare pictures of powerful kings, wearing the clothes of various periods. After trying recipes from a king's kitchen, decorate a box to keep, using 17th-century colours, before watching a play describing a 50-year-long local 15th-century battle.

- What kind of text do you have to read?
- How is question 15 different to the other questions?

TIP In Reading Part 3, there will be some questions asking about people's attitudes or opinions.

VOCABULARY: PHRASES THAT DESCRIBE OPINIONS AND ATTITUDES

1 Read the paragraph and underline all the opinions given about a holiday. Put the opinions in order, from most positive to most negative.

> The swimming pool was pretty good, and the food was absolutely fantastic. The location of the hotel wasn't too bad. It took us about 20 minutes to walk to the closest beach. We didn't go there much as we were really disappointed, because it was dirty.

2 These expressions describe how easy or difficult something is. Put them in order from 'least difficult' to 'most difficult'.

> almost impossible   extremely challenging   not too difficult
> pretty easy   quite hard   totally impossible   very simple

TIP Adverbs of degree such as *pretty* (*good*) or *absolutely* (*amazing*) are often used in Part 3 texts to give information about the strength of an opinion or attitude.

3 Write sentences showing how you can use two of the expressions from Exercise 2 together in a sentence.

Example *For me, running a five-kilometre race in the park would be pretty hard, but running five kilometres through the mountains would be almost impossible!*

TIP You might be asked questions about what someone likes best or finds the most useful.

FOCUS: EXPRESSING COMPARATIVE AND SUPERLATIVE IDEAS

4 Look at the two paragraphs and underline all the positive comments. Which activity did each writer like best or find the most useful? How do you know?

1 At the leisure centre open day, I got to try different sports. The badminton courts were pretty good and the gym was fantastic. Above all, it was the fact that the staff were so welcoming that made our visit worth it.

2 The lecture on how wind power will change the way we heat and light our homes was better than I had expected. I also thought the film we saw on new environmentally friendly methods of growing food was extraordinary. But what has really changed how I think about the planet was watching a documentary about ice levels in the Arctic.

5 Write a sentence giving your opinion about situations 1–3. Use these expressions and your own ideas to show what you liked best or least.

> (That) was the most …   more than that, …   the biggest problem …
> what really helped more than anything was …   most of all,
> … was great / OK / not bad   I really loved …

1 going to a new café
2 learning a new skill
3 joining a new sports club

Example   *The biscuits were great, but the chocolate cake I had was the most delicious I've ever eaten!*

FOCUS: DECIDING WHY AN OPTION IS WRONG

6 Look at the question and options. Read the paragraph and choose the correct option. Underline the part of the text that gave you the answer. Decide why the other options are wrong.

> Gemma was so excited about going on the helicopter trip. She remembered how nervous she'd been the last time, but how much she'd loved it – so much, in fact, that she'd managed to persuade her best friend to join her, although that hadn't been particularly easy! The region she would fly over was known for having wildlife that was almost impossible to get close to on the ground. She therefore realised this flight might give her the only opportunity to see it. Although the company charged quite a bit for the trip, she was sure it would be worth it.

11 Why did Gemma decide to go for a helicopter ride?

A She wanted to see some animals.

B Her friend had recommended it to her.

C She was offered a special price for the ticket.

D She wanted to try something new.

7 In pairs, read this paragraph and the four options. The correct answer is D. What do you think the question is?

> I went to the cinema last night to see *The Blue River*. It's the film everyone's talking about, because they love the big surprise at the end, although I have to say, I guessed pretty early on what would happen! It was filmed in Scotland, in the mountains. It looked beautiful there – although in the film, it seemed to rain quite a lot. The lead actor was pretty good, although I'm not sure this was the best film for his style. It's funny, but actually the soundtrack was the thing that impressed me above all. I'm going to download it, I think.

11 ....?

A the acting

B the story

C the scenery

D the music

Questions 11–15

For each question, choose the correct answer.

Jacob Harvey
Lead singer with the band Mason

Fans always ask how Mason started. My guitar teacher knew I wanted to be in a band and said putting posters up at school to find musicians could help. The trouble was, I knew my classmates weren't into rock, like me. In the end, I heard about a band who'd recently stopped playing. The singer had moved away, so they couldn't practise. I messaged the drummer and the keyboard player. We did some songs together, and we've been together ever since. We've become close mates: me singing, Kath on drums and Victor on keyboards.

That was eight years ago. Our audiences have increased, and we play in bigger places. We still do concerts in our home town, though, on every tour – that's important to us. I still get nervous before a concert, but once I'm on stage I feel fine. Sometimes things go wrong, but that's OK! And being in front of an audience improves our performance. The atmosphere's incredible, with everyone videoing their favourite songs on their phones!

We've recently met Gary Keen from rock band The 45s. He took us round his studio and let us record our song *Days* there! He stayed to listen and made some interesting suggestions. He even promised to take a copy to a meeting he was having with an international music company! And he's put a link to us on his on his social media. More than anything, that's what's got even more people talking about us, and it's what really changes things.

People sometimes want advice about being in a band. Well, when you get more well-known, people start offering to manage you. Don't do anything you don't want to do; don't worry about doing things yourself; it's better than being with the wrong person. You need to get your music heard, though. Giving away tickets to shows is a good way to do this. Just remember to develop your own style and be original. And maybe one day, you'll get recognised in the street! The first time that happened was amazing! And we're very happy to be in photos and chat with people. We're nothing without our fans, after all!

11 How did Jacob find people for his band?

    A He invited musicians from another band to play with him.

    B He teacher suggested a band to join.

    C He put a notice up on his school noticeboard.

    D He chose musicians who were already his friends.

Advice

Even when you are sure you have the right answer, it's a good idea to spend a little time double-checking that the other options are wrong.

12 What does Jacob say about playing music to an audience?

    A Going on stage gets easier each time.

    B Making mistakes is very embarrassing.

    C Doing a live show makes the band play better.

    D Seeing people recording the songs is annoying.

13 What did Jacob find most useful about meeting a famous musician?

    A Gary included some information about the band online.

    B Gary introduced Jacob to a new contact in the music business.

    C Jacob got help to finish writing a song.

    D Gary let them use his music studio.

14 Jacob's advice to other young bands is to

    A create a website to advertise yourselves.

    B let people see you play for free.

    C get a manager as soon as you can.

    D follow the latest trends in music.

15 What would fans of Mason say about the band?

A
> I love that all the members have great voices – it's good that they all have a chance to sing, not just Jacob!

B
> I live in the band's home town. I wish they'd play here when they're on tour – they stopped doing that as soon as they got famous!

C
> *Days* is my favourite song – I loved that the lead singer of The 45s sang on it too!

D
> The fact that Mason are always willing to talk to their fans is great. It shows they think we're important to them.

- What kind of text do you have to read?
- How many sentences are missing from the text?

GRAMMAR: LINKERS OF CONTRAST

1 Which sentences follow on best? Match sentences 1–4 with sentences a–d.

1	There are many months which are very hot and dry.	**a**	But the artist has been very successful, with exhibitions in over 20 countries.
2	The results weren't what the scientists hoped for.	**b**	However, this didn't happen and, in fact, the judges gave her second prize.
3	Everyone said that it would be impossible to make a living from painting.	**c**	Despite this, some plants still manage to grow with almost no rain at all.
4	Katie was convinced she would do badly in the competition.	**d**	Although this was a disappointment, they refused to give up and decided to do more experiments.

2 In pairs, write new sentences (or parts of sentences) to continue sentences 1–3.
Use the linkers of contrast in Exercise 1 (*although, but, despite this, however*).

1 The weather forecast was for sun and showers …

2 The friends thought they would never be able to climb the steep hill …

3 We had hardly any time to work on our presentations …

VOCABULARY: IDENTIFYING TOPIC CONNECTIONS

3 Look again at the sentences in Exercise 1. Which words in each pair of sentences are either paraphrases or connected by topic?

4 Work in pairs. Think of words which might appear in sentences about these topics or ideas.

> animals   education   fitness   the environment

GRAMMAR: PRONOUNS AND DETERMINERS

Remember

It is important to check for reference words like *it* or *they* and singular/plural agreement between the text and the options.

5 Complete the paragraph using the words from the box.

> its   their   them   these   they   this

People go to the beach for windsurfing and sailing. **(1)** .... sorts of activities have been popular for many years. Particularly in the summer months, there are lots of visitors to the area. Local business owners are always very happy to see **(2)** .... One of the most popular places **(3)** .... stay in is the Grand Hotel. **(4)** .... central location is perfect for visiting all the major sites of the city and also the beaches. With **(5)** .... beautiful sand and warm water, **(6)** .... are very popular with hotel guests and easy to reach on foot.

Questions 16–20

Five sentences have been removed from the text below. For each question, choose the correct answer.
There are three extra sentences which you do not need to use.

An incredible journey

A small boat built by high school students from the American state of New Hampshire has made an incredible journey. The boat, around 1.5 metres in length, is called *Rye Riptides*. The adventure started when a teacher at Rye Junior High School ordered a kit for a project to make a boat. The kit was supplied by a company called Educational Passages, which aims to use boat-building projects to develop children's interest in science and technology. **16** [ ] For example, because the kit includes technology which sends information about the boat's position back to a computer, they learned about how waves move around the oceans.

The students spent two years making the boat, and also chose items to send with it on its journey. **17** [ ] The hope was that anyone finding the boat later would be interested in seeing things like these from another country. After students had some help from Educational Passages, the boat was ready to start its journey. The students were very excited. Some believed it would reach European shores. **18** [ ] At first, they were able to follow *Rye Riptides* as it moved across the Atlantic Ocean and marked the route on a map.

Then, in September 2021, *Rye Riptides* stopped sending a signal. The students knew that there were huge waves in the Atlantic Ocean. **19** [ ] But this wasn't what happened. Only a few months later, another signal was received. *Rye Riptides* had landed on Smøla Island off the coast of Norway. Educational Passages helped again, using social media to contact a local school.

A boy called Karel Nuncic saw her message. Karel went to Smøla Island and found the boat. **20** [ ] Luckily, though, the objects the students had put inside were safe, and Karel took the boat back to show his classmates. The two groups of students have since connected online, making friends and learning about new cultures.

A   It was covered in small sea creatures and badly damaged.

B   The result was exactly what the students wanted.

C   These included photos and coins that were placed inside.

D   Others, however, were not so sure.

E   It hasn't been easy to decide what they should do.

F   At the same time, it helps increase their understanding of the oceans.

G   Despite this, the boat had travelled a huge distance.

H   They thought that these had destroyed the boat.

Advice

Even if you might be sure that you have already used an option in the right place, checking each one (A–H) as you work through is a good idea, so you can be absolutely sure that you're right.

Advice

As well as the overall meaning of the text, you can use certain clues to check that the option you have chosen is correct. Examples are words such as this and these, and pronouns such as it and they.

- What kind of text do you have to read?
- What do you have to do with the text?

VOCABULARY: PHRASAL VERBS

1   Complete sentences 1–7 with phrasal verbs. For each sentence, use one word from each box. Remember to make sure the phrasal verb is grammatically correct.

base	break	go	put	run	stay	take	throw

behind	for	off	on	out	up

1   I wanted to make a cake, but I realised I'd .... of eggs.
2   My sister has just .... the violin. She says it's quite hard.
3   The teacher asked us to .... after the lesson and help with a display.
4   My brother has .... all the clothes that he didn't want any more.
5   The sports coach has asked if anyone wants to join the team. I'm going to .... it!
6   I saw a film about a couple who .... It was so sad! It was .... a true story.
7   We had to .... our shopping trip because we were too busy.

VOCABULARY: FIXED PHRASES

2   Complete the fixed phrase in bold in each sentence.
1   I knew I had .... **the answer wrong** when I checked with my friend.
2   My best friend and I .... **a lot in common**.
3   **There's no** .... that she will win the race. She's so fast!
4   I really **couldn't** .... **my eyes** when I saw the size of the pizza!
5   If you don't get a ticket for the concert soon, you'll .... **the chance** to see one of the best singers in the world!
6   I really **don't** .... **like** going out tonight.
7   I know I said I was hungry, but I've .... **my mind**.
8   As long as I .... **my best**, I know that's all that matters.

GRAMMAR: DEPENDENT PREPOSITIONS

3   Some adjectives, nouns and verbs are followed by a dependent preposition. Complete each sentence with one preposition.
1   My brother is afraid .... spiders, but I'm not.
2   I'm so excited .... seeing the new *Mystery 7* film – I can't wait!
3   The difference .... you and me is that you think video games are boring, but I love them.
4   I worry .... eating too much ice cream and cake.
5   As a result .... the football team's hard work, they won the tournament.

Advice

Reading through the whole text before you look at the options will help you get a good general understanding of what it's about.

Questions 21–26

For each question, choose the correct answer.

Ancient Chinese Art

Ancient China is known for its important inventions, including paper, silk and tea. As the culture is over 8,000 years old, it is perhaps no (21) .... that Ancient China is also famous for creating wonderful art. One example is 'calligraphy', the name given to producing beautiful pieces of writing by hand. Once someone had decided to (22) .... up

calligraphy, years of practice were required before they became an expert. Drawing each part of a letter had to follow a special order, and the final piece of work had to be completely (23) ....

Another important type of art from Ancient China is painting. The paintings produced were often of the countryside and often (24) .... of scenes including birds, fish, water or trees. The pictures were also painted in a wide (25) .... of sizes, and in important buildings like palaces, a painting might even (26) .... a whole wall!

21	A	reason	B	idea	C	surprise	D	argument
22	A	bring	B	take	C	set	D	put
23	A	proper	B	exact	C	true	D	accurate
24	A	belonged	B	included	C	consisted	D	contained
25	A	range	B	total	C	amount	D	quantity
26	A	hang	B	follow	C	cover	D	appear

Advice

The words in the four options will be linked in meaning, and will be the same sort of word, for example, all verbs or all adjectives.

- What kind of text do you have to read?
- How is this part different from Reading Part 5?

GRAMMAR: AUXILIARY VERBS

1 Underline the auxiliary verbs in these examples of different tenses.

1 present simple: *Where <u>do</u> you live?*
2 past simple: *I didn't see you at school yesterday.*
3 present continuous: *They are taking photos in the park.*
4 past continuous: *She wasn't waiting at the bus stop when I got there.*
5 present perfect: *She has been my best friend for five years.*
6 past perfect: *By the time we arrived, the film had started.*

> **Remember**
>
> If the word you have chosen is an auxiliary verb, you can use a contraction, such as *(I)'m, (we)'ve, (he)'s*. You don't have to use the full form of the verb.

2 Write example sentences in these tenses using the verbs given.

1 present simple negative: *don't care*
2 present continuous question: *applying*
3 present perfect statement: *visited*
4 past simple question: *forget*
5 past continuous negative: *listening*
6 past perfect statement: *eaten*

1 **Example** *I don't care if the water's cold – I want to swim!*

GRAMMAR: USING DEFINITE AND INDEFINITE ARTICLES

◉ *B1 Preliminary* candidates often make mistakes with articles.

> **Remember**
>
> Many fixed phrases use articles, e.g. *on the other hand, at the moment, by the way, as a result, quite a few.*

3 In pairs, decide why the definite article *(the)* is used in these examples.

1 **A:** I saw a great film yesterday.
  B: Oh really? What was the film about?
2 My music teacher is one of the best guitar players I know.
3 The Pacific is the biggest ocean.
4 I looked into the sky and saw the moon shining brightly.
5 The player who has scored the most goals this season is Jon Robertson.
6 The French are always described as being very good chefs.
7 I had to go to the post office before work.
8 The brain is an incredible machine.
9 I always get the bus to school.

4 Complete the text with *a* or *the*.

I live in **(1)** .... small town. In **(2)** .... town, we have lots of things for young people to do. For example, **(3)** .... park is really lovely and because it's in **(4)** .... centre, it's always busy. It's got **(5)** .... small café, where everyone goes to get ice cream. There are other places in town that sell ice cream, but **(6)** .... ones from the café in **(7)** .... park are **(8)** .... most delicious. **(9)** .... owner of the café is a friend of my dad's, and he often lets me have one for free!

Advice

When you have completed the text, read it all again to check it makes sense. Make sure your spelling is correct too.

Questions 27–32

For each question, write the correct word. Write **one** word for each gap.

Hi Johann,

I really need your help with the history homework that Mr Wilson gave us **(27)** .... few days ago. I really need to start it. I **(28)** .... been too busy to think about it until now, I'm afraid! Mr Wilson said it might be a good idea to go through our ideas with a friend before we start doing any work on the project. What **(29)** .... you think? I know it would be really helpful to show you what I'm planning. I can look at yours too **(30)** .... you think that could be useful. **(31)** .... you know, out of all our school subjects, history is **(32)** .... one I like most, so I really want to do my best!

Let me know, and we can arrange a time, OK?

Harvey

- What kind of text do you have to write?
- How do you know what to write about?

FOCUS: UNDERSTANDING THE TASK

1 Read the exam instructions and the email below. Then answer questions 1–4.

1 Who has written to you?

2 What is the email about?

3 How many notes are there?

4 How long should your email be?

Read this email from your English teacher and the notes you have made.

✉ **EMAIL**

From: Ms Shipton

Subject: Helping a charity

Dear Students

I have some exciting news – we are going to support a charity this term! Could you please tell me which type of charity we should help? → Great!

← Tell Ms Shipton

I want to organise a fun activity for a charity that other students will pay to take part in. We'll then give the money to the charity. We could have a cake decorating contest or a disco. Which do you think would be best? → Explain

I want to advertise what we are doing for charity, so that lots of people will take part. How can you help share this information?

← Offer to …

Bye for now,
Ms Shipton

Write your **email** to Ms Shipton using **all the notes**. Write your answer in about **100 words**.

FOCUS: UNDERSTANDING THE NOTES

2 Work in pairs. Match the notes from the email in Exercise 1 (1–4) with the example sentences (a–d). How could you finish the sentences?

1 Great!

2 Tell Ms Shipton

3 Explain

4 Offer to …

a Some kind of contest would be a good idea because …

b I'd be very happy to …

c Perhaps we should support one that helps …

d I think this idea is …

FOCUS: STUDYING A SAMPLE ANSWER

3 Read the sample reply to Ms Shipton. Then answer questions 1–4.

> Dear Ms Shipton,
>
> I think helping a charity this term is an extremely good idea. Although there are many different types of charities to choose from, I think we should support one that helps animals.
>
> I believe having a disco is the best idea because lots of people will want to buy tickets to go to a dance. In my opinion, a cake decorating contest sounds a bit boring.
>
> Perhaps you could design some really cool posters to put around town, so people can see what the school is planning to do for the charity.
>
> Best wishes,
> Kerry

1 Did Kerry cover all four notes?

2 Is Kerry's reply email the correct length?

3 How could Kerry's reply email be better?

4 Is Kerry's email in formal or informal language? Find examples.

FOCUS: INFORMAL AND FORMAL STYLE

4 Does the writer of the email in Exercise 1 use formal or informal language? Find examples.

5 Which phrases (1–6) would be appropriate to start or end an email to Ms Shipton?

1 Hello!

2 All the best

3 Hey, Ms Shipton!

4 See you later

5 Dear Ms Shipton

6 Cheers

6 Which sentences (1–8) would be appropriate in a formal email?

1 Supporting a charity's such a cool idea!

2 I am very happy that our school is going to help a charity.

3 Perhaps we could support a children's charity.

4 I think it'd be awesome if we helped an environmental charity!

5 A disco would be amazing, don't you think?

6 In my view, more people would take part in a cake decorating contest.

7 I think it would be better to have a disco.

8 I could make some short videos about the event to post online.

> **Remember**
>
> Make sure you think about the person you are writing to in your reply. Decide if your email should be formal or informal, and include an appropriate greeting (*Dear/Hi* …) and an appropriate ending (*Kind regards/Bye*).

GRAMMAR: GRADABLE MODIFIERS

7 Order these words or phrases from weakest to strongest.

| a bit | a little | extremely | fairly | pretty | really | very |

1 a little / ....

2 .... / ....

3 .... / ....

4 ....

You **must** answer this question.

Write your answer in about **100 words** on the answer sheet.

Advice

Always read the email carefully to help you decide if your reply should be formal or informal. If the email is from an English-speaking teacher, write a formal reply. If the email is from a friend, write an informal reply.

Question 1

Read this email from your English teacher and the notes you have made.

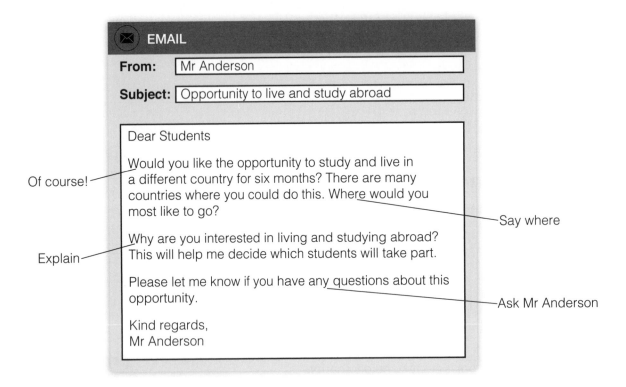

EMAIL

From: Mr Anderson

Subject: Opportunity to live and study abroad

Dear Students

Would you like the opportunity to study and live in a different country for six months? There are many countries where you could do this. Where would you most like to go?

Of course!

Say where

Why are you interested in living and studying abroad? This will help me decide which students will take part.

Explain

Please let me know if you have any questions about this opportunity.

Ask Mr Anderson

Kind regards,
Mr Anderson

Write your **email** to Mr Anderson using **all the notes**.

Advice

Write down some rough ideas beside each note to include in your email. Always check for any spelling or grammar errors in your final draft.

- How many texts do you need to write in Part 2?
- What kinds of task will you have to choose from?

Remember

Using linking expressions will help you to avoid writing short, simple sentences with only one idea in them.

GRAMMAR: LINKING EXPRESSIONS

1 **Complete the sentences with these linking expressions.**

and	as	because	so	when

1 My friend was upset .... I hadn't remembered her birthday.
2 I didn't have enough money .... I didn't go to the concert.
3 .... I wanted to get some exercise, I went to the park.
4 Adam was starting to feel nervous .... I tried to make him feel calm. It didn't work.
5 .... I got to the airport, I realised I had left my passport with me.

2 **Match the linking expressions in Exercise 1 with these functions.**

1 used to say at what time something happened or will happen
2 used to join words or ideas of a similar kind together
3 used for introducing the reason for something
4 used for introducing the result of something

Remember

We can use a range of past tenses in stories to make it clear what happened, when and for how long. Do this in your writing to show that you know a range of structures.

GRAMMAR: PAST TENSES

👁 *B1 Preliminary* candidates often make mistakes with past forms.

3 **Look at the sentences in Exercise 1. What past tenses are used?**

4 **Match the tenses (1–3) with the correct functions (a–c).**

1 past simple
2 past perfect
3 past continuous

a used to show an action that happened before another action in the past
b used to show an action that is unfinished in the past
c used to show a completed action in a time before now

5 **Complete the story with the correct past tense form of these verbs.**

asked	finish	make	manage	suggest	take	work

I have always admired how well my grandad knits things out of wool – particularly his jumpers. A few months ago, I **(0)** <u>asked</u> him to show me how to knit something fairly easy. He **(1)** .... that I start by knitting a plain scarf, which I **(2)** .... still .... on until last weekend. Ever since I **(3)** .... knitting it, I have worn it to school. I'm really pleased with what I **(4)** .... to achieve as I **(5)** .... never .... anything like this before! However, all my friends now want me to knit them something! They don't seem to realise how long it **(6)** .... me to knit my scarf!

FOCUS: CONTRASTING IDEAS

6 Match these linking expressions (1–4) with the correct information (a–b).

1 although

2 despite   **a** After this word or phrase, we can use a gerund.

3 in spite of   **b** After this word or phrase, we use a subject and a verb.

4 even though

7 Choose the correct word or phrase in each sentence.

1 *Despite / Although* spending months on my invention, it still wouldn't work!

2 I was confident I would be ready, *in spite of / even though* the competition was tomorrow.

3 I was nervous about entering my robot into the competition, *in spite of / even though* being proud of it.

4 I enjoyed learning how to build a robot, *although / despite* I would have liked a bit more time.

FOCUS: UNDERSTANDING THE TASK

8 Look at the exam task below and decide which sentences are true (T) or false (F).

1 You can include the sentence anywhere in your story.   T / F

2 Your story is meant for your English teacher.   T / F

3 Your story must be at least 100 words.   T / F

Write your answer in about **100 words** on the answer sheet.

Your English teacher has asked you to write a story. Your story must begin with this sentence:
I decided to build a robot for the science competition.
Write your **story**.

FOCUS: STUDYING A SAMPLE ANSWER

9 Complete the story with the correct expressions from Exercise 6.

I decided to build a robot for the science competition. First, I began by researching how to build one that could dance to music **(1)** .... I had never invented anything before. I really enjoyed the challenge **(2)** .... choosing something complicated to build. However, the night before the competition, my robot still wasn't working, so I was pretty worried! By the next morning, I had fixed my robot, so it danced whenever I played music! I was fairly nervous about showing it to the judges **(3)** .... I was extremely proud of what I had achieved. When they saw it dancing, they all smiled and asked me loads of questions.

10 Look at the story in Exercise 9 again and answer these questions.

1 What time linkers does the writer use?

2 Find examples of the past simple, the past continuous and the past perfect.

Choose **one** of these questions.

Write your answer in about **100 words** on the answer sheet.

....

Question 2

You see this notice on an English website for young people.

> **Articles wanted!**
>
> **WORLD NEWS**
>
> Where do you like to get your news from?
>
> Do you think knowing what is happening in the world is important? Why?
>
> The best articles answering these questions will appear on our website.

Advice

Try not to repeat the same words as in the article. Think of other words and phrases that have a similar meaning.

Write your **article**.

Question 3

Your English teacher has asked you to write a story. Your story must begin with this sentence.

I was so excited when I arrived at the music festival.

Write your **story**.

Advice

Always check your writing after you have finished, for spelling or grammar mistakes.

- What kind of texts do you listen to in Part 1?
- What do you have to do while listening?

VOCABULARY: HOLIDAYS AND ENTERTAINMENT

1 Match the activities 1–8 with the sentences a–h.

1	eating in a restaurant	a	I had a seat by the window.
2	visiting a museum	b	The sand was very hot.
3	lying on the beach	c	The match was very exciting, but we lost in the end.
4	playing volleyball	d	All the fans were singing at the same time.
5	going to a concert	e	The Roman statues were enormous.
6	going to the cinema	f	I sent him a postcard from the island.
7	writing to a friend	g	The soup was delicious, but a little cold.
8	travelling by plane	h	My favourite ones are action with a bit of comedy.

2 Complete the sentences with these words.

cap	flight	keyboard	meal	score	soundtrack	shop	voice

1 She managed to .... in the final minute, so her team won.
2 I forgot my ...., so I got a headache from the sun.
3 His .... is late, so he'll miss his connection.
4 Does the .... close early on Sundays?
5 We had a tasty .... for a good price.
6 The girl playing the .... was very talented.
7 Sending a .... message is easier than writing a text.
8 I like listening to the .... from my favourite movies.

> **Remember**
>
> The word *close* is pronounced in two ways. /klauz/ is a verb meaning the opposite of *open*. /klaus/ is an adjective meaning *near*.

3 Listen to the conversation. Which activity did the girl enjoy most? Choose the correct picture.

A

B

C

FOCUS: EXPRESSING POSITIVE AND NEGATIVE IDEAS

4 Match each sentence (1–4) with two sentences from a–h. They should show they are not true.

1 I could understand everything he said.
2 The cinema was very crowded.
3 I had a good day sightseeing in the city.
4 There were plenty of parking spaces.

a I didn't see anything interesting.
b I didn't catch his words.
c Not many people were there.
d It was difficult to park there.
e I only had time to go to one museum.
f He spoke too fast for me.
g There weren't enough places to leave the car.
h There was no one watching the film.

5 Complete the conversations with these words. Then listen and check your answers.

23

| anywhere | didn't | don't | enough |
| nobody | none | not | too |

1 I tried on three dresses, but .... of them fitted me.
2 I quite liked diving, but I .... want to do it again in the future.
3 I couldn't find my book .... in the classroom.
4 It was .... cold to stay outside.
5 My camera's .... working, so I'll leave it at home.
6 I fell on the street, but .... helped me.
7 I haven't got .... money to get the bus.
8 We .... need to buy a ticket because the concert was free.

Remember

When we use a negative word, the main verb is affirmative (e.g. *he found nothing* or *he didn't find anything*).

6 Listen to the conversation. Where did the girl find her phone? Choose the correct picture.

24

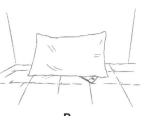

A   B   C

Advice

Don't choose the first option you hear. Listen carefully for negative and positive words and ideas.

Questions 1–7

25

For each question, choose the correct answer.

1 How did Jackson break his arm?

A

B

C

2 Which film are they going to see?

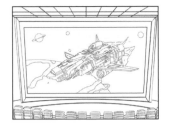

A

B

C

3 What does Martha lend her friend?

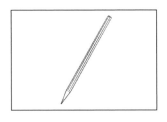

A

B

C

Advice

(3) Which things do the friends need? What is the girl going to give the boy? Which thing does she want him to give back?

4 Who is going to pick the boy up after the match?

A

B

C

5 How did the boy manage to contact his friend?

A

B

C

6 Why can't the girl go to the party?

A

B

C

7 Which place did Jacob most enjoy visiting on his trip?

A

B

C

Advice

(7) Did the boy go to all three places in the pictures? What did he think about the restaurants? Which place was best?

- What kind of texts do you listen to in Part 2?
- What do you have to do while listening?

VOCABULARY: IDENTIFYING HOW PEOPLE FEEL

Remember

Adjectives with -*ed* show feelings, e.g. *I'm disappointed*. Adjectives with -*ing* describe something, e.g. *The show was disappointing*.

1 Choose the correct option.

1 I was *sad / delighted* when I got the *shocking / shocked* news.
2 She's so *unreliable / reliable*. I can't trust her to arrive on time.
3 The skydiving was so *exciting / excited*. It was *fun / funny*.
4 He was really *cross / dull* when I broke his camera.
5 I'm *ashamed / nasty* I didn't tell you the truth, but I was *worried / worrying* about hurting you.

2 Listen and match these adjectives with how each speaker (1–8) is feeling.

26

| annoyed | confused | disappointed | exhausted | jealous | nervous | proud | relieved |

1 ....   5 ....
2 ....   6 ....
3 ....   7 ....
4 ....   8 ....

FOCUS: UNDERSTANDING THE SPEAKER'S INTENTION

3 Match the sentences (1–7) to the intentions (a–g).

1 I think you should try playing a team sport.
2 I'm tired of having to walk to school every day.
3 I'm really sorry I didn't give your book back.
4 I'd love you to come to my party at the weekend.
5 What do you think about that new game?
6 May I sit in this seat?
7 Shall I hold your bag while you take the photo?

a inviting
b apologising
c offering
d giving advice
e asking for an opinion
f asking for permission
g complaining

4 Listen to the speakers. Match each speaker with an intention (a–g) in Exercise 3.

27

Speaker 1 ....
Speaker 2 ....
Speaker 3 ....
Speaker 4 ....

5 Listen and choose the correct option.

28

You hear two friends talking about homework. The boy

A advises the girl to study harder.
B offers to help the girl.
C apologises for not helping the girl.

TIP

Listen carefully to how the speakers express their ideas. The way they say something can help you understand their intention.

Questions 8–13

29 For each question, choose the correct answer.

8 You will hear a boy telling his friend about a clothes shop.
The boy complains that
A   the shop is too crowded.
B   the staff are unfriendly.
C   there is little choice of clothes.

9 You will hear two friends talking about a train journey.
The boy thinks
A   it was interesting.
B   it was unusual.
C   it was comfortable.

10 You will hear two friends talking about making a presentation.
The friends agree
A   it'll take a long time.
B   it'll be difficult to do.
C   it'll improve their marks.

11 You will hear a girl telling her friend about helping at home.
The boy thinks the girl should
A   discuss the situation with her parents.
B   make an excuse to avoid having to help.
C   persuade her brother to do something.

12 You will hear a girl telling her friend about a tennis match.
Why was she happy?
A   She won the match.
B   She pleased her coach.
C   She played perfectly.

13 You will hear two friends talking about a new film.
Why is the boy planning to see it?
A   A friend recommended it.
B   He read good reviews of it.
C   He wants to learn something.

- What kind of text do you listen to in Part 3?
- What do you have to do while listening?

FOCUS: TOPIC VOCABULARY

1 Listen to five people. Match what each person is talking about with the speakers.

30

Speaker 1	a club
Speaker 2	a competition
Speaker 3	a hobby
Speaker 4	a trip
Speaker 5	a website

TIP In this part of the test, you will hear information about trips, clubs, jobs, competitions, places to visit, etc.

2 Listen again and choose the correct option.

30

1 The club has *50 / 80* members.
2 The bus left at *8.00 / 9.30*.
3 The website is for people who are interested in *photography / writing*.
4 She's been making models for *6 / 10* years.
5 The first prize is a *helmet / sweatshirt*.

FOCUS: DISTRACTORS

3 Match the answer options (a–d) with the questions (1–4).

1 When is the swimming competition?
2 Where do they go running?
3 Where do they have to meet?
4 What's the name of the poem that won first prize?

a *Yellow Sun / The Cave / Tall Trees*
b in a stadium / in the countryside / in a gym
c Friday evening / Sunday morning / Saturday afternoon
d in a car park / at a gate / in front of a shop

TIP You'll hear several possible options. Listen carefully to decide which one answers the question.

4 Listen and decide which option answers the questions from Exercise 3.

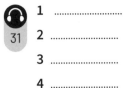

31

1 ....
2 ....
3 ....
4 ....

Questions 14–19

32 For each question, write the correct answer in the gap.
Write **one** or **two words** or a **number** or a **date** or a **time**.

Advice

In this part of the test, you'll hear the information in the same order as the questions. If you miss a piece of information, don't worry. Listen carefully for it the second time.

You will hear a teacher talking about taking part in a science fair.

School science fair

The last date for applications is **(14)** ....

This year, the topic of the fair is **(15)** ....

There will be a prize called **(16)** ....

All the team members will receive a **(17)** ....

The **(18)** .... of the team has to put the team members' names on the website.

Website to apply to take part in the fair:
(19) www. .... .com

Advice

(14) How many different ways can you say a date in English, such as 22/6?

Advice

(17) What did the students make last year? What will the organisers give everyone this year?

- What kind of text do you listen to in Part 4?
- What do you have to do while listening?

VOCABULARY: TECHNOLOGY

1 Match the words with the items in the picture.

headphones	keyboard	microphone	mouse
mouse mat	printer *1*	screen	

2 Listen and decide which of the objects in Exercise 1 the people are having problems with.

33

1 ....   3 ....

2 ....   4 ....

GRAMMAR: FUTURE PLANS

👁 *B1 Preliminary* candidates often make mistakes with future forms.

3 Decide if the underlined word is about the present (P) or the future (F).

1 We're really <u>enjoying</u> the party. Thanks for inviting us. P / F

2 I'd like to try <u>snowboarding</u> next time. P / F

3 She's <u>flying</u> to Hawaii at 6 o'clock. P / F

4 I'm going to take up <u>singing</u>. P / F

5 They're <u>having</u> a wonderful time. P / F

> **TIP** In this part of the test, the speakers often talk about their future plans. Listen carefully for references to future times.

4 Listen and choose the correct option.

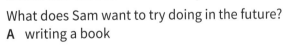
34

What does Sam want to try doing in the future?

A writing a book

B visiting new places

C creating a blog

Advice

Before you listen, find the key words in the question and the options.

🎧 **Questions 20–25**

35 For each question, choose the correct answer.

....

You will hear an interview with a young man called Jake, who works as a sound engineer in a music studio.

20 How did Jake get the job in the studio?

   A by working for free

   B by asking a friend's father

   C by studying the business

21 Jake thinks the most interesting thing about his job now is

   A meeting well-known people.

   B using modern techniques.

   C helping other people.

Advice

(21) What did he do when he first started working in the studio? And now? What word does he use to say something is really interesting? Does he often meet famous people?

22 What happened when Jake met a famous singer?

   A He didn't give her the correct gift.

   B He didn't understand her music.

   C He didn't recognise her at first.

23 What does Jake find difficult about his job?

   A the kind of people he works with

   B the long hours he has to work

   C the problems he has with equipment

24 In the future, Jake wants

   A to set up music events.

   B to work in a studio in a city.

   C to become a professional musician.

Advice

(24) What does he say he'd like to try? Does he want to play the drums as a job?

25 What advice does Jake give about finding work in the music business?

   A He recommends going to college first.

   B He suggests posting music online.

   C He says it's important to be patient.

TIP Every candidate has to answer questions about what their name is, how old they are and where they live. Make sure you know how to say these things.

- Who will you talk to in Part 1 of the test?
- What kind of questions will you answer?

1   **Match the people (1–3) with their roles in the speaking test (a–c).**

1 candidate

2 assessor

3 interlocutor

a This person asks the questions during the test.

b This person takes the test and answers the questions.

c This person listens to the test and gives the marks. They do not speak.

FOCUS: COMMON QUESTIONS

2   **Listen and complete a student's answers to some common questions.**

36

1 It's a .... school with a thousand students. It has a ...., some science labs and a big ....

2 My .... friend usually comes to my .... after school. Sometimes we go .... in the park.

3 My sister is a .... years older than me, but we get on .... She likes swimming and ....

4 I love playing .... in the school team, and I read a lot. I enjoy .... too.

5 I've .... English for three years. I think the .... Is difficult, but I like learning about grammar.

6 Actually, I really like .... and I often help my parents in the .... Home-made .... is the best!

7 I can't .... Oh, yes! I went to my cousin's .... It was a .... birthday because he's 21!

3   **Look at the answers in Exercise 2. In pairs, discuss what questions the student was asked.**

4   **Listen and write what the interlocutor says.**

37

1 ....

2 ....

3 ....

4 ....

5 ....

6 ....

7 ....

TIP In Part 1 Phase 2, try not to give very short answers. You can give examples of your experiences, for example.

5   **Now ask and answer the questions in Exercise 4 with a partner.**

TIP If you get stuck or can't think of anything to say, don't worry. The interlocutor will ask the question in another way to help you or move on to another question.

(2–3 minutes)

Phase 1
Interlocutor

To A/B	Good morning / afternoon / evening. Can I have your mark sheets, please? *(Hand over the mark sheets to the assessor.)*
To A/B	I'm .... and this is ....
To A	What's your name? How old are you? Thank you.
To B	And what's your name? How old are you? Thank you.
To B	**B**, where do you live? Thank you.
To A	And **A**, where do you live? Thank you.

Phase 2
Interlocutor

(The interlocutor may ask you one or more questions similar to the following.)

Tell us about a teacher you like.

How often do you practise English?

What do you do at the weekends when the weather is bad?

Which TV programmes do you enjoy watching? (Why?)

Who would you most like to meet? (Why?)

Do you like watching action films? (Why? / Why not?)

How long do you spend on your phone each day?

What are you going to do this evening?

Advice

Practise talking about your free time, studies, hobbies and so on before the exam. This will help you answer the questions more easily and confidently.

 Listen to two students answering the questions above.

38

- What do you need to talk about in Part 2?
- How long will you talk for?

FOCUS: DESCRIBING PHOTOS

1   Work in pairs. Look at photograph A below (see colour version on page C10) and describe it. Use some of these prompts in the box. Take turns to say one sentence each.

I can see …	In the background, there's / there are …	It looks …	It might be …	The weather is …
There are ….	There's …	They are in …	They look like they are …	They're …	They're wearing …

A

B

FOCUS: SAYING WHERE THINGS ARE

2   Look at these words and phrases of position. Complete the sentences about photograph B (see colour version on page C10) using the phrases in the box.

In the foreground / At the front   In the background / Behind / Beyond
On the right / On the left / In the middle
To the right of the photo / To the left of the photo

TIP Only describe what you can see in the photograph and try to give as much detail as possible. Keep talking until the interlocutor stops you.

1   .... there is a girl who is standing on her hand.
2   There is a school building ....
3   The girls .... of the photos are watching the girl at the front.

3   Work in pairs. What else can you say about photograph B? Think about these things.

- what the people are doing
- how they are feeling
- what they are wearing
- where they are
- what the weather is like
- why they are doing this activity

Remember
Remember to use the present continuous to describe what people are doing/wearing.

4   Listen to a student describing photograph B. Did they say the same things you said? Did they say anything different? Do you think they described the photograph well? Why? / Why not?

39

Remember
If you aren't sure what people are doing, or what something is, you can say *It looks like / It looks …, I'm not sure what the word is, but it's used for …*, etc.

5   Listen again. What does the student say to fill in time when they aren't sure what to say next?

39

Advice

Try not to leave any silences when you are talking. Use 'fillers' such as What else can I see? What is he/she doing?

(3–5 minutes)

Interlocutor	Now I'd like each of you to talk on your own about something. I'm going to give each of you a photograph and I'd like you to talk about it. **A**, here is your photograph. It shows some people **travelling on public transport**.

The interlocutor will place Exam Practice Test 2 Speaking Part 2 picture (see page C1), in front of Candidate A.

	B, you just listen. **A**, please tell us what you can see in the photograph.
Candidate A	*(Approximately 1 minute)*
Interlocutor	Thank you.

Back-up prompts (for A and B)
- Talk about the person/people.
- Talk about the place.
- Talk about other things in the photograph.

Interlocutor	**B**, here is your photograph. It shows someone **helping someone else**.

The interlocutor will place Exam Practice Test 2 Speaking Part 2 picture (see page C2), in front of Candidate B.

Interlocutor	**A**, you just listen. **B**, please tell us what you can see in the photograph.
Candidate B	*(Approximately 1 minute)*
Interlocutor	Thank you.

   Listen to students talking about Photographs A, B and C. (See pages C1, C2 and C7.)

Remember

In this part of the test, the question will always include a superlative, for example *the best*, *the most useful*, *the most fun*. Remember to use *most* before long adjectives such as *interesting* or *helpful*.

- Who do you have to talk with in Part 3?
- What kinds of thing do you need to say or do?

FOCUS: GIVING AND ASKING FOR OPINIONS

1 Look at the words in the box. Work with a partner to make phrases and questions for giving opinions and asking for opinions. Write them down.

agree	idea	opinion	prefer	sure
think	what about	would		

2 Listen to Anh and Mathilde doing Part 3 of the Speaking test and complete the conversation. Do they use the phrases you wrote in Exercise 1? Do they use any different phrases?

43

Anh: So, we have to decide which thing would be most useful for a walking trip in the mountains. Let's start with the map. I think that's **(1)** ...., especially if you don't know where you're going. **(2)** ....

Mathilde: I do, but you shouldn't really set off up a mountain if you don't know the route. But I suppose people sometimes get lost. **(3)** ...., the phone's probably the best thing to take. Then if you do get lost, you can call for help.

Anh: **(4)** .... about that. There isn't always a good phone signal in the countryside.

Mathilde: Well, that's true. Shall we talk about the raincoat now? Is it **(5)** ....? I can't decide. I mean, it's useful to carry in your backpack, I suppose. **(6)** .... it's the most useful thing to take, though.

Anh: Me neither. **(7)** .... walking boots? They're very important.

Mathilde: Yes, I think they **(8)** .... very useful. If you've got good, comfortable boots, you can walk all day and avoid getting sore feet.

Anh: You're right. I think **(9)** .... have good walking boots than a torch. You shouldn't be walking in the dark! **(10)** ....?

Mathilde: **(11)** .... And everyone's phone has a torch on it, anyway. So, what shall we say is the most useful thing to take on a walking trip in the mountains? I think it's the walking boots.

Anh: Yes, **(12)** ....

3 Work in pairs. What do you think would be most useful to take on a long car journey? Discuss these four options.

- books and magazines
- a pillow and blanket
- a tablet or laptop
- a picnic

TIP There are no right or wrong answers in this part of the exam. Just give your own opinion and don't worry if it is different from your partner's.

TIP You won't lose any marks if you do not finish discussing all the pictures. Just keep talking until the interlocutor stops you.

Interlocutor

> Now, in this part of the test you're going to talk about something together for about two minutes. I'm going to describe a situation to you.

The interlocutor will place Exam Practice Test 2 Speaking Part 3 set of pictures (see page C12), in front of both candidates.

Interlocutor

> **A group of students want to improve their second-language skills.**
>
> **Here are some things they could do to practise their second-language skills.**
>
> **Talk together about the different things they could do to improve their second-language skills and say which would be best.**
>
> All right? Now talk together.

(Approximately 2–3 minutes)

Interlocutor

> Thank you.

 Listen to two students doing the task above.

44

Advice

Practise using phrases such as Let's start with …, Shall we discuss this now?. This will help you keep the conversation going and guide you and your partner through the task.

- Who do you talk to in this part of the test?
- What do you have to talk about?

FOCUS: QUESTION FORMS

1   Look at the topics. Write three questions about each one. Use some of these question words.

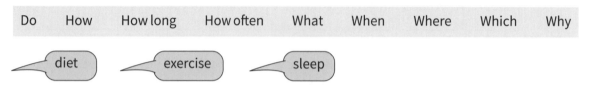

Do	How	How long	How often	What	When	Where	Which	Why

diet   exercise   sleep

2   Work in pairs. Take turns to ask and answer each other's questions.

3   In pairs, discuss the questions. Give reasons for your answers using some of these phrases.

Because	I doubt	In my opinion	It's a good idea	Personally	They should	Well

1   Do you think everyone should have eight hours' sleep a night?
2   Which form of exercise is better: swimming or walking?
3   How important is it to eat healthy food?
4   Do you like getting up early in the mornings?
5   How often do you think people should exercise?

Remember

Repeat the interlocutor's question or use 'fillers' to give you time to think if necessary. For example, you could use words and phrases such as *I'm not completely sure, but I think ...*, *That's a good question ...* or *Let me think ...* .

4   **Listen to two students answering some of the questions in Exercise 3. Complete the conversation with the words you hear.**

🎧 45

Interlocutor: How important is it to eat healthy food?

Girl: I think it's very important **(1)** .... it helps to prevent diseases. What do you think?

Boy: I agree. **(2)** .... to eat lots of fresh food and not have too much fat or salt. Those things can make you put on weight and make your blood pressure too high.

Interlocutor: How often do you think people should exercise?

Boy: Let me think ... **(3)** ...., I think they should do some exercise every day. It helps to keep you fit and it makes you feel better too.

TIP

Try not to do all the talking. It's important to give your partner the opportunity to speak as well. Make sure you each say an equal amount and encourage your partner to talk by asking questions if they are a little quiet.

Interlocutor: Which form of exercise is better, swimming or walking?

Girl: **(4)** ...., swimming is better because it exercises every part of the body. But walking's very good too.

Interlocutor: Do you think everyone should have eight hours' sleep a night?

Girl: No, I don't.

Interlocutor: Why not?

Girl: **(5)** ...., I read that between seven and nine hours is fine. **(6)** .... that everyone is the same, but as long as you get enough sleep, it doesn't matter how long you sleep for.

5   Do you think the students answered the questions well? Why? / Why not? Discuss your ideas with a partner.

(3–4 minutes)

Interlocutor
(to both candidates)

- Do you think English is a difficult language to learn? (Why? / Why not?)
- Would you like to learn another language? (Why? / Why not?)
- How do you feel when you are able to communicate with other English speakers?
- Why do you think it is important to learn other languages?
- Do you think everyone should learn another language from an early age? (Why? / Why not?)

Thank you. That is the end of the test.

46

Listen to two students discussing the questions above.

Advice

Give reasons for your answers. For example, to answer the question Do you think English is difficult to learn?, *you could say,* Yes, because the pronunciation of the words is not always similar to the spelling. *Alternatively, you could say,* No, in my opinion, English is easy to learn because the tenses are the same as they are in my first language.

Advice

Don't worry if you make some mistakes. Just carry on with the test.

Questions 1–5

For each question, choose the correct answer.

1

Jamal
If you've finished playing *Rider*, pass the game on to Rory, OK? He heard it's good so I promised he could have it next. It'll be quicker than returning it to me first!
Matt

A Matt wants Jamal to hurry up and finish playing a game.

B Matt wants Jamal to give a game directly to Rory.

C Matt wants Jamal to recommend a suitable game to play.

2

Sports centre activities

Free activity with every swimming session paid for!
See list for sports included in offer.
Hurry, limited places!

A Customers can choose any number of activities they like.

B A small number of customers can use the pool without paying.

C People wanting to take advantage of an offer must do so quickly.

3

Jenny

My guitar lesson's cancelled tomorrow. Let's meet in the park! I remember you have tennis at 9, so maybe after that? I'd like to try that ice cream place you said was good!

Sue

What is Sue doing in her text?

A giving a reason for meeting her friend Jenny tomorrow

B reminding Jenny about a change to a tennis lesson tomorrow

C suggesting that she and Jenny meet after a music lesson

4

New Message

To: Jon

About: History website

Thanks for telling me about that site – it helped me finish my project! I see what you mean about bits being rather confusing, but as you said, the diagrams were excellent.

Kenny

A Kenny wants Jon to help him complete his homework.

B Kenny agrees with Jon's opinion about some of the information.

C Kenny suggests Jon should include pictures as part of his project.

5

Jasmine

I'd like to borrow your calculator tomorrow – mine's not working!

If you're going out tonight, put it downstairs for me. I'm going to the cinema and I can't see it in your room!

David

A David hopes Jasmine can give back something he lent her.

B David needs Jasmine to tell him where to find some equipment.

C David wants Jasmine to leave something for him that he wants to use.

Questions 6–10

For each question, choose the correct answer.

The young people below all want to find a place to spend the day with a group of their friends.
On the opposite page there are reviews of eight places.
Decide which place would be the most suitable for the young people below.

 6      Jing wants to go somewhere where she can play football outside and where she and her friends can get bikes to ride. She'd like to do some cooking outdoors during the day too.

 7      Carlos hopes to take part in a team sports competition with his friends. He wants the place to have cover available if it rains, and his parents would rather not drive to the location.

 8      Ebba loves animals and wants to learn about different types, and how to make good drawings of them. Her parents want space to arrange a picnic lunch.

 9      Yusuf wants to do something with his friends connected to photography. He'd like to spend the day in an interesting building and to get to solve puzzles.

 10      Sheena doesn't like fast food, but wants a meal during her day. She'd like to do some singing with her friends and would like advice about putting on a really good performance.

Places for a day out with a group of friends

A   Adventure for All

This is a fascinating museum with displays on different subjects. It's also the perfect place for special days. Groups will love the 'escape room' – answer questions to find hidden keys and escape! There's also a list of the museum's rarest and most unusual objects – make teams and see who can take the best pictures!

B   Lomas Centre

A day out with a difference! For those coming by car, there's parking a kilometre away, then you catch a shuttle bus. Once you're there, you and your group will help an expert to look after some animals – buy photos of you all feeding penguins!

C   Fun Factory!

There's a huge hall here with plenty to do in bad weather, including volleyball courts with electronic systems to keep score. If you prefer to explore outside spotting wildlife, there are lots of nature tracks for walkers, so no bikes rushing past! The directions by road are clear, or the station's convenient too.

D   Bewley Hall

This place is great for groups of friends, as you'll write the words and music to make your own record! The staff are there to offer tips about creating a professional sound. Being creative is hungry work, and there's a wide range of healthy options on offer at the café.

E   Jack's Place

If a great day means playing sport, this might not be for you! But if you're interested in wildlife, you'll find out about some unusual examples. Then, with just a pencil and paper, you'll create something more interesting than a photo. Head to the tables by the lake if you're bringing refreshments and you want great views.

F   Newton Hollow

There's a mix of forest-based activities to entertain everyone – explore nature, whatever the weather! Those bringing bikes will find various paths, with places to stop and take perfect selfies! There's a café with hot food like pizzas, and an amazing range of ice creams for special treats too.

G   Action Hub

The place for creative teens! You'll need to go by car, although the car park's small and gets busy. There's a daily performance where musicians entertain you with songs from shows, making special memories of the day, and a photography exhibition of weird buildings – try and guess which country they come from!

H   Carley's Ground

The woods have lovely cycle routes – look out for deer! There are bicycles for hire, and you can even borrow a ball and use the pitches there. If you're hungry, choices include barbecuing your burgers in the woods for a picnic or buying snacks from the stall. Remember it's outdoors – pack suitable clothes in bad weather.

Questions 11–15

For each question, choose the correct answer.

River Cleaning Event
Report by Lily Hahn

I recently took part in an event called a River Clean, where volunteers collect rubbish from a river. I'd wanted to do one ever since I saw an online post from a school friend, describing one she'd done. Then one day, down near the river, there was a poster on the noticeboard providing details about a River Clean event. It included the phone number of the person setting it up so you could register your name. And that's what I did!

On the day, I went to the river and saw some people standing around. Despite the faces not being familiar, everyone looked friendly. Most had brought thick gloves, which the organisers had asked us to do if possible. I was pleased there were spare ones to borrow, as I realised I'd left mine at home. I'd been in a rush because I hadn't wanted to be late! We read through a list of instructions, and after being given the chance to ask questions, we started collecting.

I'm generally a sociable person, but once I started, I mostly worked in silence, probably because I had to focus so much. When we'd finished, despite there being only a small number of us, we'd filled four big trucks with rubbish. Unfortunately, I think it will keep appearing in the river in future, but seeing everything we'd removed in one place felt like an achievement and clearly showed the problem. I'd never imagined there'd be so much rubbish, and by far the most common sort was plastic packets.

We finished exactly at midday, and before we went home, we completed a short questionnaire about our top idea for solving the problem of rubbish in rivers. Everyone had useful ones, like providing more recycling bins – although I think people need to be taught to use them! There's lots of information about recycling in schools, but in people's homes, too much plastic often goes into general rubbish and can end up back in the water. Actually, though, I think that unless people start buying products that aren't wrapped in plastic, nothing we do will have an effect, even if we did a river clean weekly! So that's what I put.

11 How did Lily find out that the event was happening?

    A   from talking to someone she knew at school

    B   from speaking to the organisers

    C   from some information by the river

    D   from an advertisement on social media

12 When she arrived at the river, Lily

    A   recognised some of the other volunteers.

    B   found she'd forgotten some important equipment.

    C   listened to a talk about what she had to do.

    D   discovered the event had started without her.

13 How did Lily feel after the River Clean event?

    A   surprised by the amount of rubbish she found

    B   upset that there was still rubbish in the river

    C   amazed by the wide variety of rubbish she collected

    D   disappointed that so few people helped clean up the rubbish

14 Lily says the most important thing people can do is to

    A   teach their children to respect the environment.

    B   take part in river clean events regularly.

    C   use the bins at the river.

    D   change their shopping habits.

15 What would Lily write in a text to her friend?

    A

> I didn't like having to spend my time picking up other people's rubbish and I think I wasted my time.

    B

> I'm so glad I got to take part. It's not something I'd ever heard of before, and I think it's a great idea.

    C

> Everyone was just concentrating on their section of the river, so we didn't spend a lot of time chatting. Quite unusual for me!

    D

> The organisers are sending us a link for a form where we can suggest solutions to the problem. I think that's a good idea.

Questions 16–20

Five sentences have been removed from the text below. For each question, choose the correct answer.
There are three extra sentences which you do not need to use.

Andrew Edston: Young Chef

Andrew Edston is a 20-year-old chef with a great future. He recently won a competition called *The Future Chef*, for professional chefs in the part of the UK where he works. He's already taken part in various cooking contests but says this latest was the toughest. Even before it started, he knew he'd be competing against talented chefs. [16] As he explains, he always enters competitions convinced he's going to win!

Although competitions can be enjoyable, cooking contests are not always just for fun. Restaurant owners often enter their young chefs into competitions as part of their training. This is what happened to Andrew. In the kitchen at Garden Tastes, the restaurant where he works, he is usually in charge of one course. [17] Doing so has allowed him to gain important experience.

The people judging the food are usually top food industry experts, which is extremely useful. Andrew gets to present his food to important people and hear their comments on every dish. [18] In fact, in the restaurant, it's more likely that customers wanting to speak to the chef will be complaining about a problem! And even when customers take the time to say they like something, it's not the same as hearing this from a food expert.

Andrew's already planning to enter a national cooking competition called *Top Chef*. If he gets to the final, he'll cook live on TV. It's a huge challenge, so he's getting advice from the other chefs at work. [19] For one thing, it'll be great advertising for the restaurant! They also think he deserves success, knowing how much he puts into getting everything right. For example, one of the dishes Andrew's planning contains cheese. Rather than using something he'd cooked with before, he visited many farms and tasted hundreds of different cheeses. [20] It's attention to details like this which he hopes will impress judges!

A   They all want to see him do well.

B   The ingredients are given to the chefs.

C   In contests, though, he plans a whole menu.

D   If the dish is popular, however, he cooks it again.

E   Having the opportunity to get opinions like this is rare.

F   He kept going until he'd found one with the perfect flavour.

G   That didn't stop him aiming high though.

H   He is expecting to be quite nervous.

Questions 21–26

For each question, choose the correct answer.

Robot staff

A restaurant in a small town in the UK has just got a new employee. But rather than being the usual helpful, friendly person you (21) .... working in a restaurant, this employee is a robot!

Katie Jones, the restaurant's owner, explains why she wanted to have a robot worker. She says it was (22) .... due to how hard it is to get new staff from the local area. She also thought it might (23) .... new customers. And indeed, she has had bookings from large (24) .... of people who heard about the robot and wanted to come and see it for themselves! The robot's job is to collect food from the kitchen and take it to the tables, which it does well. However, for things like taking orders and (25) .... with problems, human waiters are still the best (26) ...., Katie admits!

---

21 A understand   B imagine   C believe   D guess

22 A nearly   B fairly   C hardly   D partly

23 A attend   B attract   C accept   D allow

24 A totals   B figures   C levels   D numbers

25 A dealing   B finishing   C answering   D solving

26 A preparation   B result   C choice   D advantage

Questions 27–32

For each question, write the correct word.
Write **one** word for each gap.

My blog

Welcome to my blog! This week I want to tell you about a photography course I joined recently. (27) .... begin with, the course is held every weekend in my local college, and there are only six of (28) .... who go. This means that Mark, our teacher, has quite (29) .... bit of time to help everyone.

Last week, we took weather photos. It was much harder (30) .... it sounds! Some people took pictures of clouds, and one person took a beautiful one of leaves that (31) .... fallen onto the ground. Mark is arranging to put on exhibition of our photos in the library soon, (32) .... gives everyone a goal to work towards. I think it'll be great and we're all really looking forward to it.

You **must** answer this question.
Write your answer in about **100 words** on your answer sheet.

Question 1

Read this email from your English-speaking friend and the notes you have made.

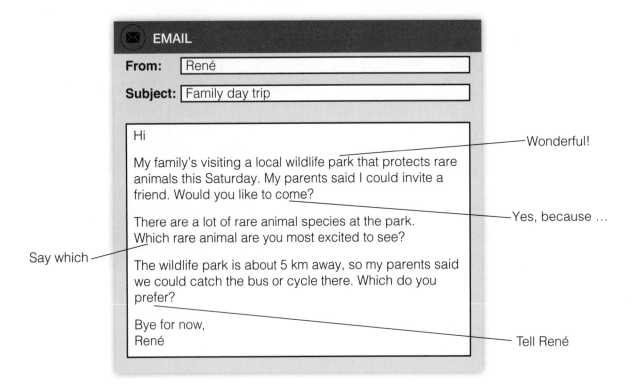

EMAIL

From: René

Subject: Family day trip

Hi

My family's visiting a local wildlife park that protects rare animals this Saturday. My parents said I could invite a friend. Would you like to come? —— Wonderful!

There are a lot of rare animal species at the park. Which rare animal are you most excited to see? —— Yes, because …

Say which —— The wildlife park is about 5 km away, so my parents said we could catch the bus or cycle there. Which do you prefer?

Bye for now,
René —— Tell René

Write your **email** to René using **all the notes**.

Choose **one** of these questions.
Write your answer in about **100 words** on the answer sheet.

Question 2

You see this notice on an English-language website for young people.

> **Articles wanted!**
>
> **NEW YEAR CELEBRATIONS**
>
> Every year, people around the world take part in New Year celebrations.
> - How do people in your country usually celebrate New Year?
> - How important is it for you and your family to celebrate New Year? Why?
>
> The best articles answering these questions will be published next month.

Write your **article**.

Question 3

Your English teacher has asked you to write a story. Your story must begin with this sentence.

The two friends couldn't believe their luck!

Write your **story**.

Test 3   Listening Part 1

🎧 **Questions 1–7**

47   For each question, choose the correct answer.

1   Which ride has the boy already tried?

A

B

C

2   Where did the girl leave her laptop?

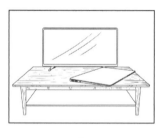

A

B

C

3   Which instrument is the boy learning?

A

B

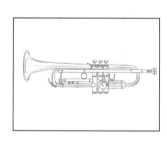

C

4 How much did the game cost?

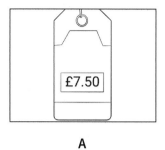

A

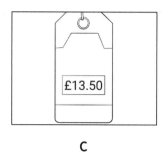

B

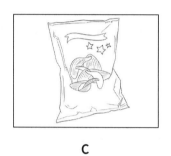

C

5 What has the boy brought to eat on the bus trip?

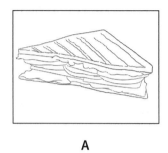

A

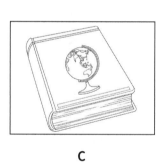

B

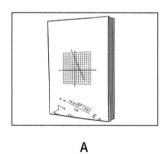

C

6 Which class have they got first?

A

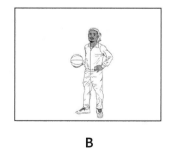

B

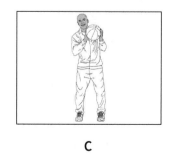

C

7 What does the new PE teacher look like?

A

B

C

Questions 8–13

48 For each question, choose the correct answer.

8 You will hear a boy telling his friend about some new shoes.
   Why is he disappointed with the shoes?

   A   They are uncomfortable.

   B   His teammates have better ones.

   C   He dislikes the colour.

9 You will hear a girl talking about someone she met on holiday.
   How did she feel about him at first?

   A   pleased that he was generous

   B   angry that he was rude

   C   surprised that he was friendly

10 You will hear two friends talking about dogs.
    The girl thinks that having a dog

    A   becomes boring after a while.

    B   requires more effort than she expected.

    C   is the responsibility of the whole family.

11 You will hear a boy telling his friend about a school trip.
    What does he complain about?

    A   The students couldn't always do what they wanted.

    B   The students didn't have time to rest.

    C   The students didn't see all they had planned.

12 You will hear a girl telling her friend about an action series.
    Why does the girl recommend it?

    A   The special effects are amazing.

    B   The story is realistic.

    C   The acting is good.

13 You will hear a girl talking about her uncle's work.
    What's his new job like?

    A   It's satisfying.

    B   It's well paid.

    C   It's relaxing.

Questions 14–19

49   For each question, write the correct answer in the gap.
Write **one** or **two words** or a **number** or a **date** or a **time**.

You will hear a teacher talking about a visit to a chocolate factory.

Chocolate factory trip

The visit is going to take place in the factory near the **(14)** ....

In the factory, **(15)** .... chocolate eggs were produced last month.

Visitors will see the new way they **(16)** .... the chocolate to make animal figures.

There's also a special chocolate **(17)** .... that visitors can see.

Students should remember to take some **(18)** ....

Students will be given free **(19)** .... when they leave to remember the visit.

Questions 20–25

50 For each question, choose the correct answer.

....

You will hear an interview with a young man called Alex, talking about his experience working with turtles as part of a project that protects sea creatures.

20 Alex went to Costa Rica because

   A   it would lead to a new job.

   B   he knew a lot about it.

   C   a friend agreed to go with him.

21 How did Alex feel when he arrived there?

   A   lonely because he was away from home

   B   worried about having an accident

   C   tired from the journey

22 The people Alex worked with

   A   had previous experience.

   B   came from many different countries

   C   were mostly older than him.

23 What special memory does Alex have of the trip?

   A   eating a special meal on the beach

   B   having a night swim

   C   watching animal behaviour

24 What surprised Alex about Costa Rica?

   A   the variety of animals

   B   the number of protected areas

   C   the hot weather

25 What would Alex like to do next?

   A   learn how to dive

   B   study a science degree

   C   work with other animals

PART 1

(2–3 minutes)

Phase 1

Good morning / afternoon / evening.

What's your name?

How old are you?

Where do you live?

Phase 2

(possible examiner questions)

Tell us about the town where you live.

How often do you listen to music?

Do you like playing video games? (Why? / Why not?)

What are you going to do on your next holiday?

Which city would you most like to visit? (Why?)

What kind of weather do you like? (Why?)

Where do you usually spend time with your friends?

Tell us about your favourite hobby.

 Listen to two students doing the task above.

51

PART 2

(3–5 minutes)

Now I'd like each of you to talk on your own about something. I'm going to give each of you a photograph and I'd like you to talk about it.

A, here is your photograph. It shows some people **in an art class**. (See page C3.)

B, you just listen.

A, please tell us what you can see in the photograph.

B, here is your photograph. It shows some people **spending time at the beach**. (See page C4.)

A, you just listen.

B, please tell us what you can see in the photograph.

 Listen to two students doing the task above.

52

PART 3

(4–5 minutes)

Now, in this part of the test you're going to talk about something together for about two minutes. I'm going to describe a situation to you.

Some friends want to go on a trip for the weekend together. They would like to go to a **place** that everyone will enjoy.

Here are some **places** they could go to. (See page C13.)

Talk together about the different **places** they could go to together and say **which would be best**.

All right? Now, talk together.

 Listen to two students doing the task above.

53

PART 4

(3–4 minutes)

Have you ever been on holiday to another country? (Where did you go?)

Where would you most like to go on holiday? (Why?)

What kind of accommodation would you like to stay in? (Why?)

What's a popular place for holidays in your country? (Why do people go there?)

Do you think it's important for people to take holidays? (Why? / Why not?)

What can you learn by visiting other cities or countries?

 Listen to two students doing the task above.

54

Questions 1–5

For each question, choose the correct answer.

1

Hana
I have to take pictures for a photography competition. The topic's 'family fun'. I'm wondering if the beach is a good place to try. I'd love your opinion – you take brilliant pictures!
Debbie

A Debbie suggests Hana should take part in a photography competition.

B Debbie needs Hana to accompany her on a trip to get some creative ideas.

C Debbie wants Hana's advice on how suitable a location is for taking photos.

2

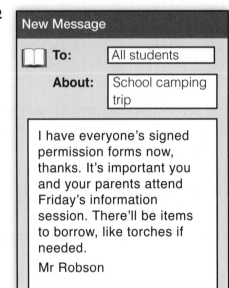

New Message

To: All students

About: School camping trip

I have everyone's signed permission forms now, thanks. It's important you and your parents attend Friday's information session. There'll be items to borrow, like torches if needed.

Mr Robson

Mr Robson's email tells students to

A bring their camping equipment in on Friday.

B make sure they are available to attend an event.

C ask their parents to return a completed document.

3

Library members

Thanks to everyone who completed the questionnaire about our services. The results will be on the website tomorrow.

What does this notice provide?

A details of when any changes suggested in the survey will be made

B an explanation of why members were asked to do the survey

C information on where to see the views given in the survey

4

Liam

I'm queuing at the café. It's taking ages. Everyone wants ice cream! If I reach the front before you arrive, shall I order something? I'll send a picture of the menu if so!

Billy

A Billy can let Liam know what food is available.

B Billy thinks the café will run out of certain items.

C Billy is annoyed that Liam hasn't arrived at the café yet.

5

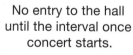

Audiences

No entry to the hall until the interval once concert starts.

Check tickets carefully for seat numbers.

Hall staff

What information is the notice giving people who are going to a concert?

A Staff will advise them which seats are available to sit in.

B When leaving the hall for the interval, they mustn't forget their tickets.

C If they arrive late, they need to wait before entering the hall.

Questions 6–10

For each question, choose the correct answer.

The young people below are all interested in finding a website about animals.
On the opposite page there are descriptions of eight websites about animals.
Decide which website would be the most suitable for the young people below.

6 Nessa likes finding out about rare animals people don't often see, and she'd love the chance to watch some of them online. She'd like to play fun games too.

7 Bradley wants to know about different projects to help animals worldwide. He's hoping to find out about how to support animals where he lives, and to understand how nature programmes film the animals they follow.

8 Sofia wants to read about animals that help humans. She'd also love to learn about a job where people protect different species and is interested in organising a nature club in her area.

9 Ishaan wants to know what animals he can see in his garden. He also needs information for a school project about how animals survive in difficult conditions and would like some photos to include.

10 Fatima hopes to learn about how climate change affects wildlife, and what happened to animals that no longer exist. She also thinks communicating with other young nature-lovers around the world would be good.

Websites about animals

A   **Shared Planet**

Follow the daily life of a researcher with interactive games – make decisions that save elephants and tigers! Although it's fun, there's a serious side – you'll discover important work experts do in real life. There's advice about setting up a local wildlife group, and articles with true stories about people being rescued by dolphins!

B   **Discovery Zone**

Animals survive in nearly every area of our planet. FInd out about those living in the highest mountains, the hottest deserts and the coldest oceans. You can watch videos sent in by young people, showing animals they have filmed out and about in local parks – you're sure to see something new!

C   **All About Animals**

Our site's perfect for nature-lovers. Read an article about how a professional cameraman records videos of unusual animals, and see updates from international organisations on work to save creatures in danger. Feel inspired? Get ideas for things you can do, from making animal feeders for your garden to noting insect numbers.

D   **Animal Centre**

Learn how global warming is leading to decreasing numbers in some species and see pictures from this year's Nature Photography competition. As well as working dogs that help farmers find lost sheep, there's a film of the competition winner taking pictures of whales in Antarctica's icy seas.

E   **World of Wildlife**

Learn about wildlife you won't find in your back garden and find sections on species which are not very common, including those in danger of disappearing. With links to live cameras, you could spot some for yourself! Report what you've seen to directly help scientists with their work. With exciting puzzles and quizzes, there's lots to enjoy.

F   **Amazing Animals**

Discover incredible wildlife by reading reports from international scientists working in the Arctic. Together with pictures to download and film clips to watch, you'll learn what makes it possible for creatures to live in such a challenging location. But you'll find there's plenty to see closer to home, with tips on identifying wildlife where you live.

G   **Incredible Nature**

From huge dinosaurs to tiny insects, our planet is home to incredible animals. You'll learn how researchers are discovering new species, and what they do to make sure they are protected. You can follow links to documentaries and programmes about various animals – a great source of information.

H   **Wildfacts**

Millions of years ago, huge numbers of species disappeared from the planet. Find out why and discover the effect that rising temperatures are having on animals. There's a chat room, so you can enjoy sharing ideas with young people of all nationalities.

Questions 11–15

For each question, choose the correct answer.

My hobby: cycling
by Zack Matthers

All my family are into sport; in fact, my older brother is an excellent runner. When he started going out on training runs, I accompanied him on my bike because I knew I couldn't run as fast as him! When he went away to college, I missed my cycle rides, so Dad suggested I joined a cycle club. The only one nearby was the Three Hills cycle club. His friend's son had been a member once and enjoyed it, so that's what I did!

I went and signed up, and was invited on a group cycle ride. Because it was my first time, I was given a special jacket and shorts to wear, which was useful. I wasn't sure what to expect; I'd thought everyone would be quicker than me, but everything was fine, and I managed to stay near the front! Because there were different abilities in the group, we kept stopping for breaks. I didn't mind, because it meant I could chat to the leader, although I was happy to keep going! She knew someone in the national cycle team, and it was interesting hearing about his experiences.

That was six months ago, and I've been on various group rides since then, and some two-day trips. They're fun, and exploring fantastic scenery is a bonus. The next ride's taking place in a city. We're careful on roads, and there's always a safety talk before we set off, plus we can deal with flat tyres and things. But we'll still need to pay attention in heavy traffic – it'll be fine – it's just not something I'm familiar with. I'm excited about trying out the bike I got recently. I've not had time yet.

For anyone new to cycling, I'd say try your local club for reasonable second-hand bikes as you can spend loads on brand new ones. There's also information online from experts on the latest equipment, but I've found the best thing is to just ride; but don't push yourself too hard. You're supposed to be having fun, so if you feel like stopping for a bit, then do. And if you pack a snack, you'll have more energy to enjoy yourself!

11 Why did Zack decide to join a cycle club?
    A   He wanted to improve his cycling speed.
    B   He knew other people in the club at the time.
    C   He realised he preferred cycling to doing another sport.
    D   He wanted the opportunity to continue doing an activity.

12 When Zack did his first cycle ride with the club, he was
    A   surprised by how well he did compared to the others.
    B   pleased he'd bought the right cycling clothes.
    C   relieved at how many times they stopped for a rest.
    D   excited to be in a group with a well-known cyclist.

13 What is Zack looking forward to doing on the club trip?
    A   cycling in some beautiful countryside
    B   using a new bicycle
    C   learning some basic repairs
    D   practising riding in busy places

14 What advice does Zack have for people just starting cycling?
    A   Keep going, no matter how tired you feel.
    B   Spend money on the best bike you can.
    C   Prepare food to take with you on rides.
    D   Watch professional cyclists for tips on technique.

15 What would Zack write in a letter to his grandparents?

    A
    I love the whole-day rides my cycle club organises. If we could do ones that lasted even longer, I'd be the first to sign up!

    B
    I like my club because I'm always cycling with people of similar levels. It means no one gets left behind.

    C
    I'm so glad I chose Three Hills, rather than choosing a closer club. It's definitely the right one for me.

    D
    Don't worry about me – every time we go on a ride, someone from the club reminds us what we need to do to stay safe.

Questions 16–20

Five sentences have been removed from the text below. For each question, choose the correct answer.
There are three extra sentences which you do not need to use.

Playing board games

If you think about games people enjoy playing, you'd probably say video games, or sports like volleyball. But many people love playing board games. There are different reasons for this. For a start, board games can usually be enjoyed by anyone who happens to be home at the time. **16 [   ]** That's because although people might have a favourite one, there is usually something for various generations to enjoy in almost any board game!

You might think that video games being so hugely popular would make board games less so; they might seem boring compared to the options available on computer. **17 [   ]** Although this may seem rather surprising, the number of people playing video games has helped make game-playing in general a greater part of our lives. This has encouraged people to explore different games for their entertainment.

There are many reasons to play board games, including certain health benefits. For example, playing board games reduces the time people spend looking at screens. **18 [   ]** It can also cause particular issues such as reducing how well people can concentrate. And by not looking at laptops or phones, families spend more quality time together, some even organising regular 'games nights'.

Studies show playing games can also have the result of making events like parties or work training activities easier for shy people. They can find it simpler to get to know each other when they are involved in a game. **19 [   ]** As everyone is concentrating on the same thing, rather than trying to make conversation, it is less stressful.

Games can help with confidence in other ways too. There are many decisions to be made during a game. **20 [   ]** The longer we play, the more likely we are to develop a good plan for winning. With every successful turn, we see our plan is working and our confidence grows.

So what are you waiting for? Go and play a board game!

A   We know doing so affects the ability to sleep.

B   Some people, therefore, are naturally better than others.

C   Actually, the opposite is true.

D   Also, they are often suitable for different ages to play together.

E   Board games are easy to take to different places too.

F   The better someone is at making them, the more successful they will be.

G   Because board games have rules, such issues are avoided.

H   It prevents people from running out of things to say in these situations.

Questions 21–26

For each question, choose the correct answer.

The Batu Caves

If you visit Malaysia's capital city, Kuala Lumpur, you really should visit the Batu Caves. They are only about 11 kilometres from the city and are easy to (21) .... by bus, train or taxi. There are plenty of transport (22) .... available.

At the entrance, there's a 43-metre high gold statue. Just past this, visitors will see 272 stairs to climb up to Temple Cave, one of the most popular tourist destinations in the world. In 2018, these stairs were painted bright colours and they now provide (23) .... for fantastic photos. Most people climb the stairs in around 15 minutes. The climate is (24) .... hot and humid however, so it is a very (25) .... idea to arrive early, when is it cooler. This also means you can avoid the worst of the crowds. Whenever you visit though, be (26) .... for the groups of monkeys which live there. They sometimes run off with visitors' phones or bags!

21 A reach   B travel   C arrive   D connect

22 A enquiries   B options   C ways   D decisions

23 A appearances B descriptions C times   D opportunities

24 A extremely   B totally   C exactly   D completely

25 A serious   B realistic   C sensible   D essential

26 A advised   B prepared   C planned   D organised

Questions 27–32

For each question, write the correct word.
Write **one** word for each gap.

Review: the Maple Café

Last week, my friends and I visited the Maple Café which opened recently. Cafés are places teenagers like to visit, and that is (27) .... I decided to write a review about it! The café is in a nice location, next to the river. It is in a building that (28) .... to be a bike shop, and the new owners put some old bikes on the walls, which is really unusual!

There is plenty of space inside, or (29) .... you prefer, there are tables outside, too. When we visited, there was a special offer to celebrate the café opening. We (30) .... given a free slice of chocolate cake and we all agreed that the Maple Café chocolate cake was better than anything we (31) .... ever tried before! There are the normal hot and cold drinks you would expect to see, and (32) .... prices are good. I would certainly recommend that everyone visits!

You **must** answer this question.

Write your answer in about **100 words** on the answer sheet.

Question 1

Read this email from your English teacher, Mrs Rashid, and the notes you have made.

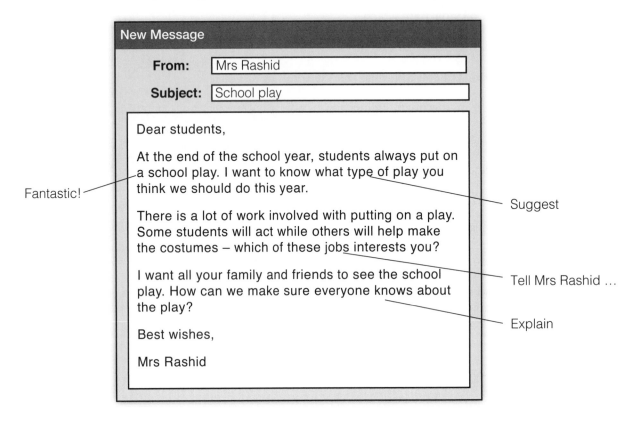

New Message

From: Mrs Rashid

Subject: School play

Dear students,

At the end of the school year, students always put on a school play. I want to know what type of play you think we should do this year.

There is a lot of work involved with putting on a play. Some students will act while others will help make the costumes – which of these jobs interests you?

I want all your family and friends to see the school play. How can we make sure everyone knows about the play?

Best wishes,

Mrs Rashid

Fantastic!

Suggest

Tell Mrs Rashid …

Explain

Write your **email** to Mrs Rashid using **all the notes**.

Choose **one** of these questions.
Write your answer in about **100 words** on the answer sheet.

....

Question 2

You see this notice on an English-language website for young people.

> **Articles wanted!**
>
> **REALITY TV**
> Do you enjoy watching reality
> TV programmes? Why?
> Can young people learn
> anything useful from watching
> reality TV? Why?
> The best articles answering
> these questions will be published
> next month.

Write your **article**.

Question 3

Your English teacher has asked you to write a story. Your story must begin with this sentence.

The twins discovered a box of old letters in their grandad's garage.

Write your **story**.

Questions 1–7

55   For each question, choose the correct answer.

1   What's the girl's coat like?

A

B

C

2   Where are the friends waiting?

A

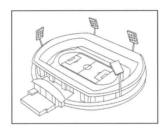

B

C

3   Which is the oldest thing in the museum?

A

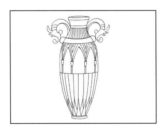

B

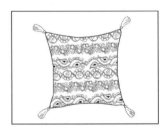

C

4 What's Liam unhappy about?

A

B

C

5 What do the friends need to fix?

A

B

C

6 What does Sophie need for her presentation?

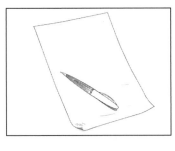

A

B

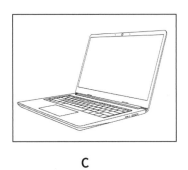

C

7 Which club is the most popular?

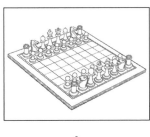

A

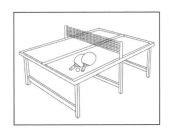

B

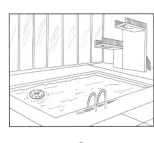

C

Questions 8–13

56   For each question, choose the correct answer.

8   You will hear two friends talking about a visit to a castle.
The friends agree that
A   the park area was pleasant.
B   the guide was helpful.
C   the art was surprising.

9   You will hear a girl telling her friend about her part-time job.
Why did she take the job?
A   She needed some extra money.
B   She had a lot of free time.
C   She wanted to learn something.

10   You will hear two friends talking about a party.
They need to
A   ask some more people.
B   arrange the food.
C   decorate a room.

11   You will hear a boy telling his friend about a new phone app.
The boy advises the girl to
A   use it for a school project.
B   protect her identity.
C   share it with a friend.

12   You will hear two friends talking about a news report.
The girl is disappointed that
A   she missed an event.
B   someone is unable to perform.
C   a concert has been cancelled.

13   You will hear a boy telling his friend about a dance video.
The boy disliked
A   the way the picture looked.
B   the quality of the sound.
C   the dancers' movements.

Questions 14–19

57 For each question, write the correct answer in the gap.
Write **one** or **two words** or a **number** or a **date** or a **time**.

You will hear a student called Oliver telling his class about a new shopping centre.

Silverton Shopping Centre

The fastest way to get to the shopping centre is by **(14)** ....

Oliver thinks the **(15)** .... is the best part of the shopping centre.

Clothes shops for young people can be found on the **(16)** ....

Oliver bought something to eat in a **(17)** ....

Oliver was surprised there was a **(18)** .... in the shopping centre.

The shopping centre is open from 9.30 to **(19)** ....

🎧 **Questions 20–25**

58   For each question, choose the correct answer.

....

You will hear an interview with a young woman called Emma who is a sports reporter.

20   Emma started working on TV
   A   through a contact in a TV company.
   B   after doing reports on the internet.
   C   because she was a sports star.

21   Why does Emma enjoy reporting on football matches?
   A   She admires a lot of the football players.
   B   She used to play football herself.
   C   She can talk about different details of the team.

22   What is difficult about Emma's job?
   A   remembering people's names
   B   concentrating on the game
   C   giving information quickly

23   What does Emma do to relax?
   A   go out with people from work
   B   get some exercise
   C   spend time in nature

24   Emma's favourite moment is when
   A   a team does well.
   B   she prepares before a game.
   C   she meets important players.

25   In the future, Emma wants to
   A   give people advice about jobs.
   B   help people become sports stars.
   C   travel to another country.

PART 1

(2–3 minutes)

Phase 1

Good morning / afternoon / evening.
What's your name?
How old are you?
Where do you live?

Phase 2

(possible examiner questions)

What are you going to do next weekend?
Tell us about a friend you enjoy spending time with. (Why?)
What are your favourite foods?
Do you like rock music? (Why?)
What do you usually do in the afternoons after school?
Which do you prefer, staying at home at the weekend or going out? (Why?)
Tell us about the area where you live.
How often do you eat at someone else's house?

 Listen to two students doing the task above.

59

PART 2

(3–5 minutes)

Now I'd like each of you to talk on your own about something. I'm going to give each of you a photograph and I'd like you to talk about it.

A, here is your photograph. It shows some people **playing a board game**. (See page C3.)

B, you just listen.

A, please tell us what you can see in the photograph.

B, here is your photograph. It shows some people **studying at the library**. (See page C4.)

A, you just listen.

B, please tell us what you can see in the photograph.

 Listen to two students doing the task above.

60

PART 3

(4–5 minutes)

Now, in this part of the test you're going to talk about something together for about two minutes. I'm going to describe a situation to you.

A teacher wants her class to **learn more about geography**.

Here are some ways to learn about geography. (See page C14.)

Talk together about the different **ways of learning geography** and say **which students would enjoy most**.

All right? Now, talk together.

 Listen to two students doing the task above.

61

PART 4

(3–4 minutes)

Do you enjoy learning about geography? (What do you most enjoy learning about?)

What is an interesting natural area in your country? (What is interesting about it?)

Where would you most like to visit in the natural world? (Why would you like to see it?)

Do you prefer cities or the countryside? (Why?)

Why is it important for people to learn about geography?

Is it useful to learn facts about other countries? (Why? / Why not?)

 Listen to two students doing the task above.

62

Questions 1–5

For each question, choose the correct answer.

1

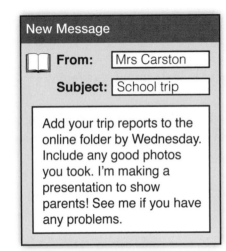

Students need to contact Mrs Carston if

A   they want to attend an event on Wednesday.

B   they need pictures to add to their work.

C   they require help uploading some files.

2

Marcus is texting Lenny to

A   inform him about a change to an arrangement.

B   give the reasons for a choice of refreshments.

C   check that the selected film is acceptable.

3

> **Cinema Club**
> No fee to join.
> Get money off tickets, plus
> free snacks of your choice!
> Click here for further details.

You should use the link to

A   download tickets for a film.

B   receive information about a special offer.

C   get a discount on the registration cost.

4

Jamie
Mum said you've taken my bike because of your flat tyre. Don't forget, I need it to get to band practice straight after dinner. I'll help you fix yours tomorrow if you like!
Sam

A   Sam is complaining that Jamie took something without asking.

B   Sam is making sure Jamie knows when he has to return something.

C   Sam is reminding Jamie that something has to be repaired.

5

> **New Message**
>
> 📖 **To:** Amanda
>
> **Subject:** Mum's birthday
>
> I want to get a book called *Silver Rose* for your mum. Can you look on the bookshelf to make sure she hasn't got it? But don't let her know – it's our secret!
> Grandma

Amanda's grandma is emailing her to

A   check that Amanda hasn't already bought a particular present.

B   suggest something that Amanda can buy as a surprise.

C   see if a present is a suitable choice for a birthday.

Questions 6–10

For each question, choose the correct answer.

The young people below all want to go on a tour of a city.
On the opposite page there is information about eight city tours.
Decide which city tour would be the most suitable for the young people below.

6 Matthew wants to learn about the history of the city in a fun way, on an easy walk around the city with a guide. His family would like to buy interesting souvenirs during the tour.

7 Jaya wants to do a boat trip to see the sights. She'd also like to try the special desserts that are made in the area and get to meet the people who make them.

8 Ari hopes to see some art during the day, and his family want ideas for somewhere good to have lunch. They'd also love advice about where to listen to some live music.

9 Hua and her family want to spend the whole day exploring famous museums, seeing the most important items in each place. They'd like to explore parts of museums tourists don't usually see.

10 Filip and his family hope to join a small tour, where they are driven around the city. He'd like this to include some of the locations described in popular stories that were set there.

City Tours

A Fanton Tours

Come and learn about the history of shipping in the area. Our guides will show you around the harbour, and if you're lucky, you'll be there when the fishing boats come in – choose something for lunch! Booking essential as each guide can only take a maximum of ten.

B Excel Tours

You can't leave the city without trying its famous lemon cream cakes! Travel by river to one of the oldest – and smallest – family kitchens, where they still use the same 100-year-old secret recipe. You can ask the chefs for it, but they won't tell!

C Sally's Tours

For a different experience, join our daily minibus tours. You'll have the chance to get out and explore tiny streets or cafés you'll recognise from some well-known novels, then relax in air-conditioned comfort as guides take you to the next stop, showing you beautiful parts of the city. Groups limited to five.

D Newton Guides

See the most famous places in the city, from the concert hall where the world's best musicians have performed, to mansions belonging to film stars and famous writers! We'll finish the tour at the historic Creative Quarter, where local artists sell their work. You can even watch them painting in their studios.

E City Explorer

Most tourists head to the shops in the city centre, but there's more to see, like the latest attraction – a sculpture trail created especially by local artists. As you walk around the various locations, our guides can give suggestions on the best places for traditional food or where to go for fun entertainment, including live bands.

F Billy's Tours

Whether you choose a longer bus or boat tour, or a shorter gentle tour on foot, our guides bring the past to life with amusing stories. All river tours include lunch, and walking tours include a stop in the central market, where you'll find wonderful items made here in the city.

G Big Day Out

Discover why the city is a centre for culture and creativity. Join your guides at City Museum, with its fun interactive games, then take a short walk through the park for coffee and cake by the river. You'll explore the old city with its little galleries and cafés that only locals know about!

H GK Tours

With GK tours, jump on and off our buses from early morning until evening. Tickets give access to exhibits which aren't on public display in some attractions and also entry to a 4D cinema. There are routes to all main museums and art galleries, with lists of what you mustn't miss.

Questions 11–15

For each question, choose the correct answer.

Class trip to Harston Forest
by Ellie Simpson

Last week, my class went to Harston Forest as part of our science course. We're lucky because we've done a few trips to places this year. Our teacher, Mr Jones, told us to find out about the wildlife we might see. Because the books in our library aren't very modern, we accessed online nature sites instead, with links Mr Jones gave us. He also said to consider some questions to ask at the visitor centre, as guides were giving a talk and could provide answers. I didn't have any, but other students did.

Then we went to the forest. On a previous family visit, my dad forgot a map, and I remember how relieved we were to find the car again! This time was completely different, as we were just following the guides. We closed our eyes and listened for birds. At first, everything was silent. But soon, we heard birds singing. I couldn't believe the range of sounds, from really quiet to pretty loud! Our guides knew what each one was, and before long I did too, which was great – everything sounded so similar before.

Our teacher put us into groups, ready to do an experiment, and luckily, I was with my friends. We counted different plant species in one hour. That might seem like ages; we were really hurrying by the end, though! Being careful not to stand on any plants, we measured a five-metre square on the ground. We put stones down so we knew where to work, and recorded the plants inside that area. We used a list with plant pictures on it – the photos weren't brilliant, but we managed well.

After a picnic – we avoided barbecues as they could cause fires and damage the forest – we were shown holes in trees. We had to guess which animals make their homes inside, and how they survive hot and cold weather. It was a lot to remember, but of course, we were only looking at local species – if you're studying different forests, there'd be hundreds of them!

Mr Jones has asked us to create displays to share what we learned with our families. They should be very interesting!

11 What did Ellie do before the day of the trip?

    A   got information from a website

    B   read some up-to-date textbooks

    C   listened to an expert who knew the area

    D   thought about what to ask when she got there

12 How did Ellie feel about being in the forest?

    A   anxious about getting lost

    B   surprised at how little noise there was

    C   excited about visiting somewhere new

    D   pleased to be able to identify some wildlife

13 What did Ellie find difficult about the experiment?

    A   not damaging the plants

    B   completing the task in time

    C   working out which area to search

    D   taking clear enough pictures

14 In the afternoon, the students did an activity to

    A   show them how to protect forests.

    B   help them learn about different sorts of forests.

    C   teach them about the places creatures live in.

    D   remind them about problems caused by climate change.

15 What would Ellie say to her grandparents about the trip?

A

We all enjoyed ourselves. It was the first time our science class has had a day away from school!

B

It was fun having the chance to cook outside in the forest – I didn't know we were going to do that!

C

I was pleased that we could decide who we wanted to be in a group with for the activity to count plants.

D

I've told mum all about the trip of course, but she'll like seeing my presentation on it.

Questions 16–20

Five sentences have been removed from the text below. For each question, choose the correct answer.
There are three extra sentences which you do not need to use.

Zara Rutherford: young pilot

Zara Rutherford is currently the youngest female pilot to fly around the world alone. In 2022, when she was 19, Zara completed her 52,000-kilometre flight in a microlight, a type of plane that is small but very fast. **16 [   ]** It was one that took her through five continents and 31 countries. Before her amazing achievement, the record was held by Shaesta Waiz. Shaesta, an Afghan-born American, completed her flight at the age of 30.

Zara's parents are both pilots and took her up in planes from an early age. It wasn't long before she began learning to fly and eventually started wondering about doing a round-the-world trip. She knew it wouldn't be easy. **17 [   ]** It also costs a lot and can be dangerous. When Zara was finishing school, however, she decided the time was right to attempt the journey.

After completing her preparations, she started from Belgium, flying west over countries including the UK and Russia. She then flew to southeast Asia, India and the Middle East, before returning to Belgium. One of the biggest issues was that on a round-the-world flight, conditions change depending on location. **18 [   ]** The mild climate in Belgium hadn't provided opportunities to practise in different weather. The freezing temperatures of Alaska and Russia and the sandstorms in the Middle East were huge challenges. **19 [   ]** In addition, she sometimes had to get her plane repaired, or collect documents to give her permission to cross certain countries.

Nevertheless, she completed her journey and felt extremely proud of herself. She is keen for other young women see her achievement, as there are not enough girls and women looking to go into subjects like engineering and technology. There are also very few female pilots. **20 [   ]** After all, when people see what she has done, they might be inspired to follow her!

A Her achievement could help change this in future.

B This made it perfect for the huge journey she went on.

C It can therefore change quickly between hot and cold.

D However, she had done most of her training in Belgium.

E They helped her prepare well for the trip.

F These conditions meant she often had to land and wait for longer than planned.

G In addition, there are other reasons for this too.

H For one thing, organising everything is very complicated.

Questions 21–26

For each question, choose the correct answer.

Henry Ford

Henry Ford was an American engineer. He is best (21) .... for making cars. He started producing them in 1896, and (22) .... up the Ford Motor Company in 1903. The first car he made was called the Ford Model T. At the time, only the very wealthy could afford a vehicle of any sort.

Ford's (23) .... was to change that, so he made his Model T design as simple as possible. In 1908, a Model T cost $850. While this was a lot for (24) .... people, the Model T cars were still (25) .... popular. In fact, Ford was (26) .... it difficult to make enough of them, so he developed a new, quicker system to use in his factory. Cars moved slowly along a line of people. Workers added the same part to each car that passed by, finishing with a completed car at the end.

21 A understood   B known   C accepted   D heard

22 A set   B made   C put   D ended

23 A reason   B ability   C custom   D goal

24 A familiar   B usual   C ordinary   D basic

25 A incredibly   B nearly   C completely   D absolutely

26 A realising   B admitting   C getting   D finding

Questions 27–32

For each question, write the correct word.
Write **one** word for each gap.

Running Blog

Hi and welcome to my blog! It's all about my

hobby, **(27)** .... is running! I joined a running

club a few months ago. Since then, I **(28)** ....

already been on lots of longer runs with the group.

As well as helping us improve **(29)** .... running

technique, the coaches also give lots of really useful

information about different types of kit. Good shoes are important, but **(30)** .... they can cost a lot of

money, it's useful to get advice before you buy any.

Last session, we heard about a big race in a few weeks' time. I am wondering whether or **(31)** .... to

enter. There's plenty of time for me to improve my speed before the race. In fact, I **(32)** .... given a

running plan last week which should help me get quicker. It will be good experience, even if I come last!

You **must** answer this question.

Write your answer in about **100 words** on the answer sheet.

....

Question 1

Read this email from your English-speaking friend Mark and the notes you have made.

Tell Mark

Yes,
but …

EMAIL

From: Mark

Subject: School garden

Hey

Guess what? Our school's going to create a garden this
year! What do you think we should grow in it?

Students can decide what happens to all the food
we grow in the garden. Do you think we should sell
everything?

There's a meeting in room 104 about the school garden
at noon. Do you want to go with me?

Let me know soon!

Mark

Cool!!

No,
because …

Write your **email** to Mark using **all the notes**.

Choose **one** of these questions.
Write your answer in about **100 words** on the answer sheet.

....

Question 2

You see this announcement on an English-language website for young people.

> **Articles wanted!**
>
> **ONLINE VERSUS
> FACE-TO-FACE**
>
> Do you prefer chatting to your friends
> face-to-face or online? Why?
>
> Do you think spending lots of time
> online each day is a good idea? Why?
>
> Write an article answering these
> questions, and we will publish the most
> interesting articles on our website.

Write your **article**.

Question 3

Your English teacher has asked you to write a story. Your story must begin
with this sentence.

I was walking in the forest when I heard a loud noise.

Write your **story**.

🎧 **Questions 1–7**

63 For each question, choose the correct answer.

1 Which book did the boy buy?

A

B

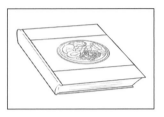

C

2 What problem did Jessica have with her surprise lunch?

A

B

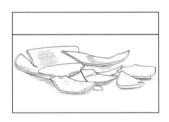

C

3 What do the students need to bring for the experiment?

A

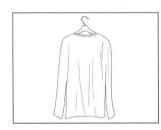

B

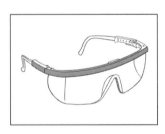

C

4 What did the divers find?

A

B

C

5 Where will James be next week?

A

B

C

6 What time do all the friends have to be at the station?

A

B

C

7 What does the doctor recommend?

A

B

C

Questions 8–13

64   For each question, choose the correct answer.

....

8   You will hear two friends talking about getting fit.
     What does the girl want to try?

     A   doing an activity with a friend

     B   training for a competition

     C   going back to something she did before

9   You will hear a boy telling a friend about a talk on cycling.
     What did the boy learn?

     A   what he needs for mountain biking

     B   how to cycle safely on roads

     C   a rule about where cycling is forbidden

10   You will hear two friends talking about a birthday gift.
     The girl suggests the boy should

     A   ask someone for advice.

     B   buy something similar to last time.

     C   get ideas on the internet.

11   You will hear two friends talking about a new sports centre.
     What does the girl like best about it?

     A   the convenient location

     B   the range of facilities

     C   the classes they offer

12   You will hear a boy telling a friend about a history lesson.
     The boy was

     A   confused about a date.

     B   surprised by the information.

     C   interested in learning more about it.

13   You will hear a boy talking about a hotel.
     The boy is pleased because

     A   he'll have his own room.

     B   he's going with a friend.

     C   he'll be in a new place.

Questions 14–19

65   For each question, write the correct answer in the gap.
Write **one** or **two words** or a **number** or a **date** or a **time**.

You will hear a visitor to a school talking about helping in an animal rescue centre at the weekend.

The Small Animal Rescue Centre

The animal centre opened in **(14)** ....

The animal centre cannot look after **(15)** ....

You may be able to borrow **(16)** .... if you don't have your own.

On Saturdays, before giving the animals water, helpers clean their **(17)** ....

Another way to help is to give information to **(18)** .... about the animals.

To apply to help at the centre you should go to the website, www.**(19)** .... .com

---

Questions 20–25

66   For each question, choose the correct answer.

You will hear an interview with a young woman called Tara Mitchell, who is an international chess champion.

20   Tara became interested in playing chess
A   because her family encouraged her.
B   when she started competing.
C   while she was at primary school.

21   What does Tara enjoy most about travelling to international competitions?
A   going sightseeing
B   learning new things about the game
C   meeting new people

22   How did she feel about her last competition?
A   confident she was well prepared
B   pleased she was improving
C   impressed by the other players

23   What does she do to relax?
A   read books
B   do a team sport
C   play an instrument

24   Why does Tara teach children to play chess?
A   to help very intelligent children
B   to learn more herself
C   to earn more money

25   What does Tara plan to do next?
A   learn a new language
B   work in computing
C   study at university

PART 1

(2–3 minutes)

Phase 1

Good morning / afternoon / evening.

What's your name?

How old are you?

Where do you live?

Phase 2

(possible examiner questions)

What did you do yesterday?

Tell us about a shop you like going to.

Which hobby would you like to try in the future? (Why?)

How often do you go for a walk?

Do you enjoy extreme sports like waterskiing or snowboarding? (Why? / Why not?)

Which do you prefer, visiting people or having visitors to your home? (Why?)

Who do you spend most of your day with?

Tell us about your English classes.

 Listen to two students doing the task above.

67

PART 2

(3–5 minutes)

Now I'd like each of you to talk on your own about something. I'm going to give each of you a photograph and I'd like you to talk about it.

A, here is your photograph. It shows some people **taking a photo of themselves**. (See page C5.)

B, you just listen.

A, please tell us what you can see in the photograph.

B, here is your photograph. It shows some people **shopping for clothes**. (See page C6.)

A, you just listen.

B, please tell us what you can see in the photograph.

 Listen to two students doing the task above.

68

PART 3

(4–5 minutes)

Now, in this part of the test you're going to talk about something together for about two minutes. I'm going to describe a situation to you.

A family wants to celebrate a special occasion. They would like to **do something special** to celebrate the occasion.

Here are some **things they could do** to celebrate. (See page C15.)

Talk together about the different **things they could do** to celebrate and say **which would be best**.

All right? Now, talk together.

 Listen to two students doing the task above.

69

PART 4

(3–4 minutes)

Which special occasions do you celebrate? (What do you do to celebrate?)

Who do you usually celebrate special occasions with? (Why?)

Have you celebrated a special occasion in another country? (How did people celebrate?)

What special celebration have you particularly enjoyed? (Why did you enjoy it?)

Do you think people need to spend a lot of money to have a fun celebration? (Why? / Why not?)

Is it important for people to celebrate special occasions? (Why? / Why not?)

 Listen to two students doing the task above.

70

Questions 1–5

For each question, choose the correct answer.

1

Visitors must not touch
the displays.
Pay particular attention
if carrying backpacks.
Exhibition items are
valuable and easily
damaged.

This notice tells people

A how they must behave while at the exhibition.

B why some items have had to be removed.

C which bags are not permitted near the museum objects.

2

New Message

📖 **To:**　Brianna

About:　Book

I've decided to get the book
you mentioned. What was
the name again? I know
you'd lend me your copy,
but I'm planning to take it on
holiday – I'd hate to lose it!

Shelly

A Shelly hopes she can borrow a book of Brianna's to read on holiday.

B Shelly wants to get Brianna's ideas about choosing a good book to read.

C Shelly needs some information about a book Brianna has recommended.

3

Lily
Your football kit's still on the table! Didn't you have a match today? Perhaps it was cancelled, but in case it wasn't, I'll leave it at reception on my way to the office later.
Dad

A Lily's dad thinks that a sports event is no longer taking place.

B Lily's dad would like to know whether or not she needs some sports clothes.

C Lily's dad will bring something she might need for a school sports event.

4

New Message

To: Violin Group

About: Tomorrow's practice

We're starting at 1.30 not 1.15, but finishing at the normal time – you won't be late for classes. I've got suggestions for music to perform at the end-of-term concert.
Mr Turner

A The practice session for violin students will be a bit shorter tomorrow.

B Violin students are told why they mustn't be late for tomorrow's practice.

C Mr Turner wants violin students to bring ideas about suitable concert music tomorrow.

5

Sally
I'm working late. I'll bring something home for dinner – maybe chicken, or salmon? I'm happy either way – it's up to you, just let me know. If you're hungry before then, remember there's fruit!
Mum

In her note, Sally's mum is

A explaining why she hasn't left Sally anything to eat.

B asking Sally to make a final decision about what to eat.

C reminding Sally that they are going to eat out later that evening.

Questions 6–10

For each question, choose the correct answer.

....

The young people below all want to visit a skateboarding park.
On the opposite page there are descriptions of eight skateboarding parks.
Decide which skateboarding park would be the most suitable for the young people below.

6

Heike hopes to have a private skateboarding lesson and can only go later in the day. She needs to buy a new skateboard but doesn't want to spend too much.

7

Anton wants to find a skateboard park that's free to use. He's interested in how the place he visits was designed and wants to buy snacks there.

8

Camille is an experienced skateboarder and hopes to try some challenging runs. She wants to visit a park when it's not too busy, and her parents want to see her skateboarding.

9

Jiiang needs to hire everything for a day's skating. He's hoping to get skateboarding tips from other skateboarders, and to buy some skateboarding clothes while he's at the park.

10

Akari knows some skateboard parks have live music, which she'd enjoy. She wants advice about the latest boards and the chance to see a skateboarding competition.

City skateboarding parks

A   Board Central

Whether you're new to skateboarding or want expert tips on technique, you can book a lesson with one of the friendly Board Central staff members. You can hire basic skateboards and helmets from the park shop – staff can advise you about what you need before your lesson.

B   Station Skate

As well as being expert teachers, staff at Station Skate can answer questions on the newest equipment or clothes. Every afternoon there are great prizes offered, from T-shirts to free snacks for those with the best skills or fastest times – fun whether you're watching or taking part! With bands performing daily, there's a party atmosphere.

C   Skate56

Even if you're not a skateboarder, with no entry charge and the music on the park's loudspeakers, Skate56's a popular place to come and watch talented skateboarders. And with refreshments available, stay until late! It was the first in the area; check out the shop's display showing how Skate56 was planned and built.

D   Renton Place

Renton Place first became famous when it appeared in a viral music video. It can get busy at weekends because that's when all the best skateboarders arrive to practise for competitions, but you'll find that watching them is a really great way of picking up tips!

E   Barton Hill

Barton Hill is the region's newest skateboard park. With a range of skateboarding equipment on offer for very reasonable prices, there's everything you need for a great day out. You can arrange an individual session with an instructor, and the park's lighting system allows skateboarding well after sunset.

F   Stanford Park

Perfect for all abilities, Stanford Park has a safe area to learn the basics with a one-to-one lesson, or you can try runs used in national competitions for something more advanced! There are various places to get great views of the action. To avoid the crowds, come earlier in the day when it's quieter.

G   Jones Road

Looking at Jones Road today you would never guess its history – it used to be a large car park! Today, it's very popular, with lots of separate areas, including some with very challenging sections, and a café serving great food. There's an entrance charge, but there's plenty to keep you busy!

H   Liv Park

Liv Park is known as the friendliest skateboard park around, and the other skateboarders are happy to teach you new skills. You can borrow equipment for a small hourly charge, and there's a range of the latest designer sweatshirts and caps from skateboarding companies at good prices.

Questions 11–15

For each question, choose the correct answer.

Monika Alson: kart racing driver

I drive karts: small racing cars. I started aged 10, and although that's young, I'd already been in a bike-racing club for two years! Another member was into kart racing, and a conversation with her convinced me to have a go. I persuaded my brother to come along. I thought he'd enjoy it – he'd started at the bike club with me, but got bored. Unfortunately, the same happened with karts. I really loved it though, and even spent hours watching kart videos online!

Soon, I was asked to enter a competition. It was a big event, with prizes presented by well-known sportspeople. I personally hadn't heard of them, but I was looking forward to taking part. Because I was the youngest competitor there, I was entering for the experience – when I came fourth, I couldn't believe it! Afterwards, there were interviews from sports channels, and I was amazed anyone would want to know so much about me! I got a medal for taking part, but the winner got a huge silver cup!

Kart racing's important in my life, and in my family's. If one of my parents is working, the other always comes to watch me compete. Because I'm still at school, I'm very busy. I can cycle to my race training sessions straight after school and still be home to get my homework done because I live close to the kart training track. Then I get to bed so I have enough sleep before being up early, ready to start again. I'm careful I don't get too tired, which means unfortunately I sometimes have to refuse party invitations from classmates. Hopefully it'll be worth it, but I don't like doing that.

I've got a big race soon. I'm preparing by continuing the gym sessions I've always done, but with extra strength-building classes. I'm seeing benefits already. All tracks are different, and as the one where the race takes place is six hours' drive away, practising there isn't an option. I've seen videos of people racing there. It's not the same, though. Luckily, my coach knows it well, and even won as a new driver there years ago. Hopefully, I'll do the same!

11 Monika decided she wanted to try driving karts after
   A   she watched a film about the sport.
   B   she talked to a young female driver.
   C   she got bored with another activity she was doing.
   D   she saw how much her brother enjoyed the activity.

12 When Monika did her first competition, she felt
   A   excited about meeting some celebrities.
   B   impressed by the prize she received.
   C   surprised by the media interest.
   D   confident that she would win.

13 What does Monika find difficult about her life?
   A   missing social activities with her friends
   B   feeling exhausted at school after a big race
   C   having to get up early to practise kart driving
   D   managing to complete schoolwork on time

14 What has been useful preparation for Monika's next race?
   A   studying previous race winners
   B   starting training with a new coach
   C   trying some new fitness exercises
   D   visiting the track where the race takes place

15 What would Monika say in a text to a friend?

A
> Sometimes I feel a bit sad because when my parents have to work, it means no one from my family can see me race.

B
> I can't believe how lucky I've been – I've always finished in the top three in my races!

C
> I'm lucky my parents are happy to spend so long taking me to the practice track. They can't wait until I can drive there myself, though!

D
> I'm so pleased that I didn't have the same opinion about kart racing as my brother! It's been such a positive experience for me.

Questions 16–20

Five sentences have been removed from the text below. For each question, choose the correct answer. There are three extra sentences which you do not need to use.

An incredible holiday

For our last holiday, mum and I went to South Africa on safari – a tour where you go in a vehicle to see different animals. We started the experience by staying the night in a wooden house, where we met our safari guide, Mandisa. The house was by a lake and I was worried there might be fighting among the animals coming to drink. **16** [____] Mandisa explained that getting water was usually the most important thing for the animals when they were there. She also explained that although they looked relaxed, each one was always looking out for danger.

The next morning, we set off in a big car. There were six seats in the back, and the sides were open, so there were no windows. It made us feel closer to the animals. **17** [____] Mandisa was great at suggesting what would make good ones! She also taught us all about all the animals in the area.

Early in our drive, Mandisa pointed to a springbok. Springboks look like deer. She explained they are very common and are South Africa's national animal. **18** [____] Later, however, we saw some elephants under trees. After a while, the largest one started staring at us. Mandisa explained that there are certain types of behaviour to watch out for. **19** [____] She told us that because the elephant wasn't displaying any of the signs of this, we weren't in danger. Having Mandisa there explaining everything was really helpful.

We didn't just learn about different animals. There were special plants growing in the area too. Mandisa got us to try the leaves of one, to explain how they tasted of salt. **20** [____]. Mandisa told us that many animals get some of the salt they require from eating plants. All too soon, we had to leave. It was an experience I'll never forget!

A   Knowing which one helped us get the best view.

B   Therefore, we realised we had to be patient.

C   However, there wasn't and everything seemed very peaceful.

D   This is something animals need to stay healthy.

E   Despite this, we didn't see any more that day!

F   These can show when an animal is feeling stressed.

G   As a result, animals quickly learn to avoid it.

H   It was also good because it made it easier to take incredible pictures.

Questions 21–26

For each question, choose the correct answer.

Spending time outside

Many of us spend more time indoors than we do outside. But did you know that being inside too much can have a negative **(21)**.................... on our health? There have been a number of scientific studies which have **(22)**..................... that being outside is good for us, even if it is just for a short **(23)**..................... of time. One of the issues with being inside a lot is that we often sit watching a screen, like a TV or a laptop. Over time, this can damage our eyes. When we walk around in a natural environment like a forest, however, we **(24)**..................... looking at objects which are nearby and others which are some **(25)**..................... away. This exercises our eye muscles, helping them stay healthy. What's more, scientists claim that looking at green plants can make us feel more creative, as well as **(26)**..................... us with the perfect chance to switch off from our busy lives.

21	**A** problem	**B** effect	**C** condition	**D** conclusion
22	**A** approved	**B** sorted	**C** persuaded	**D** confirmed
23	**A** period	**B** age	**C** total	**D** level
24	**A** hold	**B** remain	**C** stay	**D** keep
25	**A** distance	**B** length	**C** amount	**D** range
26	**A** offer	**B** give	**C** provide	**D** deliver

Questions 27–32

For each question, write the correct word.
Write **one** word for each gap.

To: Katie

About: Shopping trip!

Hi!

Guess what – I went to that new shopping centre in town this afternoon with Mum! We had a really good time. You should go if you can because I know you **(27)** .... love it. Do you remember my favourite blue shirt, the one with flowers on it? Well, I found another similar one with leaves instead **(28)** .... flowers and I decided to get it. It's really nice! There were **(29)** .... many clothes shops that even I needed to have a rest after a bit. Luckily, there were quite a few really nice cafés for lunch. Then, while Mum **(30)** .... having a coffee, I went into the video game shop and bought a new game **(31)** .... the money I got for my birthday. **(32)** .... don't you come over at the weekend so we can play it together? And we can go shopping too, of course!

Mandy

You **must** answer this question.
Write your answer in about **100 words** on the answer sheet.

Question 1

Read this email from your English-speaking friend Avery and the notes you have made.

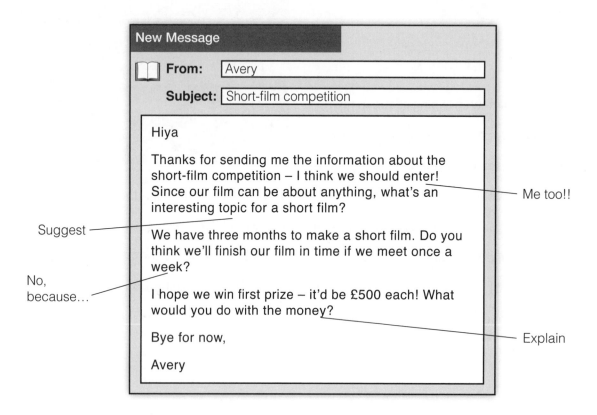

Write your **email** to Avery using **all the notes**.

Choose **one** of these questions.

Write your answer in about **100 words** on the answer sheet.

....

Question 2

You see this notice on an international website for young people.

Articles wanted!

ENJOYING YOUR FREE TIME

Tell us about the leisure-time activity you most enjoy doing.

Why do you like it so much?

Is it important for you to do lots of things in your free time? Why?

The best articles answering these questions will be published next month.

Write your **article**.

Question 3

Your English teacher has asked you to write a story. Your story must begin with this sentence.

I looked at my best friend, and we both started to laugh.

Write your **story**.

Questions 1–7

71   For each question, choose the correct answer.

1   Which is the girl's favourite painting?

A

B

C

2   What new series do the friends decide to watch?

A

B

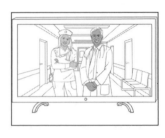

C

3   Where can the visitors to the museum get information from?

A

B

C

4 Which video game does the girl prefer?

A

B

C

5 Why did the boy go to the match by train?

A

B

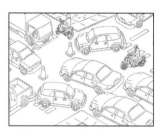

C

6 What did the boy buy for the holiday?

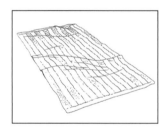

A

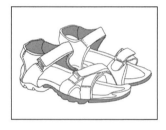

B

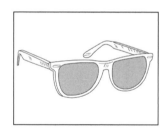

C

7 What is the girl famous for?

A

B

C

Questions 8–13

72   For each question, choose the correct answer.

8   You will hear two friends talking about a band.
     What does the girl think is most original about the band?

     A   what they sang about

     B   how well they sang

     C   how they were dressed

9   You will hear a boy talking about a restaurant.
     Why did his family decide to go to the restaurant?

     A   The food was a reasonable price.

     B   There was lots of space.

     C   They could park there.

10   You will hear a boy and a girl talking about recycling.
     The boy is trying to convince the girl to

     A   join an activity.

     B   support his plan.

     C   give up a habit.

11   You will hear two friends talking about their classroom.
     What do they have to do next week?

     A   move the furniture

     B   decorate the walls

     C   remove their books

12   You will hear a girl telling a friend about a job advertisement.
     How does she feel about it?

     A   hopeful she'll get work

     B   shocked by the wages

     C   keen to work hard

13   You will hear a boy talking about a photograph.
     What was difficult about taking it?

     A   It became too dark.

     B   The weather was bad.

     C   The location was hard to get to.

Questions 14–19

73   For each question, write the correct answer in the gap.
Write **one** or **two words** or a **number** or a **date** or a **time**.

....

You will hear a student talking about a roller-skating club.

My roller-skating club

The club offers classes for beginners on **(14)** ....

At the weekends when the weather is good, they skate in **(15)** ....

When they are skating in the city, they have to wear a **(16)** .... and a helmet.

At the National Championships, the club members were surprised to get special
(17) ....

The class wants to learn to **(18)** .... on skates.

The club training sessions take place in a **(19)** .... in a school.

For each question, choose the correct answer.

You will hear an interview with a young man called James Clark, who designs clothes.

20 How did James first learn about making clothes?

    A He went to classes.

    B He watched other people.

    C His mother taught him.

21 What kind of clothes does James like designing now?

    A dresses

    B trousers

    C T-shirts

22 James thinks he's successful because

    A his clothes are a good price.

    B his ideas are original.

    C his designs are for young people.

23 How did James feel about showing his designs in the London fashion show?

    A nervous about speaking in public

    B certain it would improve his career

    C surprised he was chosen to be there

24 What does James like most about his work?

    A drawing

    B travelling abroad

    C meeting people

25 James thinks it's important to

    A help the planet.

    B keep learning.

    C protect fashion workers.

PART 1

(2–3 minutes)

Phase 1

Good morning / afternoon / evening.

What's your name?

How old are you?

Where do you live?

Phase 2

(possible examiner questions)

What did you do last night?

What school subject would you like to learn more about? (Why? / Why not?)

Tell us about your favourite day of the week.

Do you like reading? (Why? / Why not?)

What job would you like to do in the future? (Why?)

Who makes you laugh the most? (Why are they funny?)

How long do you study English each week?

Tell us about how you spend time with friends.

 Listen to two students doing the task above.
75

PART 2

(3–5 minutes)

Now I'd like each of you to talk on your own about something. I'm going to give each of you a photograph and I'd like you to talk about it.

A, here is your photograph. It shows **some people with an assistance dog**. (See page C5.)

B, you just listen.

A, please tell us what you can see in the photograph.

B, here is your photograph. It **shows some people playing music**. (See page C6.)

A, you just listen.

B, please tell us what you can see in the photograph.

 Listen to two students doing the task above.
76

PART 3

(4–5 minutes)

Now, in this part of the test you're going to talk about something together for about two minutes. I'm going to describe a situation to you.

A class wants to plan an event. They would like to **do something fun** to celebrate the end of term.

Here are some **things they could do** to celebrate. (See page C16.)

Talk together about the different **things they could do** to celebrate and say **which would be best**.

All right? Now, talk together.

 Listen to two students doing the task above.
77

PART 4

(3–4 minutes)

What special occasions does your school celebrate?

Do you go to any clubs at your school? (What do you do?)

What kind of club would you like your school to have, for example, an art club? (Why?)

Is it important for schools to have sports teams? (Why?)

What kind of activities can bring students closer together at school? (How do they help students develop better friendships?)

Does school help students to learn useful skills? (What skills do you learn at school?)

 Listen to two students doing the task above.
78

LISTENING PART 1

Training

1 I put my guitar in the wardrobe in my bedroom, but now it's not there.

2 Why did you leave all those plates in the sink? The kitchen's a mess!

3 I think it's dangerous to go diving in very deep water.

4 I heard her new recording on a website. It was amazing!

5 There was a tiny cottage at the bottom of the hill.

6 Can you help me put this tie on? It's really difficult.

1 *Man*: How was work today?

Woman: I'm exhausted. I've been working on Mr Harrison's motorbike all day and I didn't even start on Mrs Brown's car. She won't be happy that she can't pick it up tomorrow. I'll have to do it as soon as possible.

2 *Girl*: Hi Jess, I just wanted to let you know that the match on Saturday has been cancelled. Kelly was injured in the game yesterday, so we won't have enough players. We won, though, and I scored a lot of points!

3 *Boy*: What's that noise?

Girl: Oh, it's my brother. He's just taken up the violin and he hasn't stopped practising all morning!

4 *Boy*: Did you hear about Chrissie?

Girl: No, what's she done?

Boy: She's become a windsurfing champion. In fact, she's out at sea right now.

5 *Woman*: How's your project going, Ben?

Ben: It's fun. We've got all the things we need now and I'm looking forward to doing the experiment in the exhibition at school at the end of term.

6 *Girl*: What happened to you this morning?

Boy: I nearly missed the bus. I was a bit late and it was just leaving, but luckily the driver stopped and let me get on.

Exam Practice

1 *Man*: Danny! Are you ready to go? It's getting late.

Danny: I'm just coming. Where are my shoes?

Man: They should be in your sports bag, or under your bed where you left them last time.

Danny: Well, I definitely had them in my bag, but it's not <u>on the hall table where I normally put it</u>.

Man: What about in the wardrobe in your bedroom?

Danny: I'll have a look.

Man: OK, but hurry up or you'll miss the bus.

2 *Boy*: So, Tammy, how was the trip to see your grandparents last weekend?

Tammy: It was OK, but I made a big mistake. My grandmother gave me a T-shirt for my last birthday. You know, the one with pink and green stripes, which is the one I wanted to wear, but I'd lent it to Lily the day before in exchange for <u>her plain one</u>. It matched the spots on my skirt, but I think my grandmother was a bit upset because I was wearing Lily's T-shirt instead of the one she'd bought me.

Boy: Oh dear!

3 *Girl*: Hi Carl. Have I shown you the photos I got from my brother yesterday?

Carl: No. Let me see! Wow, that one of the huge waves is amazing!

Girl: Yes, he went to the north coast last weekend with some friends and <u>they introduced him to surfing</u>.

Carl: That sounds fun. He really loves the sea, doesn't he?

Girl: You're right. We used to go a lot with my father when he was into fishing. I've got some great pictures of the sea from that time as well.

4 *Boy*: Finally, you're here! What happened?

Girl: I'm sorry. I took a taxi to the station, but when I got to the ticket office, I realised I'd lost my purse. I'd been in the sweet shop before, so I went back there, but the assistant said she hadn't found it. I thought of going to the police, but then <u>the taxi driver called me. She'd found my purse</u> with my phone number in it, so I ran to the taxi stop and there it was! But I missed the train!

Boy: Well, I'm happy you got here!

5 *Girl*: How was your sister's birthday party?

Boy: It was fun. We went to that café that she loves. She goes there a lot with people from work and she's friendly with all the waiters, so they looked after us very well, but <u>what I think is really wonderful is the band</u> that plays there on Friday night. They sang a song specially for her, which was great. The food there is quite ordinary, though. They only have sandwiches and cakes.

6 *Boy*: Hey Grandma. Can you help me?

Grandma: Sure, what do you need?

Boy: Well, the school play's next month and I need something for my costume.

Grandma: So how can I help? Last time you needed your grandfather's helmet!

Boy: I remember! No firefighting this time! The main character's a detective and wears a suit and tie, but I'm a mad scientist. I know you used to work in a laboratory, so I was wondering …

Grandma: Ah, so <u>you need a lab coat</u>. I'm sure mine is somewhere. I'll find it for you.

Boy: Thanks Grandma!

7 Metropolitan railways apologises for the delay to the 8:15 train to Stockbridge. This is due to the storm we had last night. While we have managed to clear a fallen tree from the line, <u>there are a number of farm animals that escaped through a broken gate and are still on the line</u>. Fortunately, the heavy snow predicted early this morning hasn't happened, so we don't expect further delays today.

LISTENING PART 2

 Training

04

1 I've got to give a presentation in front of the whole class next week and I'm really nervous about forgetting what I want to say.

2 That wildlife programme was really good. That tiger was sweet. I loved the way she looked after her babies.

3 Wait a second for the bell and when it rings, run as fast as you can.

4 When we got to the top of the tower, I couldn't believe how high we were. We could see the whole city.

5 Although he speaks very slowly, the stories he tells are really funny.

6 The park in the city centre is surprising – you wouldn't think it could be as huge as it is.

 Jemma: How was the summer camp?

05 *Fred:* Well, I only stayed a week in the end.

Jemma: Oh! What happened?

Fred: Actually, it was good fun and I was happy because I'd just finished all my exams before we left. But then my coach called me and said there was an important game and I had to be there for the team, so I came back. Luckily, I was feeling fit and ready for it.

 Exam Practice

06

8 *Mia:* Danny, what's our homework for tomorrow?

Danny: It's on the school website. I'll show you where to find it ... Here!

Mia: Ah yes, of course. I'd forgotten where to find it, but it's actually quite easy. Oh, look at these. Articles about next year's trip to Scotland. I'd love to go, and all of this information is exactly what we need to know in advance.

Danny: You're right. It looks like they did a lot of exciting things on last year's trip. And there are some pictures. Ha ha, this one is terrible! It's raining!

Mia: I quite like it. It shows you what to expect.

9 *Tess:* Harry, you'll be really interested in what I saw last night.

Harry: What's that?

Tess: It was a programme about space and I know you love that. They talked about a project to send people back to the Moon. I hadn't realised that it's been 50 years since any human has been there. I know some people have been to space as tourists, although they have to pay a lot of money, but I thought they might have been to the Moon as well. Anyway, they've been planning this for ages, which I suppose is normal. You must watch it!

10 *Bea:* Hi Freddy, what have you been up to lately?

Freddy: You won't believe it, but I've started a cookery course.

Bea: That sounds fun! What's it like?

Freddy: Well, it was only the first day, but the teacher was really friendly and we made a strange sort of cake. There are a lot of different people on the course. I was one of the youngest, but my partner was a woman who's a professional photographer and she took some photos of us cooking. That was the best bit, actually. She got a great one of me covered in flour!

11 *Richard:* Are you nervous about the concert this weekend?

Jasmine: A little. I mean, I think we've practised enough, but that section where each group has to sing a different part at the same time is difficult. I think I might get it wrong when we perform.

Richard: Yeah, that part makes me anxious too. And remember, we have to wear something formal. My Dad got me a new black suit.

Jasmine: Yes, I haven't had time to organise that yet, but I think my black trousers will be perfect. I'll have to buy a white shirt, though.

12 *Jon:* I'm so happy. I passed the maths test! I thought I was going to fail!

Flora: How did you manage to pass?

Jon: Well, what I did was find lots of extra problems and then try to solve them. I think that's much more useful than just using the book we have for class. There aren't enough examples. There's this great app that I used. My friend Joe told me about it. I'll show you, if you like.

Flora: Oh yes please. Maths is so difficult this year and I've got my test next week.

13 *Joe:* How was your weekend in the mountains?

Bella: Amazing! The snow was fantastic, so I got lots of practice with my new snowboard. It's great for jumping so I don't regret spending so much money on it, but I did have a few falls at first.

Joe: I hope you didn't hurt yourself!

Bella: No, but once I was in such deep snow that I almost lost the board. It's white, so it's not easy to see! Ha ha! Anyway, I hope I'll improve because I'm going to join the snowboarding team next month.

Joe: Good luck with that!

LISTENING PART 3

 Training

07

1 I think I've got everything for the exam. Let me check ... Oh no! My calculator's not here! I'd better ask my brother if he can lend me his.

2 We looked everywhere for a place to eat. Eventually, we found the only café that was open. It wasn't very good!

3 Well, I'm happy with the result. Although I wasn't one of the winners, I did finish in fourth place.

4 I had to find a job for the summer. When I saw a sign in the shop window, I immediately went in to ask.

5 The interview was last week. It took me a long time to prepare for it because I had to give a presentation.

6 I really didn't fancy going to the party because I'd had a busy week and I was so tired.

7 I knew I had to find out more about the expedition because the documentary I saw about it was so interesting.

8 It was a fantastic trip. It took us a long time to get there, though. I've never spent two days on a train before.

 1 We thought about going to see a play at the theatre, but we decided to go to the cinema, despite the bad reviews of the 08 film, because it was cheaper.

2 I couldn't decide if a backpack or a suitcase would be better for when I go on holiday this summer. Although backpacks are cheaper, I thought a suitcase would be more comfortable to carry, so I ended up getting one of those light ones.

3 We wanted to meet up this weekend and we both love sport, so the obvious choice was to play tennis. However, the courts were all booked so we went for a run instead.

4 I've done all my homework, so I've got the afternoon free. Mum told me not to make a mess in the kitchen, otherwise I'd make a cake, so I think I'll clean my bike outside.

5 The concert wasn't too expensive. There was a special offer for students so actually, I only paid £10 rather than £15, which was the full price.

Exam Practice

09

Hi, I'm Aidan, and on this week's podcast I'll tell you about my kayaking trip last weekend. I'd wanted to do this for ages, since my brother went on the same trip last year. So, I persuaded my <u>cousin</u> to come and my parents took us to the beach early in the morning.

The coast there is really interesting. It's not just sandy beaches. There are lots of really incredible rocks and beautiful little islands. We saw some <u>caves</u> too, and those were the most exciting part as it was quite dark. We had head torches so we could see when we were inside.

In fact, that's why you need something warm to wear because if you just have a swimming costume you can get quite cold there, so you need at least a T-shirt. I was glad I hadn't forgotten my <u>sweater</u>.

Outside it was better. I mean, you can't expect high temperatures in spring, but it was <u>sunny</u> the whole day! Although we thought it might be rainy, it wasn't. We just got wet from the waves!

If you're interested in a trip like this, it's best to organise a group because they have special prices. If you go on your own, it's £26.50 for the day, but if there are ten of you, you only have to pay <u>£15.50</u> each.

I'd recommend this trip to everyone. However, be prepared to feel really tired afterwards. I imagined that my arms would ache at the end of the day, but it was my <u>hands</u> that were sore from holding the paddle so tight.

LISTENING PART 4

Training

10

Interviewer: So why did you decide to have a year off before starting university?

Sylvie: Well, I've always been adventurous and when Julia suggested I go with her to India, I thought it would be good to have some time off before I began my degree. But <u>it was the chance to find out about the wildlife there that made up my mind for me!</u>

Exam Practice

11

Presenter: Good morning. Today we're talking to Jessica Shore, the winner of the Young Scientist prize. Hello Jessica. What did you win the prize for?

Jessica: I won it for making a robot cat!

Presenter: Where did you get the idea for this invention?

Jessica: Well, my brother and I used to make models together, so I've always been interested in how machines work. Last year I had a great IT teacher who encouraged us to experiment and get ideas from websites. <u>We also went to science exhibitions. In one of those, there were robot animals, so I thought a cat would be the perfect thing to try.</u>

Presenter: So, are you proud of your work?

Jessica: Although I won the competition, actually I think <u>my best project was with a friend after that. It's a cleaning robot that helps people</u> who can't reach high windows. We tried it out at my grandmother's and she was so impressed she didn't want to give it back!

Presenter: All this must keep you very busy. What do you do in your free time?

Jessica: I have a lot of school work to do. But I do like getting out at the weekends as well and recently, I joined a local group that promotes cycling. We have a small workshop where <u>we fix bikes for people. It's a free service for anyone</u>, so I'm often doing that when my friends are shopping or away somewhere for the day.

Presenter: So, what projects are you working on now?

Jessica: I'm in my final year at school. I'd like to go to university and do something like programming, but my technology teacher suggested I could make some money from what I do now. <u>She's helping me start a small company</u>, so next year I'll be giving advice to other teenagers about robotics.

Presenter: I'm sure that'll be popular. Do you think all teenagers should learn about technology?

Jessica: Well, not everyone likes that kind of thing, but <u>I think it's important to know about the world around us</u>. I mean, we all use technology and if we understand how it works, then it's easier to use and even repair sometimes!

Presenter: So, what do you feel about robots in the future?

Jessica: Of course, robots are useful, but we mustn't become too dependent on them. They should make our lives easier, not replace human contact. I hope they'll give us more free time to enjoy ourselves with family and friends, and to improve life, <u>not have a negative effect on it. I'm worried that might happen</u>.

SPEAKING PART 1

Training

12

1 What do you like doing in your free time?

2 How often do you exercise?

3 Tell us about a teacher you like.

4 Which do you prefer, going to the cinema or watching a film at home?

5 How long have you studied English for?

6 When do you practise speaking English?

Exam Practice

13

Interlocutor: Tell us about the town where you live.

Maria: Well, I come from a village in the mountains in Italy. It's very pretty, but there isn't much for young people to do. Like, there's no sports centre or clothes shops. But we go horse riding and swimming in the river. And everyone's very friendly.

Interlocutor: Where would you most like to visit in the world?

Ivan: Australia.

Interlocutor: Why?

Ivan: Because I'd like to see kangaroos and go on a long road trip. I think it would be fun. My country's very small and it rains a lot. I think I'd like to experience the really hot weather in Australia.

Interlocutor: What do you enjoy learning about at school?

Maria: Sorry, I don't understand.

Interlocutor: What do you enjoy learning about at school?

Maria: I love maths because for me it's easy. In maths, I can always get the right answer. I can't do that with all my subjects.

Interlocutor: And you?

Ivan: I like art best. I love drawing and painting, and my teacher says I'm pretty good at it. One day, I'd like to be an artist maybe.

Interlocutor: Do you like playing team sports?

Maria: No, I don't.

Interlocutor: Why not?

Maria: I'm not very good at sports like football or basketball. It isn't interesting for me. I prefer things like dancing and walking.

Interlocutor: What did you do in your last school holidays?

Ivan: I went camping with my best friend and his parents. We stayed near the beach and it was really good. My friend's dad hired a boat and we went fishing. And we cooked food on the fire for dinner every day.

SPEAKING PART 2

Training

In the photo, I can see two people sitting at a table in a kitchen. It's quite a small space and there are lots of dishes on the table. It looks like they're having a tasty meal, but I'm not sure what they're eating. It could be small plates of snacks, and I think there's some cheese. The girls could be relatives or friends, and it looks like they're having an interesting conversation. I think the girl on the right is telling the girl on the left a funny joke because she's laughing. The kitchen's very tidy. I can see some baskets and the thing you get water from – I've forgotten the name for that. Tap? I There are some things on the shelves between the cupboards. I'm not sure what they are – jars maybe? One girl's got a top with stripes on and the other's wearing a headscarf. The girls look relaxed and I think they're having fun.

Exam Practice

 A In the photo, there are four people – it's a family, I think. There are two children. I'm not sure how old they are, but they're very young. They're looking at some plants, or maybe they're planting them. I think they could be growing some food to eat. I'm not sure what the plants are, though. I think they're in a garden because there are some trees and other plants. They're wearing comfortable clothes. The boy's wearing a cap and sandals. I think it's warm but not hot because the people have got long sleeves, but they haven't got coats on. The man is holding one of the plants and the woman and man are watching what the children are doing. Maybe they're teaching them about the plants, or perhaps the children are picking them. They look interested in what they're doing, and the woman is smiling.

 B In the photo, I can see a man and two children. He's probably their dad. They're in the living room – there's a sofa and tables, a plant and some shelves. There's a nice rug and there's a lot of wood. It looks like a comfortable room where the family enjoys spending time together and relaxing. The people are cleaning together. The girl's cleaning the TV – she's wearing gloves and she's got a cloth and something to clean the screen with. She's concentrating on her job. The man's got a small brush and he's brushing the rug. The boy's looking at him and laughing. He's got a larger brush, and I think he's helping his dad. The boy's wearing headphones, so maybe he's listening to music. They're all wearing comfortable clothes and it looks like they're enjoying what they're doing.

 C In the photo there are four people. It looks like a small family and they're watching something on TV. It could be a film night because the children – I think they're both girls – are wearing their pyjamas. They all look very comfortable. The woman is lying on a red sofa and the man's on the floor with the two girls. They've all got drinks. I think the girls have glasses of juice and the parents have got cups of coffee or tea. I think there's a snack on a plate on the floor – some crisps maybe? The girl on the right of the picture is holding a toy bear, and there's another bear on the sofa. I think they're watching something fun because they're laughing. It's dark. I think they've got low lights to create a kind of cinema atmosphere.

SPEAKING PART 3

Training

Boy: What do you think would be a good gift for a friend who's in hospital?

Girl: Well, the flowers make the room look nicer.

Boy: I'm not sure about that. They're pretty, but not very useful.

Girl: Well, I think the magazines are a good idea. Being in hospital is boring, so they give the person something to read.

Boy: I agree. But it can be noisy in hospitals and it might be hard to concentrate on reading.

Girl: You're right. What about the fruit? That doesn't seem very useful.

Boy: I don't agree. Hospital food isn't always very nice! Fruit would be lovely and fresh.

Girl: Well, maybe the meal would be better? Home-cooked food is always good.

Boy: Yes, perhaps. What about a card? That would show your friend you're thinking about them.

Girl: I don't know about that. You only look at cards once or twice.

Boy: How about the tablet, then?

Girl: I think that would be best. Then the person can keep in touch with friends and family.

Boy: That's a good idea! OK, so why don't we say that the tablet would be the best gift for someone in hospital?

Girl: Great.

Exam Practice

Susie: OK, so we have to decide which places the friends could visit. I think somewhere outside might be nice, like the countryside. They could go for a walk and get some fresh air.

Leo: I'm not sure about that. It might be a bit boring. There are only fields and trees… What about the art gallery? Lots of young people like art.

Susie: I don't know about that. Not everyone likes it. I don't because I don't understand it. Maybe a trip to the castle would be better. It looks amazing!

Leo: It's very big and old. But if you don't like history, I'm not sure it would be very interesting. It's just looking at rooms and walls.

Susie: OK, so do you think a city would be a good place to visit? Most people live in cities, so I don't think it would be especially nice.

Leo: I agree. We see big buildings and lots of traffic every day. It would be nice to go somewhere different. How about the museum with the trains? That might be fun. Maybe they could go on a train ride or something.

Susie: You're right. That might be interesting, but I think the stadium tour would be best. Most young people like sport and maybe they could get to meet some of their favourite players!

Leo: That's a good idea! And maybe they can watch a match there.

Susie: I think that would be better than going to the seaside. There's nothing much you can do there, especially if the weather's not very good. And not everyone likes going to the beach.

Leo: No. And I think the sea's usually too cold to swim in!

SPEAKING PART 4

Training

Olivia: So, I think it's lovely to receive gifts that people have obviously put a lot of thought into. Like, I collect old records. If someone buys me one they know I'll like, I think that's brilliant.

Tomasz: Yes, that would be good.

Olivia: I like food as a gift too, for example nice chocolates or snacks. You can enjoy them, but you don't need to find somewhere to put them in your house. What about you? What do you really like?

Tomasz: I like lots of different things. My brother always gets me an interesting book for my birthday and I love that. But I think my favourite kind of gift is something that someone's made. A friend gave me a wooden box that he made for me to keep all my cables and things in. That's the kind of thing that I prefer to receive.

Interlocutor: Do you prefer to visit places that are indoors or outdoors?

Boy: I prefer to be outdoors, so I like visiting the mountains and the seaside. It's nice to be in the fresh air and get some exercise.

Girl: Me too! I love taking photos of spectacular scenery. But I like some indoor activities, as well, like going to museums and palaces.

Interlocutor: What's an interesting place that you've been to?

Girl: I went to Prague.

Interlocutor: Why was it interesting?

Girl: I think it's really great. The buildings were very different to the city I live in. I loved travelling around the city on the trams – we don't have trams where I'm from, only buses. And we had some delicious food.

Boy: I've never been there, but I've been to London. It's a huge city and there's so much to do. It's great for young people like us.

Girl: I agree!

Interlocutor: How do you prefer travelling to new places?

Boy: It depends. If it's a long way you need to go by plane, but that's not good for the planet. I'd rather use public transport instead of cars.

Interlocutor: Why?

Boy: Because it's cleaner and if you go by train, it's often faster too.

Interlocutor: What do you think people can learn from visiting new places?

Girl: I'm not sure. What about you? Do you think people learn things in new places?

Boy: I think so. It's a good way to find out more about other countries and other people. Do you agree?

Girl: I guess so. But it's hard to talk to people in other countries when you don't know the language. I suppose a lot of people speak English, but not everyone does.

Boy: But when you *can* speak to people, you find out about new ways of life and different opinions about things.

Girl: That's true. And that can help you to understand other people better.

Boy: Exactly!

Interlocutor: Do you think younger people and older people like visiting different kinds of places?

Girl: Yes, probably.

Boy: Really? I think it depends on what kind of person you are and what interests you've got. Like, if you're into sailing or shopping or whatever, you'll always like those things and the places you do the activities in, whether you're 19 or 90!

Girl: I don't know about that. I think people change during their lives and that includes what they're interested in. Also, when you get older, maybe you don't want to travel as far, or be uncomfortable.

Boy: Maybe you're right.

Test 2

LISTENING PART 1
Training

Johnny: So how was the summer camp? They had a lot of activities you enjoy, like sailing and hockey, didn't they?

Grace: Yes, and table tennis too. In the evenings we had different competitions and I played with a girl who was a real expert with a bat and ball. <u>What I really loved was being out on the water almost every day</u> and most of the time there was plenty of wind. There weren't enough players to do team sports, but I didn't miss playing hockey. I do enough of that at school.

1 *Man:* How did your shopping go?

Woman: OK. I tried on three dresses but none of them fitted me, so I bought a skirt instead.

2 *Girl:* So what was the experience like?

Boy: I quite liked diving, but I don't want to do it again in the future. It was a bit scary.

3 *Boy:* Come on, we're late!

Girl: Sorry, I couldn't find my book anywhere in the classroom, so I had to look in the library.

4 *Boy:* Did you do a lot of walking?

Girl: No, it was too cold to stay outside, so we spent the afternoon playing board games.

5 *Woman:* Have you got all you need?

Boy: Yes, my camera's not working, so I'll leave it at home. I can take photos with my phone.

6 *Boy:* What happened to you?

Girl: I'm so angry. I fell on the street, but nobody helped me. People are so selfish.

7 *Boy:* Oh no, I haven't got enough money to get the bus. I'll have to walk.

8 *Girl:* Was it expensive?

Boy: No, we didn't need to buy a ticket because the concert was free.

 Girl: Mum, have you seen my phone? I haven't used it since I left school yesterday.

Mum: Did you leave it in your room?

Girl: I don't think so. I've looked everywhere in the house.

Mum: What about in the bathroom?

Girl: I didn't have it this morning when I was cleaning my teeth.

Mum: You didn't look hard enough. <u>It's here under your pillow</u>!

Girl: Oh, thanks. I thought maybe I'd left it on the bus yesterday evening.

Exam Practice

25 **1** *Girl:* Hi Jackson. What happened to you? Have you broken your arm?

Jackson: Yeah, I did it last week.

Girl: Oh, I remember you were going on holiday.

Jackson: Yes, I was going skiing, but the day before we were supposed to go, I had an accident. I was cycling home from the climbing club when I hit a rock on the road and fell.

Girl: Did you hit your head?

Jackson: Luckily, I was wearing a helmet, so it's only my arm.

2 *Boy:* Emma, I've been looking at films on this week. What do you fancy going to see? There's an action film about fast cars or one about a basketball team.

Emma: Hmm, I was looking too. We could go to see the new science–fiction film. I've seen the first two in the series and they were really good.

Boy: I haven't seen them, so I'd rather wait till I can. Shall we go for the sports one?

Emma: I think the first one you said would be the best.

Boy: OK, that's decided then.

3 *Boy:* Hey Martha. Are we going to go to the park to do some work for our biology project?

Martha: OK. Let's go this afternoon.

Boy: Can I borrow a notebook to draw the plants and write where we found them?

Martha: I can give you one. I don't want it back if you've written in it!

Boy: Thanks! I'll need a pencil as well. I haven't got time to go home and get one.

Martha: Sure, but I *will* want that back. We won't need a calculator, will we?

Boy: Not this afternoon, no.

4 *Girl:* Do you need a lift home from football practice today? Your dad's away, isn't he?

Boy: Yes. His flight is tonight, but it'll be too late so my mum's going to leave work early and pick me up. I asked my aunt if she could come, but her shop doesn't close till 8 o'clock, so I'd have to wait for an hour and it's freezing!

Girl: Well, next time, ask me. My dad's always free in the evenings.

Boy: Thanks!

5 *Girl:* I haven't seen Tommy for ages. Have you?

Boy: No, since he changed schools, we haven't seen each other much. In fact, I sent him a message the other day and we're going to meet at the weekend. It wasn't easy though, because it looks like his phone's not working, so he didn't answer my call and of course texting was no good either. In the end I wrote a note and left it at his house on the way to school and he called me on his mother's phone.

6 Hi Megan. I'm really sorry, but I won't be able to go to the party tonight. I really want to, but I can't get rid of this headache I've had all day. Maybe I spent too much time studying on the computer yesterday and it's my eyes, but also I didn't sleep well because my baby sister was up all night crying, so I helped my parents with her. I'm so sorry to miss it!

7 *Girl:* Hi Jacob. You're back! Did you have fun?

Jacob: It was amazing. I thought the trip was going to be a bit boring, you know, sightseeing and museums, that kind of thing, but the city's actually really interesting. We ate a lot of food, although some of it was a bit strange and the restaurants close very early. It's a very green city too, with loads of parks. There was one with a lake in the middle and the best thing was we could take a boat out on it.

LISTENING PART 2

 Training

26 **1** I thought I'd lost my notebook, but Jason found it. Thank goodness.

2 My brother's got a new phone. I wanted one too! It's not fair!

3 I expected to do better in the test, but I didn't. I'm a bit sad about that.

4 I've never been so tired in my life.

5 The woman behind me in the cinema didn't stop talking. It made me quite angry.

6 I hope we won't be late to the airport. I'm worried we're going to miss the plane.

7 I don't understand these instructions. They just don't make any sense.

8 You did really well! I'm going to tell everyone how clever my sister is!

 1 Hi Marty, I've just heard that that new band is giving a concert next month in the city. I'd be so happy if you'd come with me. Please say yes!

27

2 I think the pictures are the wrong way round. You could try putting the one of the horses first, before the one of butterflies.

3 I didn't mean to do it. I'm so sorry. Will you forgive me?

4 That was the worst film I've ever seen. I don't know why you persuaded me to go!

 Girl: I've got no idea how to do this geography homework!

28 *Boy:* Let me see. Oh yes, it's that one about weather and comparing different countries. It's not difficult, but it took me a long time.

Girl: Oh dear! I don't know where to start.

Boy: Well, I'm sorry, but if you'd done the exercises we had to do last week, you'd already have all the information. You should try to make more effort.

 Exam Practice

29 **8** *Girl:* Did you get a new shirt for the party?

Boy: Not yet. I went to that new clothes shop in the shopping centre and I thought I'd definitely find something there, but I was disappointed.

Girl: Why's that? I heard they have a good variety of clothes.

Boy: Maybe they have, but even though there weren't that many people there, the assistants didn't seem to have time to help me and I couldn't work out the sizes, so I left without buying anything.

Girl: That's a pity. I'll go with you next time.

9 *Girl:* Finally, we're here. What a long journey!

Boy: It certainly was! I'm exhausted. I couldn't believe it when they told us there would be a two-hour delay when we changed trains.

Girl: Me neither, although the trains are often late these days.

Boy: You're right, they are.

Girl: It was quite dull, wasn't it?

Boy: Well, actually, I enjoyed talking to some of the other passengers. We had a good laugh and I think I've made some new friends.

Girl: Hmm, while you were chatting, I was sleeping. I can't remember much!

10 *Boy:* Come on. Let's get this presentation done. I thought we could finish it this evening.

Girl: Do you think so? There's still a lot to do. I've been having problems finding the right photos for the slides.

Boy: You'll be happy to hear I found a website where you can download some good ones for school work, so I've got quite a few to show you.

Girl: Wow, that'll save us a lot of time. We'll get a good grade if we do it well.

Boy: I'm sure we will! Shall we make a start?

11 *Boy:* Are you coming to the party today?

Girl: I can't. My brother and I take turns to clean the house on Saturdays and this week it's my turn.

Boy: Yeah, we do that on Sundays. But last week <u>my parents let me go</u> to a football match after <u>I explained how important the game was</u>. Your brother's coming to the party too, so he won't want to change with you.

Girl: What if say I have to do homework at a friend's house?

Boy: I'm not sure that would work. <u>Maybe try doing the same as I did</u> and they'll let you come.

12 *Boy:* How was your weekend?

Girl: I had a good time, actually. You know I had that important tennis match and I wasn't looking forward to it much, but in the end it was fun.

Boy: I'm glad to hear it. You hurt your wrist a couple of months ago, didn't you?

Girl: Yes, my performance hasn't been as good as usual after my injury so I only got to the semi-finals, but <u>my trainer said I'd definitely improved since last month</u>, despite making some silly mistakes in the first game.

Boy: That's great. I'm sure you'll just get better and better!

13 *Girl:* What are your plans this weekend, Carl?

Carl: I'm going to see a film that's just come out.

Girl: What's it about?

Carl: It's a real-life story about a family living in the 18th century.

Girl: I thought you didn't like historical films.

Carl: I normally don't. I prefer something that is entertaining and easy to watch, but <u>Laura mentioned that it's worth going to see</u>. She's seen some positive reports on that teenage website about films. I might have a look at them before I go, to find out more.

Girl: Well, I hope you enjoy it!

LISTENING PART 3

 Training

1 There are over 50 members who joined last year, so there are 80 of us now, which means we can have three teams.

2 I was a bit late, so I only got to school ten minutes before the bus went. We set off from school at eight and we arrived at half past nine.

3 You can upload your pictures and then change them as well as posting your work on social media. Other people can write comments.

4 I learned to make models when I was ten years old, but since then, in the last six years, I've improved a lot.

5 We've changed the prize this year as there aren't any helmets available, but there'll be a sweatshirt for the winner.

 1 As many of you have other activities on Friday evening, we were going to arrange for the competition to be on Saturday afternoon, but the pool will be closed then, so we've changed it to Sunday morning.

2 We normally meet at the weekend and the day starts in the gym with some exercises to warm up our legs. We go out of the stadium to run in the countryside after we've run a few times around the track.

3 At the end of the day, we'll need to get the bus back. It won't be at the gate where it left us in the morning. Everyone should go to the car park, but if you want to buy a gift, make sure you go to the shop inside the theme park before you leave.

4 The judges gave a special certificate to the boy who wrote the poem called *Yellow Sun*, although the one written by the winner was by far the best. It was called *Tall Trees* and was followed by *The Cave* in second place.

Exam Practice

 Right, now listen everyone. I want to give you the details about the science fair next term. It would be great if you all could take part if possible. You've got a couple of months to prepare because it'll be on June 24th, but you need to send in your ideas with an application by the end of this week, which is <u>April 21st</u>. So I want you to organise your groups and talk to me about your ideas on Thursday 20th. The most exciting news is the subject is something we've been working on all year and I'm sure you'll all have lots of ideas. We did quite well with the space ideas before, but I'm sure <u>recycling</u> will be interesting for many of you this time. There are several schools taking part, including the previous year's winners of the Best Invention prize. We'll have to work hard to win the <u>Improve Earth</u> prize on this occasion. I'm sure you can do it! If you fancy making T-shirts again this year that's fine, but the organisers will give everyone a <u>backpack</u> for taking part as well.

So, some practical details. You need to be in groups of four people. Everyone can help, but you should choose a captain to lead the team and one person on the team should be the <u>secretary</u> and write the report. That person should go online and put in everyone's names. The website is www.<u>scarborough</u>.com because <u>Scarborough</u> School is organising the fair this year. I'll spell that for you: S-C-A-R-B-O-R-O-U-G-H. You need to go to the section related to secondary-school science projects. So, let's decide on the groups for this …

LISTENING PART 4

 Training

1 *Seth:* Katie, can you help me? I'm trying to move this picture, but every time I click on it to drag it to a different place, it won't move.

Katie: Have you checked the battery in your mouse?

Seth: Ah! Of course, I need to change it.

2 It's so annoying. I'm trying to record my voice for a presentation, but the sound is terrible. I think I'll have to get a new microphone.

3 *Natalie:* It's taking me ages to type the report because the letter A on my keyboard is always getting stuck.

Seth: I think you need to clean it!

4 I turned my laptop on this morning and it's making noises, but the screen is blank. I think it's broken.

 Interviewer: What are your plans for the future, Sam?

Sam: Well, writing has always been my hobby and I'm happy that I've been able to earn some money with my first novel. I'm not sure I want to do that again, but it would be interesting to do something online, <u>maybe write about my travel experiences and tell people about all the cities I've been to.</u> It would be great to hear what other people think about the information.

Exam Practice

 Presenter: Welcome Jake, Thank you for coming in today to tell us about your experience working in GBT music studio. How did you get the job?

Jake: Well, I used to play the drums in a band at school with some mates. The guitarist's dad owns the studio, and we often went there at the weekend to hang out and learn about recording. One Saturday, they asked me if I could <u>give them a hand setting up the equipment, so I did and then they offered me a paid job</u>.

Presenter: What's interesting about your work?

Jake: When I started, I just moved stuff around and got things people needed. That was often cold drinks and sandwiches! But I did a course in sound engineering and now I'm in charge of the actual recording part. <u>It's amazing what you can do with the sounds nowadays and I love</u>

the different methods available now to make good music, even if the musicians aren't perfect. We mostly work with unknown bands, but I did meet a famous singer once.

Presenter: Did anything interesting happen when you met the singer?

Jake: Well, it was a bit embarrassing actually. This woman came in with some flowers. I thought she was just delivering them, so I ignored her when in fact she was a famous jazz star and had been given the flowers at the entrance. I only realised when she began singing her amazing song!

Presenter: What do you think is most difficult about your job?

Jake: It's quite simple to prepare the microphones and other things, but while recording we always have to repeat the same sections again and again which means we're there till late every evening. I don't have much free time, which is hard, although the other members of the team have become good friends, so my social life is at work!

Presenter: Have you got any plans for the future?

Jake: I don't think I'll be working here forever. It's a small studio so there aren't a lot of opportunities to do anything different, but I don't really fancy moving to London. I think organising live concerts would be interesting. The possibilities with light shows and big screens are fantastic nowadays, so I'd like to try that. I'll keep playing the drums as a hobby too.

Presenter: What advice can you give young people who want to work in the music business?

Jake: Some people think you only have to upload your work and someone will notice you, but you have to be prepared to start at the bottom and slowly get experience. Few people are instantly successful, even if they have studied the right course or created a great song.

SPEAKING PART 1

Training

1 It's a large school with a thousand students. It has a gym, some science labs and a big library.

2 My best friend usually comes to my house after school. Sometimes we go running in the park.

3 My sister is a few years older than me, but we get on well. She likes swimming and climbing.

4 I love playing hockey in the school team and I read a lot. I enjoy drawing too.

5 I've studied English for three years. I think the pronunciation is difficult, but I like learning about grammar.

6 Actually, I really like cooking and I often help my parents in the kitchen. Home-made food is the best!

7 I can't remember. Oh, yes! I went to my cousin's party. It was a special birthday because he's 21!

1 Tell us about your school.

2 Where do you like to spend time with friends?

3 Tell us about a member of your family.

4 What do you do in your free time?

5 How long have you studied English for?

6 Which do you prefer, eating at home or eating at a café?

7 What did you do yesterday after school?

Exam Practice

Interlocutor: Tell us about a teacher you like.

Boy: I like my Maths teacher at school. His classes are fun and he's very patient.

Interlocutor: How often do you practise English?

Girl: I have English classes at school and sometimes I read websites in English or watch films in English.

Interlocutor: What do you do at the weekends when the weather is bad?

Boy: I do sport indoors, like I go swimming and I sometimes play football at the sports centre. Or I play video games with my brother.

Interlocutor: Which TV programmes do you enjoy watching?

Girl: Science-fiction programmes.

Interlocutor: Why?

Girl: They're interesting and take you away from ordinary life. I like to think about what the future could be like.

Interlocutor: Who would you most like to meet?

Boy: Erm, I don't know.

Interlocutor: Would you like to meet a famous actor or sportsperson, for example?

Boy: No, not really. I like the people I know.

Interlocutor: Do you like watching action films?

Girl: Yes, sometimes. I think they're more exciting than romantic films or whatever.

Interlocutor: And you?

Boy: I'm not keen on them.

Interlocutor: Why not?

Boy: They're all the same. I prefer unusual films where you can't guess the ending.

Interlocutor: How long do you spend on your phone each day?

Girl: About two hours. It's not as much as my friends! I play games or check social media.

Interlocutor: What are you going to do this evening?

Boy: I'll probably relax with my friends after this test!

SPEAKING PART 2

Training

In the photo I can see a group of girls who are dancing. They're outside and I think they might be in a school playground because the building in the background looks like a school. There's something on the ground – I'm not sure what it is. It might be an old box opened up or something like that. Why is it on the ground? Well, I think it's to protect the girl's hand. I think they're doing hip-hop or street dance. They're wearing jeans and trainers, and sweatshirts, I think. What else can I say …? They look like they're having a lot of fun. I think they're playing some music because there are some speakers on the ground.

Exam Practice

🎧 40 **A** In the photo I can see four people. In the foreground, there are two young people sitting down. It looks like they're looking at something together – a magazine maybe? I don't know what kind of magazine it is. I think they're on a bus or a train. It might be the underground because you can see it's dark outside the windows. The guy on the right is wearing some kind of hat – I don't know what that's called. A cap, I think. The girl's got long hair and they're both wearing casual clothes. They look happy. They might be going to visit a friend or going home. Maybe they're brother and sister because they look a bit like each other. In the background there's a man standing up. He looks a bit bored or tired. He's looking at the floor. Maybe he's on his way home from work. There's another person on the train. I don't know if it's a man or a woman because they seem to be walking away from the camera.

🎧 41 **B** In the photo there are two children. The boy is older than the girl and it looks like he's helping her to do something. She looks too young for homework, so he might be helping her to read. They're looking at something on a tablet, but you can't see what it is. There are some papers in front of them. I'm not sure what they are. Perhaps they're sitting at a desk that someone else in the family uses to work or study at. They're both wearing casual clothes. I'm not sure what's in the background. It looks like shelves with some kind of boxes on them – maybe it's to keep the room tidy. I'm not sure what else to say … Well, the boy looks patient with the little girl, who I guess is his little sister. They both look interested in what they are doing.

🎧 42 **C** In the photo there are three people – a girl and two boys. I think they might be students because the boy on the left and the girl in the middle have both got backpacks. The boy to the left of the photo has got a book in his hand – it looks like the kind of book you use in class. The girl has a phone in her hand. They're both looking at the boy on the right and smiling. They look like they're having a fun conversation. The boy on the right has got something on his back but I don't really know what it is … Oh! I think it's a guitar or another kind of musical instrument in a case. They're wearing casual clothes – T-shirts and shirts with jeans. There are some steps behind them and a building in the background. It could be a college or a university building perhaps. There are some plants in pots going up the steps.

SPEAKING PART 3

🎧 43 **Training**

Anh: So, we have to decide which thing would be most useful for a walking trip in the mountains. Let's start with the map. I think that's a great idea, especially if you don't know where you're going. Do you agree?

Mathilde: I do, but you shouldn't really set off up a mountain if you don't know the route. But I suppose people sometimes get lost. In my opinion, the phone's probably the best thing to take. Then if you do get lost, you can call for help.

Anh: I'm not so sure about that. There isn't always a good phone signal in the countryside.

Mathilde: Well, that's true. Shall we talk about the raincoat now? Is it a good idea? I can't decide. I mean, it's useful to carry in your backpack, I suppose. I don't think it's the most useful thing to take, though.

Anh: Me neither. What about walking boots? They're very important.

Mathilde: Yes, I think they would be very useful. If you've got good, comfortable boots, you can walk all day and avoid getting sore feet.

Anh: You're right. I think I'd prefer to have good walking boots than a torch. You shouldn't be walking in the dark! What's your opinion?

Mathilde: I think so too. And everyone's phone has a torch on it, anyway. So, what shall we say is the most useful thing to take on a walking trip in the mountains? I think it's the walking boots.

Anh: Yes, I agree.

Exam Practice

🎧 44 *Boy:* So, the students want to practise their second-language skills. I think that's probably their English.

Girl: Yes, so we have to decide which way of practising English is best. OK, so let's start with this picture. They've all got headphones on. I think they might be in their English class. The teacher's probably given them some listening exercises to do.

Boy: Yes. I think it's a good idea to practise listening. It's hard to understand people in another language when they talk fast or use words you don't know.

Girl: I agree.

Boy: What about talking to other people? I think that's better than listening because you get to practise saying all the things you've learned.

Girl: Yes, if it's with someone who speaks English well, it's a really good way to improve. But it can be a problem if the other person doesn't speak English as a first language because you don't know if they're saying things in the correct way.

Boy: True. Shall we discuss this picture now?

Girl: What do you think they're looking at? Is that a dictionary?

Boy: Yes – and maybe a textbook like we use in class. I think classes are really useful but it's boring to do exercises on your own.

Girl: I like it – you can work when you want to and check the answers at the back.

Boy: Mm. What's your opinion about using websites? I prefer to use websites than look at books. You can play games and that helps you remember new words and grammar.

Girl: I agree. The people in this picture are reading magazines. They must be in the second language. Do you think that's a good idea?

Boy: I'm not sure. Maybe. If you read car magazines, you might learn lots of words about cars, but that's not very useful for general conversation in English!

Girl: You're right. What about this picture? They're on a trip to London, I think, in England. I don't think that's very useful – they'll talk together in their own language and there are lots of tourists in London, so they might not even talk to an English-speaking person!

Boy: What about the final picture – watching a film or TV show in the second language. Would you like to do that?

Girl: Yes, but actors speak really quickly. But sometimes you can see the words in your own language on the screen and that helps.

Boy: So, which way of improving their second-language skills do you think is best for the students? I think speaking is best – with someone who speaks English very well.

Girl: So do I. Let's say that.

SPEAKING PART 4

🎧 45 **Training**

Interlocutor: How important is it to eat healthy food?

Girl: I think it's very important because it helps to prevent diseases. What do you think?

Boy: I agree. It's a good idea to eat lots of fresh food and not have too much fat or salt. Those things can make you put on weight and make your blood pressure too high.

Interlocutor: How often do you think people should exercise?

Boy: Let me think … So, personally, I think they should do some exercise every day. It helps to keep you fit and it makes you feel better too.

Interlocutor: Which form of exercise is better, swimming or walking?

Girl: In my opinion, swimming is better because it exercises every part of the body. But walking's very good too.

Interlocutor: Do you think everyone should have eight hours' sleep a night?

Girl: No, I don't.

Interlocutor: Why not?

Girl: Well, I read that between seven and nine hours is fine. I doubt that everyone is the same, but as long as you get enough sleep, it doesn't matter how long you sleep for.

 Exam Practice

46 *Interlocutor:* Do you think English is difficult to learn?

Girl: Well, some things are hard for me, like grammar. But I like learning vocabulary. Some of it is similar to my first language.

Boy: I think it's really difficult to remember new words and spelling in English isn't easy for me. But I like having conversations in English – it's nice to be able to communicate in another language.

Interlocutor: Would you like to learn another language?

Boy: Yes, I'd like to learn Chinese, or maybe Hindi.

Interlocutor: Why?

Boy: Because they will be very useful in the future, I think that lots of people speak them.

Interlocutor: And you?

Girl: Personally, I'd like to learn English better first. You can speak to people around the world in English and I think learning another language at the same time might be confusing.

Interlocutor: How do you feel when you are able to communicate with other English speakers?

Boy: That's a good question. Sometimes people who speak English as a first language speak really quickly and then I have to understand what they say and translate what I want to say into English.

Girl: Yes. My teacher says it's better not to translate and just try to use the English words we know, but it's difficult to do that! I like it when someone tells me when I've made a mistake because it helps me learn.

Interlocutor: Why do you think it is important to learn other languages?

Girl: In my opinion, it isn't just the language that you learn, but you learn about other countries and cultures too. Like, there are words in English that don't exist in my language, and that's because it's something about the UK or the US that we don't have in my country. I can't think of an example now. What do you think?

Boy: I think it's a good idea to learn other languages. It helps you to understand your own language and you can talk to people when you travel.

Interlocutor: Do you think everyone should learn another language from an early age?

Girl: I'm not completely sure, but I think maybe it's too hard for little children who can't speak their own language properly yet.

Boy: They should only teach words that they already know in their own language maybe.

LISTENING PART 1

1 *Girl:* This park is great, isn't it?

Boy: Yeah, there's so much to do, but I didn't expect so many people here. I got in the queue for the car driving ride, but I soon left because they said I'd have to wait for an hour. The queue for the big wheel was shorter so I went on that instead. I hope there aren't too many people waiting for the boat ride, because that's where I'm going next.

Girl: I'll come with you.

2 *Girl:* Dad, I forgot my laptop. Could you bring it to school for me?

Dad: Alright. I have to go into town this morning. Where is it?

Girl: Well, I had it on the sofa when I was watching TV last night and then I put it on the table in the living room to charge the battery. Before breakfast, I remembered to put it in the hall, but I'd put it under the chair so I didn't notice it when I was leaving.

Dad: OK. I'll bring it later.

Girl: Thanks, Dad!

3 *Girl:* Are you enjoying your music classes?

Boy: Yeah, but they're quite difficult. You know, when you start to play an instrument very young, like I did with the piano, it's much easier than taking up a new one when you're a teenager. The sound I make with the trumpet is awful, but I'll continue with the classes this year. I think playing a guitar is simpler though, so maybe I'll try that after the summer.

4 *Boy:* So, you got the new videogame in the end!

Girl: Yeah, I'm really happy. My brother and I bought it together. I'd saved £7.50 which was more than enough, and although it usually costs £13.50, they had a special offer last Saturday with great reductions so we got it for £11.50. Do you want to come over to play it? It should be fun with the three of us.

Boy: That's a great idea!

5 *Girl:* Did you bring something to eat on the bus?

Boy: Yeah, but we didn't have anything at home, so I went to the shop on the corner near school. It's a small one so they don't have much choice. I usually like to have fruit, but they only had bananas and I can't stand them, so I thought one of those big packets of crisps would be great to share. It cost too much so I had to go for a sandwich instead. You can have half if you like.

Girl: Thanks!

6 *Boy:* I'm really nervous about the biology test today.

Girl: Me too. I want to look at the section about plants if I have time in the break.

Boy: But it's before that. Don't you remember? The maths teacher isn't coming in first thing today, so they changed her class to later. That means we have biology in the second period after the geography class.

Girl: Oh no! I'd forgotten about that.

7 *Girl:* Have you met the new PE teacher? He's going to do the basketball training for the team.

Boy: I saw someone in the teachers' room yesterday. He's bald, isn't he, and quite tall?

Girl: That was the new physics teacher. Actually, he's smaller than me and I'm not very tall. I was surprised because they say he plays basketball very well. You can't miss him. He's got his hair tied back.

Boy: I hope he's a good coach!

LISTENING PART 2

8 *Girl:* Did your shopping trip go well yesterday?

Boy: More or less. I was looking for some new running shoes for this season. There's a new design that everyone in the athletics club is getting nowadays.

Girl: I know the ones you mean. They're very light.

Boy: Yes, so they may help you run faster. I tried some on, but they weren't comfortable at all so I got some others. They fit fine, but there wasn't much choice and I had to get green ones, which I'm not keen on. Anyway, I had to get something for training this week, so I bought them.

9 *Boy:* How was your holiday?

Girl: Great! I thought it was going to be boring because I had no friends there, and on the second day this boy ran past me on the beach and sand went all over me. He didn't even say sorry at the time, but later he came back and apologised saying he hadn't noticed at the time. He offered to buy me an ice cream and then we played football with his friends, so I wasn't annoyed any more. After that, I was busy every day and I'll see them again, because my parents want to go back there next year.

10 *Boy:* I'm so excited. We're getting a dog! I'm going to take it for a walk every day.

Girl: That's what I said when we got a dog, but in the end, I haven't had enough time, so my parents usually take him out.

Boy: I thought you loved your dog!

Girl: I love playing with him for a bit when I get home from school, but in the end, he's my parents' dog because they're the ones who look after him. I didn't realise that a dog needs so much training and you have to spend ages doing that.

11 *Boy:* I'm sorry I can't go out tonight. I've been walking for hours today on a school trip to the city.

Girl: You must be exhausted.

Boy: Well, it wasn't that bad. We managed to visit everything on the programme, but I thought the teacher would let us go off by ourselves for a while. We hoped to have a little more free time for our own things.

Girl: Well, at least you were with your mates.

Boy: I suppose so and the park was awesome. I'd never been before and they let us relax there to have lunch.

12 *Boy:* No exams next week! I'm going to start watching a new series this weekend.

Girl: You should see *The Spy Game*.

Boy: What's that like?

Girl: Well, if you like action series, then there's a lot of that, mostly the typical chasing criminals and police cars with flashing lights. What's really worth it though, is the main character. It's played by Tom Barton, who's just perfect for the part. The first few episodes are brilliant, although I'm not sure I'll watch the second season because the story is becoming hard to believe in the later programmes.

Boy: OK, I'll try it!

13 *Girl:* My uncle came to visit this weekend, you know, the one who's a pilot. He told me all about his new job, which sounds amazing.

Boy: What's the job?

Girl: Well, he used to work for an airline that carried passengers going on holiday, but now he's joined a transport company. He flies from Europe with medicines, tents and food to countries that have had problems, like environmental disasters.

Boy: He must earn a lot for that.

Girl: Not really, but he says he loves the fact that he's helping people and doing something useful.

LISTENING PART 3

Before we start class today, I just want to tell you about the trip to the chocolate factory next week. We'll be there all morning, but it won't take long to get there because we're going to see the new factory which is by the park instead of the old one near the swimming pool where last year's fourth year group went.

The new factory is much bigger; you'll be surprised how much chocolate they make. Last month, they made 13,765 chocolate eggs as well as all the usual varieties of chocolate bars and the hundreds of gift boxes for birthdays. Don't worry, you'll be able to taste some chocolate while you're there!

We'll be looking at all the machines they use in the factory. There are the usual ones to heat the chocolate and also a brand new one used to cool it to create a mix of different animal shapes. It's a totally new method!

You may have heard about the wonderful model they made of the Eiffel Tower from chocolate bars but, sadly, this has been removed. Maybe someone ate it! However, in its place they now have a new attraction for visitors which is an incredible fountain. And of course, it's been created using chocolate!

I think you'll be allowed to try some of the chocolate there so don't forget to have tissues in your pocket to clean your hands afterwards. We all know that chocolate makes people thirsty, so they provide water for everyone.

After the tour of the factory, we'll be able to visit the shop where you can buy sweets or boxes of chocolates to take home and they've got biscuits for all visitors which you can pick up at the exit if you don't want to spend any money but still have a souvenir.

LISTENING PART 4

Presenter: Alex, you've just got back from a trip to Costa Rica where you worked with turtles. Why did you go to Costa Rica?

Alex: A mate of mine told me he did something similar in an Asian country a couple of years ago. I used to work cleaning cages at the weekend in a wildlife park so when the zookeeper suggested I could go there and they would pay me to talk about the experience when I got back, I couldn't miss the opportunity.

Presenter: How did you feel when you arrived there?

Alex: When I arrived, they picked me up and we drove about six hours into the jungle. I knew that it'd be very different to being in my own country and, although I wasn't anxious about that, there were moments when I thought the car would go off the road, which was full of holes and seemed dangerous!

Presenter: What were the people you worked with like?

Alex: I made some very good friends there. Most of them were from Costa Rica, but everyone spoke some English, which was great. I was actually one of the youngest there, but it didn't matter because we were all in the same situation, learning about turtles for the first time.

Presenter: What's your most special memory of the trip?

Alex: It was one evening when we all went down to the water. Suddenly, we saw the turtles come out of their eggs and go towards the sea in the moonlight. It was incredible to see such tiny animals all moving in the same direction. After they'd gone, we went back to the house for a barbecue to celebrate.

Presenter: What did you learn about Costa Rica on your trip? Did anything surprise you?

Alex: Before I went, I found out as much as possible, so I knew that this country is home to a lot of different wildlife, but I didn't realise that there are so many national parks where environmental projects take place. The climate there is tropical, so it's quite warm most of the year.

Presenter: So, what is the next thing you'd like to do?

Alex: Before I left for Costa Rica, my aim was to do physics at university, but I've changed my mind now and I'd like to concentrate more on turtles. If I want to observe them in their natural surroundings, <u>I need to get a diving certificate. I'm going to do a course in that</u> because I'd love to be able to tell people more about these amazing animals.

SPEAKING PART 1

Interlocutor: Tell us about the town where you live.

Girl: I live here, in Edinburgh. It's a big city, but I like it. It's very busy and there's lots for young people to do. Sometimes it's cold, but I don't mind.

Interlocutor: How often do you listen to music?

Boy: I listen to music a lot because I walk to school and it takes me half an hour. I like listening to rock and pop music.

Interlocutor: Do you like playing video games?

Girl: Not really.

Interlocutor: Why not?

Girl: I prefer to be outdoors. I like playing sport and going for walks in the woods near my house.

Interlocutor: What are you going to do on your next holiday?

Boy: I don't know yet. Usually in summer, I go camping with my family. It's fun. We cook food on the fire and sing songs. My mum plays the guitar.

Interlocutor: And you?

Girl: I am going to visit my grandma. She lives in Spain. I'm going with my brother and sister. We go every summer for two weeks.

Interlocutor: Which city would you most like to visit?

Girl: London, I think.

Interlocutor: Why?

Girl: Because it seems exciting. I'd like to do some sightseeing.

Interlocutor: What kind of weather do you like?

Boy: I like rain! I like walking in the rain and I don't mind getting wet.

Interlocutor: Where do you usually spend time with your friends?

Girl: Sorry, I don't understand.

Interlocutor: What do you do when you see your friends?

Girl: Oh. We go to the park or ride our bikes. Sometimes we have a picnic. If it's cold, we go to someone's house and watch a movie.

Interlocutor: Tell us about your favourite hobby.

Boy: I like painting. I'm not very good, but I don't think about school or problems when I'm painting.

SPEAKING PART 2

A So, the people in the picture are in an art class. They are doing sculpture, I think. There's a teacher and five students. The teacher's showing the class how to do something, I think. I'm not sure what she's got in her hand, but maybe it's a knife or something like that? There are some brushes in a pot on the table, so it could be a brush. At the front of the picture on the left, there's a sculpture of a head with a face on it. Maybe the teacher's showing the students how to create a realistic face. The students are concentrating on what the teacher's doing. They're wearing casual clothes – T-shirts and shirts. I think they're in a classroom. There are shelves behind the group with jars on them. They look like coloured paints or something. That's all.

B My picture shows some people on the beach. It looks like a family – there's a mum and dad and two children – both girls. They're very young, but I don't know how old they are. They look like they're having fun. On the right of the picture, the woman is helping the girl do something. I think she's filling the bucket with sand. She's in a wheelchair. It's got big – what do you call them? Like, wheels? Tyres. They're good for going on the sand because it's soft. The man is looking at the girl on the left. They're having fun. The man is smiling at her. He's got glasses on. All the people are wearing coats and boots, so I don't think it's very warm. The sea is in the background – it looks grey! It's a cloudy day.

SPEAKING PART 3

Girl: So, the friends want to go somewhere together that everyone will enjoy. Shall we look at this picture first – they're in a city centre. I think that would be fun because there's lots to do in a city, so there's something for everyone.

Boy: Yeah, like shopping or looking at the old buildings. Maybe the boat trip would be even more fun, though.

Girl: I'm not sure about that. Some people feel sick on boats!

Boy: That's true – I didn't think about that. OK, so what about going to the countryside and staying in a little house together? Do you think that's a good idea?

Girl: Maybe, yes. They could make as much noise as they want to without bothering the neighbours!

Boy: It might be difficult to get there, I suppose. Not many teenagers our age can drive and there might not be trains.

Girl: True. What about camping, then? I love camping and being outdoors. I like the idea of swimming in the river. Not everyone thinks it's a fun thing to do, though.

Boy: I agree – some people think it's uncomfortable. It can be cold and wet if you go camping in this country.

Girl: You're right. This picture shows the friends in a forest, having a picnic. I like that idea. They could go for a walk or even collect some things to eat.

Boy: I don't know about that. There can be insects and stuff in the forest, but picnics are always good.

Girl: What about the seaside? That would be nice. They can stay at the house and go to the beach. They can eat and play games and swim or go on boats.

Boy: Exactly – there's something for everyone. In my opinion, it's better not to stay in a big hotel like this one. You have to follow the rules in a hotel, like go for breakfast when they say – or miss it!

Girl: So, I think the seaside is the best place for the friends. What do you think?

Boy: I agree.

SPEAKING PART 4

54

Interlocutor: Have you ever been on holiday to another country?

Boy: Yes. I've been to Turkey and Canada. I liked both countries. In Turkey, we spent a lot of time at the beach and visiting ancient monuments, and in Canada, we did a road trip – we travelled a long way and saw lots of different places.

Interlocutor: Where would you most like to go on holiday?

Girl: Let me think … Maybe Egypt or Italy.

Interlocutor: Why?

Girl: Egypt's got lots of historical sites and I think it would be really interesting to see those. I like history. And I'd like to go to Italy because my cousin lives there, so he could show me around. It looks exciting.

Interlocutor: What kind of accommodation would you like to stay in?

Girl: A wooden cabin!

Boy: Me too! In the mountains. I'd love to go somewhere that's really cold and snowy in winter, and then go inside and be next to the fire and drink hot chocolate.

Girl: Yeah, like in the movies!

Interlocutor: What's a popular place for holidays in your country?

Boy: Lots of people go to an area where there are lots of lakes.

Interlocutor: Why do people go there?

Boy: It's great for water sports, like sailing and waterskiing. It's a really beautiful area too.

Girl: In my country, people like to visit the capital. It doesn't have lots of beautiful old buildings, but there are lots of restaurants and cinemas. Most of the other towns are quite small and don't have a lot of things to do for young people.

Interlocutor: Do you think it's important for people to take holidays?

Boy: I think it's important to take time off from work or school, so you can have a rest. But I don't think it's necessary to go somewhere else for a holiday. Not everyone can afford to do that, anyway. But I like going to new places with my family.

Girl: I do too! But I agree, you just need time to relax, and you can do that at home or in your own town.

Interlocutor: What can you learn by visiting other cities or countries?

Boy: You find out about how other people live. My country's quite big and there are lots of different landscapes. People speak different languages too, so you can find out about their language and lifestyle.

Test 4

LISTENING PART 1

55

1 *Boy:* I love your new coat! Where did you get it?

Girl: In that shop on the high street. I wanted to get one with big pockets, but the last one they had in the store was the wrong size for me. The shop assistant showed me this one with big buttons and I liked it much more. Even better, it'll keep my head warm.

2 *Woman:* Freddy, where are you? I've been driving around looking for you. You said you were going to be outside the stadium.

Freddy: Sorry Mum. There was a lot of traffic there and we thought you wouldn't be able to stop, so we walked down the high street. We're just at the clock tower on the road going out of town. You know, the one that's before you get to the grocer's. Can you pick us up here?

Woman: OK, I won't be long.

3 Now, this is a display of objects from the royal bedroom. Here you can see the chest of drawers that the queen used to keep her personal objects in. It was made two centuries ago and many queens used it before her. On the armchair you can see the fine cushion that was given to her in 1970 by the French president for her wedding. The vase on the right comes from more recent times. It was given to her by her husband on her birthday.

4 *Girl:* What's the matter, Liam?

Liam: I feel terrible. I borrowed my sister's phone to look something up for my homework project. I put it on a chair while I went to get a notebook and forgot it was there. At that moment, Mum came home early from work because she had a bad headache, so I told her to sit down while I got her some water and you know what happened? She knocked it on the floor and the screen broke! Sally's going to be so annoyed with me!

5 *Boy:* Do you want to go out?

Girl: I'd love to, but I promised Dad that I'd help him first. Do you want to give me a hand?

Boy: Sure, what can I do? Is your scooter broken again?

Girl: I think we'll have to take that back to the shop to get it mended. No, this time the wheel on my skateboard came off so Dad's gone to buy a new one. He asked me to repair the brakes on that old kid's bike we've got so my sister can start learning.

6 *Boy:* You look worried, Sophie!

Sophie: I am. I've got to get this school work finished for Friday. It's a report on that geography trip we went on.

Boy: How many words do you have to write?

Sophie: That's not the problem. I'm happy to give in a written report, especially if I can do it on the computer, not by hand, but this time it's a recorded presentation and they'll play it in front of the whole class. I'm anxious that I'll sound really boring!

7 *Girl:* Are you going to join an afterschool club this year?

Boy: I haven't decided which one yet. What about you?

Girl: Well, I thought swimming might be fun for a change. I like to do some exercise.

Boy: Me too. I wanted to do table tennis, but there are no spaces left because everyone likes that one. I'm not keen on swimming, so it'll probably be the chess club for me this year, not so many people do that.

Girl: You won't be doing much physical exercise there!

LISTENING PART 2

8 *Girl:* Did you enjoy the castle? It was my first time there.

Boy: Me too. It was fun, although I thought there were too many of the usual old paintings. But I learned a lot from the woman who gave the tour. I took some useful notes for our history project.

Girl: I did think that her explanations were easy to understand. Oh, and I loved those amazing statues.

Boy: It was just a shame we couldn't spend more time outside sitting under the trees.

Girl: I was happy to go back in. It was getting very hot and there were too many insects!

9 *Boy:* How's your job going?

Girl: Not too bad. It's harder than I imagined and I'm not really finding out much about plants. All I do is cut grass and the machine I have to use is really heavy so it's quite tiring. My plan was to be better prepared for my degree in biology, but the hours are long, and I was already busy with school work before this anyway. They pay me quite well, which I hadn't expected, but that's not the most important thing. I'll probably have to give it up next term.

10 *Boy:* Only one day till the party! Is everything ready?

Girl: I think so. My dad's put all the stuff we got at the weekend in the freezer, and you've got the snacks, haven't you?

Boy: I've ticked that off the list! Did you tell the kids from the football club about it?

Girl: I completely forgot! Can you text Mark? And I'll send a message to the rest. I hope they'll be able to come. Oh, did the others finish putting up the balloons and setting up the music?

Boy: I thought they wouldn't have time, but Harry's just called me to say it's all done.

11 *Boy:* I've just started using a great app my friend Leo recommended.

Girl: What's it like?

Boy: You can record videos and then add sound or music afterwards to tell a story. He showed me how he used it for a presentation he had to give in class. You should do that for the one we've got next week.

Girl: Can anyone use it?

Boy: If you're over 12. The videos can be shared, but the good thing is that anyone who appears in a video has to allow you to use it, so nobody will see you if you don't want them to.

12 *Boy:* Did you hear the news? Our favourite band played a surprise concert in town last night.

Girl: Oh, I thought they were doing a concert this weekend. I know they changed it to the sports stadium so more people could go and I've got a ticket.

Boy: Don't worry, they're still doing that.

Girl: That's good.

Boy: But the real news is that in the middle of a song, the singer lost her voice, so the band will have to play without her on Saturday.

Girl: Oh no, she's the best part of the group!

13 *Girl:* How did you get on in the dance video competition? Did they like your dance?

Boy: We came third, but I really wasn't happy with the final version of our show.

Girl: What happened?

Boy: We'd worked really hard on the routine and our steps went well, but you couldn't hear the tune properly. It seemed as if we weren't in time to the music even though we'd used my uncle's video camera, which is brand new, so the audience could see us perfectly. The winners obviously used a better recording than us.

Girl: Never mind. Coming third was still pretty good.

LISTENING PART 3

Hi everyone. Today I'm going to tell you about Silverton Shopping Centre, which has just opened.

It's really easy to get to because there's an underground stop right there but you can also get a bus from the city centre, which takes a bit longer. I went with my family in Mum's car, but that was definitely slower.

Of course, there are lots of shops there and an area with restaurants, including some of my favourites such as a burger place and an Italian. What's absolutely brilliant is the games area. For fans of video games, like me, it's got everything you can imagine.

They've put the same kind of shops together, so you just have to go for the area you're interested in. The teenage fashion section is on the second floor. My mum got me this really cool T-shirt and then we went down to the first floor so that my parents could look at furniture.

The shopping centre is very spacious with wide hallways and there are plenty of little shops where you can buy snacks as well as a small market. I got a bag of popcorn there as I always feel hungry when I'm shopping!

When we got to the top, I couldn't believe what I saw. There's a garden there where you can walk around or sit and have a coffee. The glass roof meant it was a bit hot, though.

We got there late morning, so there were already a lot of people there because the shopping centre opens at 9.30. It got busier in the afternoon. Some of the shops started closing around 7.30, but the shopping centre itself doesn't close until 11 pm because of the restaurants. We left at around 8. We'd had enough by then.

LISTENING PART 4

Presenter: Emma, You've been working as a sports reporter on TV for a few years now. How did you start working on TV?

Emma: I've always loved sport and I used to work with a basketball team organising their advertising. This meant doing blogs about their matches. A TV station saw them and got in touch with me to say they liked what I did, and they offered me a job.

Presenter: You mostly report on football matches now. Do you enjoy it?

Emma: Well, it is the most popular sport in the country! It wasn't my sport when I was young, but it's exciting and there's lots to say because the ball is always moving. There are many famous players, so I like to let people know what each one is doing and facts about them.

Presenter: What's difficult about your job?

Emma: I've had to learn the names of lots of sportsmen and women, but I have a good memory, which helps. The challenge is when I'm talking in a live game. I have to follow what 22 players are doing and they move so fast. I have to pay attention all the time. It's easy to miss something important.

Presenter: It must be a bit stressful sometimes. How do you relax in your free time?

Emma: My job is hard work so I decided I need a complete change from sport. So, instead of going to the gym, I've taken up art. I often go out with an art group to the countryside to draw animals and plants. They're not into sport, so we talk about everything except that!

Presenter: So, what's the best moment for you in your work?

Emma: I'm happy because it's quite varied. The mornings are often less interesting because I'm just searching for information on the next game. Getting the opportunity to chat to well-known people from time to time is great, but there's nothing like the noise of the crowd when a goal is scored.

Presenter: So, what would you like to do in the future?

Emma: I've thought about going abroad to work in a different sport, like baseball, which is much more popular in places like Japan and the USA, but that's quite hard. Recently, a friend suggested giving talks in schools to encourage teenagers to get involved in other areas of sport, not just dream of being a great player. They can do things like sports medicine, organising events or being a trainer. I'd prefer to stay here and do something like that.

SPEAKING PART 1

59

Interlocutor: What are you going to do next weekend?

Girl: I'm going to a festival with my family. It's a music festival and there will be lots of good bands. We're going to camp and I'm really looking forward to it.

Boy: I don't know what I'm going to do, yet. I usually visit my grandparents, so I'll probably do that.

Interlocutor: Tell us about a friend you enjoy spending time with.

Boy: My friend, Artem.

Interlocutor: Why?

Boy: He's funny and we both like video games and cycling.

Interlocutor: What are your favourite foods?

Girl: I like everything! But I think Thai food is probably my favourite. I love Thai curries. They're delicious. And I love Italian ice cream as well.

Interlocutor: Do you like rock music?

Boy: Yes, I do. It's difficult to explain why. It just makes me feel happy and excited. I play rock music on my guitar too.

Interlocutor: What do you usually do in the afternoons after school?

Girl: I do my homework as soon as I get home. I like to finish it so I can have my free time without thinking about it. Then I help Dad prepare dinner and we watch TV together.

Interlocutor: And you?

Boy: I never do my homework until I have to. I like being outside if the weather's good. We don't have a garden, but I go to the park.

Interlocutor: Which do you prefer, staying at home at the weekend or going out?

Girl: I like both things. Sometimes we go to the seaside because it's nearby. But I like being at home and just relaxing as well.

Interlocutor: Tell us about the area where you live.

Boy: I live here, in the city. I like it. It's got plenty for young people to do. I go to a sports club and the cinema. It's very busy and noisy, but I don't mind.

Interlocutor: How often do you eat at someone else's house?

Girl: Not very often. I sometimes have lunch at my grandparents' or my aunt's house. And sometimes people come to our house for a barbecue.

SPEAKING PART 2

60

A: So, the people are playing a board game. I'm not sure what the game is, but it looks like it's made from wood and each person has something they go round the board with – I'm not sure what they're called. I think it's probably a family – there's a man and three c0hildren. There's a boy and two girls. The boy's older than them – they could be twins, perhaps? There's a large cup with a snack in it – it's popcorn, I think. The people are in a place with wooden walls. What's it called? … A cabin. Yes, they're in a cabin. It might be in the woods because you can see trees outside the windows. Not many people live in that kind of place, so they could be on holiday. They look happy and they're smiling and having fun.

B: In this picture, there are two people studying together in a library. On the left, there's a boy and there's a girl on the right. They might be classmates or even brother and sister or cousins. They look like they're a similar age. They're looking at something on the desk in front of them. Maybe pictures in a book. I think they're doing some homework because there's a laptop and a thick book which could be a dictionary. There's the thing you put pens and pencils in as well – a kind of case. In the background, there are shelves of books. The children look like they're concentrating and they seem interested in what they're doing. They're wearing casual clothes.

SPEAKING PART 3

61

Boy: OK, these are ways to learn about geography, and we have to decide which one students would enjoy the most. The first picture shows the students looking at maps. I love maps! It's interesting to see where places are in your own country and in the world.

Girl: Yes, I like maps too. And they show lots of interesting things, like rivers and towns and mountains. I think students would enjoy learning about geography like that.

Boy: Me too. What about this picture? They're at a – what do you call that? I've forgotten.

Girl: A waterfall. And there are big rocks around it. It's good to get out into the natural world, instead of just learning in a classroom.

Boy: I think so too. And you can take photos and explore.

Girl: Exactly. So, they're in the classroom in this picture. It looks like they're just reading books. I don't think that's the most interesting way to learn about geography.

Boy: Me neither. But it can be useful. I'd prefer to watch a film. I love films about other places.

Girl: Right. Especially ones you can't visit because they're too far away or too expensive to go to.

Boy: The next picture shows the teacher giving a talk. It's all notes. I'm sure the teacher is interesting, but I think it's easier to understand geography by looking at pictures, so I'm not so sure about this way of learning. Do you agree?

Girl: Yes, I do. It's a good idea to use the internet to do some research. You can find almost anything you want to know about the world.

Boy: True. But it's not interesting to work on your own at school – you can do that at home and spend as long as you want to.

Girl: You're right … And here, the students are in a museum. Are there special geography museums?

Boy: I think they're called 'natural history' museums. That looks like a fun thing to do. They've got notebooks and pencils, so maybe they're doing a quiz about the displays or taking notes.

Girl: It would be better to go to the places, but maybe they can't, like we said before.

Boy: Yes. In my opinion, going into nature to look at it would be the most fun thing to do. I think all the students would enjoy that.

Girl: I agree. Let's say that visiting places is the most interesting way of learning about geography, then.

SPEAKING PART 4

Interlocutor: Do you enjoy learning about geography?

Girl: Yes, I do.

Carlos: Yes.

Interlocutor: What do you most enjoy learning about?

Girl: I love things like volcanoes and exciting landscapes that you don't see in this country. What about you?

Boy: Yeah, me too. And I like to find out about people who live in different places around the world. They're geography too! It's interesting to find out about people who have completely different lifestyles to us.

Interlocutor: What is an interesting natural area in your country?

Girl: The mountains. They're really high and there's always snow on top. A lot of people go to look at them, but only climbers get to the top.

Interlocutor: And you?

Boy: The rainforest. There's a huge river and people like to go on boats down that. But you have to be careful because there are some dangerous creatures in the water! It's really beautiful and peaceful there, though.

Interlocutor: Where would you most like to visit in the natural world?

Boy: Iceland.

Interlocutor: Why would you like to see it?

Boy: There are so many fantastic things there. Like, there are volcanoes and there's an ice lake – they call it the land of fire and ice. It sounds really exciting.

Girl: Yes, I'd love to see that too. There's a place where there's natural hot water and it all comes out of the ground and into the air. That must be amazing to see.

Interlocutor: Do you prefer cities or the countryside?

Girl: Probably the countryside. You can relax and forget about school and any problems you have. I like walking and seeing birds and insects.

Boy: Really? I prefer cities. There's still nature in cities, but you have to look a bit harder for it. And I love people, so my favourite thing to do is watch people and see how they live their lives.

Interlocutor: Why is it important for people to learn about geography?

Girl: It helps you understand our planet and the issues that affect it, like climate change and global warming, and how that can be a problem for wildlife and future generations.

Boy: Yes, and I think if you learn about other places and other people, you accept people's differences more. You can also learn about what you can do to help other people and protect animals and plants.

Interlocutor: Is it useful to learn facts about other countries?

Boy: It depends. I'll never remember how many people there are or what the size is. But some facts are helpful. What do you think?

Girl: Yes. I think facts about the environment are useful. That helps countries to help each other and understand problems that affect us all.

Test 5

LISTENING PART 1

1 *Jenni:* Did you get something for your dad's birthday?

Saul: Yes, I bought him a book. It wasn't easy to find something he might like. You know he's really into nature and wildlife, but he's already got loads of books about that. I saw a good one about planes with some amazing pictures and then another one about Chinese cooking. He likes to try different recipes, but I think he gets them from the internet, so I ended up getting the first one.

Girl: I hope he likes it.

2 *Eduardo:* You look upset. What happened?

Jessica: I wanted to give my parents a surprise lunch and I decided to make chicken and pasta. I was frying the chicken when some hot oil went on my hand and it really hurt. It looked really red. Anyway, I managed to finish the cooking alright, but when my parents came home, they were quite shocked. In the end, the food tasted pretty good and at least I hadn't burned it or broken anything, but I'll have to be more careful next time.

3 OK everyone. Tomorrow we're going to do the chemistry experiment we've been reading about. We'll be using some dangerous things, so you must make sure you're all wearing the correct equipment. Apart from something to protect your eyes, which the school provides, there will be gloves for you all to wear. It's important to wear a long-sleeved shirt as well. In fact, if you don't wear one, you can't take part, so remember to bring one to school.

4 I watched a really interesting documentary yesterday about a group of divers who were looking for valuable objects from a ship that sank two centuries ago. They were trying to find gold coins that were on the ship. It was an ancient ship just like the one in that mystery story about the magic necklace. Sadly, they didn't get what they wanted, but they found a box with old documents and personal objects in it like an 18th-century watch, which probably belonged to the captain. And it still worked!

5 *Suzie:* So, you're off on holiday next week!

James: Yeah, I've been looking forward to it for ages. I've never been to that part of France before. It's our big holiday this year. Instead of going to the coast, we're off to the mountains. I hope the weather's good because last time we went sightseeing in the capital and it rained all the time. I can't wait to try a new winter sport this time.

6 *Miriam:* So what are the plans for tomorrow? Are we all meeting in the station?

Jan: Yes, we are. Mark's dad is picking you and me up and taking us to the station at quarter past nine because he has to get to work. It's a bit early for the train, which leaves at eleven thirty, but I thought that it'd be nice to have breakfast in the station before we leave. So I've told the others to meet us there at a quarter to ten. I hope they're not late!

7 *Cindy:* So what can I do about my backache?

Doctor: I've looked at your test results and there's nothing serious, so I don't think you need to spend so much time resting in bed now. In fact, some gentle exercise would be good, so you could try going for a short walk every day. It's also better to sit on a chair rather than lying on the sofa for too long.

LISTENING PART 2

8 *Lucie:* I've been studying so much this year I've got really unfit.

Stan: Well, now your exams have finished, you should do something.

Lucie: But I'm not sure what. I used to play in a basketball team, but I don't fancy that anymore. My teammates were really into competing and when we lost, everyone was upset.

Stan: <u>You could come to my swimming club. I go twice a week</u> and the coach is really nice. She's really helped me improve my style. We practise different things every class.

Lucie: That sounds much more relaxing. <u>I think I'll join you!</u>

9 *Teresa:* Where have you been?

Harry: I stayed after school to listen to a policeman telling us about cycling.

Teresa: Was it interesting?

Harry: Actually, it was. We often go cycling in the mountains and I know that it's important to be able to communicate with someone if there's an accident, so I always have my phone with me. We're also careful when we cycle wherever there are cars and we've got lights if it's dark. But <u>I didn't realise that you're supposed to get off your bike on a pedestrian crossing in a town.</u>

10 *Fred:* I don't know what to get my sister for her birthday and I can't ask her what she'd like because I want it to be a surprise. Do you think she'd like a book?

Hadley: Well, that's what you got her the last two years. Maybe you should think about something different.

Fred: That's true. Perhaps I should ask her friend Emily.

Hadley: I wouldn't do that; she can't keep a secret! But there's <u>a great online shop for teenagers where I got my sister's present last month. That might be the best place to look.</u>

Fred: I'll have a look at it. Thanks.

11 *Ben:* Have you been to the new sports centre yet?

Alyson: Yeah, I went last weekend. It's amazing. There's a gym, a pool, courts for basketball and even a rock climbing wall. I'm interested in learning to climb and they've got several beginner groups so I might sign up for that.

Ben: Yeah, I've heard the teachers are good. You live nearby, don't you?

Alyson: I do, so it's only a few minutes' walk, so for me it's better than the one on the other side of town. <u>It's great that there are so many things to do there. That's what impressed me most.</u>

12 *Zara:* I missed the history class today because I had to go to the doctor. What did you do?

Liam: It was all about travelling to the Americas hundreds of years ago. It was fun because we had to imagine we were going to explore and what we needed for the journey. <u>I couldn't believe how long the journey across the Atlantic took in those days.</u> The teacher explained when it all happened really well. I won't forget the year 1492! So, we've finished this period, I think we've learned a lot this term.

Zara: Could I borrow your notes?

Liam: Of course!

13 *Olivia:* What are you doing this summer?

Seb: We're off to the beach. I can't wait.

Olivia: Where are you going?

Seb: To a hotel near the coast with my family. We've been there a couple of times already and I love going there because I've made a few mates who also go every year and it's right on the beach. Now that I'm older, I can go down to the beach whenever I want and <u>I can sleep by myself so I don't have to share with my parents any more.</u>

Olivia: That's sounds awesome. I hope you have a good time.

Seb: Thanks!

LISTENING PART 3

65 Good morning everyone and thanks to your school for inviting me to talk to you about the Small Animal Rescue Centre and what we're going to do there.

You may know that the centre's located in the town and we need people to help. The building was finished at the end of April so we took the first animals in <u>May</u>, and we're expecting a lot more in the summer months. So, in July and August we're looking for extra people to give us a hand.

The animal centre takes different kinds of animal, but mostly cats. Occasionally, there might be a lost snake but in general they are typical small animals you might have at home. Unfortunately, <u>birds</u> require special cages so we aren't able to take them.

We provide most of the equipment. There are brushes and buckets for cleaning and we'll give you a T-shirt. You should wear old trousers and make sure you have strong shoes, although we can lend you some <u>boots</u> if we have ones the right size.

We're hoping you'll offer to help us at the weekends because there's always a lot to do. For example, Saturday morning starts with collecting the animals' <u>bowls</u> in order to clean them before filling them. Then, you'll clean their cages.

It's not always dirty work, though! You'll also help show <u>visitors</u> around the centre. To do this you should know the animal's name and a little bit about their story if we know where they came from. There is always a vet present to report on the animals' health.

So, if you're keen to join us and learn more about animals please go online to our webpage and complete the application form. The address is www.pawshome.com. That's P-A-W-S-H-O-M-E. We'd be happy to hear from you!

LISTENING PART 4

66 *Presenter:* Hello Tara. Can you tell us something about when you became interested in playing chess?

Tara: We used to play all the time at home, but I wasn't that keen because being the youngest child, I always lost. It wasn't until I was a teenager that I discovered that I could actually play quite well and <u>they chose me for the school team. It was much more fun to be able to win school championships, and I was soon really into it.</u>

Presenter: Now you travel a lot for international competitions. Do you enjoy it?

Tara: It's great to go to new places, although it's not often easy to see much of the city I'm in because the competitions can last all day and even into the evening. I also need to spend a lot of time studying the other players, and I watch their games when I haven't got a match, so it's hard work. But <u>the best bit is getting to know them socially afterwards.</u>

Presenter: What about your last competition. How did you feel about it?

Tara: I was a bit disappointed because I didn't play as well as I did last year. I realised I hadn't spent enough time getting ready for it. To do well you need to practise and learn from past games. Anyway, this time, <u>the other players were so much more talented than me that I knew I wouldn't win.</u>

Presenter: It sounds very hard. What do you do to relax?

Tara: I'm an active person so I like to go out for a run most days. After a stressful day studying, I like <u>to pick up a novel</u> for a while because it makes me feel calm, or listen to jazz music. I love the sound of the trumpet, for example.

Presenter: You also teach children to play chess. Why do you do that?

Tara: It's actually a way to support children who find school difficult. It isn't about the money, which is always useful, but not the most important reason, I simply enjoy it and <u>I get lots of ideas from them for my own techniques for my game as well.</u>

Presenter: And what about the future?

Tara: I'd like to use my skills in a different area. I've been offered work with programming for online chess games, but it's not something that interests me much. I've signed up to do a degree in maths, which requires similar thinking. Maybe I'll learn Japanese as well, but that'll have to wait until I have more time.

SPEAKING PART 1

Interlocutor: What did you do yesterday?

Boy: I went to school as usual. When I got home, I went to play basketball with my friends in the park. Then I had dinner and watched a film with my mum.

Interlocutor: Tell us about a shop you like going to.

Girl: I don't like shopping, so I don't really have a favourite shop.

Interlocutor: And you?

Boy: I'm into skateboarding and there's a cool shop in my town which has lots of skateboarding stuff. I like that shop best.

Interlocutor: Which hobby would you like to try in the future?

Girl: Sorry, I don't understand.

Interlocutor: Is there a new activity that you would like to do?

Girl: Oh, I'd like to go climbing.

Interlocutor: Why?

Girl: It looks like a challenge and I like challenges! Also, you can go to interesting places and learn something new.

Interlocutor: How often do you go for a walk?

Boy: Never! My mum is always asking me to go for walks in the countryside near our house, but it's not my kind of thing.

Interlocutor: What about you? How often do you go for a walk?

Girl: I like walking. One day I want to walk up the highest mountain in the country.

Interlocutor: Do you enjoy extreme sports like waterskiing or snowboarding?

Boy: I've never tried an extreme sport, but I'd like to go on a winter holiday and try skiing or snowboarding. It looks fun.

Interlocutor: Which do you prefer, visiting people or having visitors to your home?

Girl: That's a difficult question … erm … I like both. I like going to my cousins' house because they've got a big garden and we play football. But I like it when people come to our house as well.

Interlocutor: Who do you spend most of your day with?

Boy: It depends. During the week, I spend most of the day at school, so I see my classmates the most. At the weekend, I'm usually with family.

Interlocutor: Tell us about your English classes.

Girl: I like my teacher a lot. He makes the classes fun – we play games and watch clips in English. We do grammar and speaking too, which is hard, but usually I like our classes.

SPEAKING PART 2

A My photo shows people taking a photo of themselves – I think that's called a selfie! They both look really happy and they're smiling at the camera – well, it's the camera on their phone. There are two people. They look like they might be father and daughter or uncle and niece for example, because the man is a lot older than the girl. It looks as though they're standing on the side of a mountain because there are rocks all around them. It's quite steep, I think. They must be going for a walk. The man's got a backpack and maybe they've got a picnic in it. It looks like the girl's wearing a backpack too. Behind them, there are some trees and beyond the trees is a mountain. It looks quite high! It's a sunny day, but maybe not too warm because the people are wearing sweaters or T-shirts with long sleeves.

B In my photo, the people are shopping for clothes. There are three young people who I think are probably friends. They look like they're having fun because they're all smiling and seem happy. To the left of the photo is a girl. She's got red hair and she's wearing a T-shirt and some kind of jacket – I don't know what you call that style. In the middle, there's a boy. He's wearing a shirt. It looks like he's got a backpack on. He's showing a black T-shirt to the girl on the right. She's looking at the T-shirt but I don't know if it's for him or for her. She's got very short hair and is wearing casual clothes like the others. She's got an orange bag. Behind them are more clothes – I can see some T-shirts or tops.

SPEAKING PART 3

Boy: Right. The family want to do something for a special occasion and these are things they could do – is that right?

Girl: Yes, and decide which would be best. Look, here, they're in a restaurant, having a meal. I think that's always a nice way to celebrate. What do you think?

Boy: I agree. Everyone can choose what they want to eat and they can all chat together.

Girl: What about giving each other gifts? I suppose it depends what the occasion is. Like, people give presents on people's birthdays.

Boy: Yes, or on a special holiday. That's nice but it's difficult to decide what to get someone. And if they don't like the gift, maybe that's embarrassing.

Girl: That's true. What about going on a boat?

Boy: It's a great idea. People can relax and talk, and look at what's around them.

Girl: I don't know about that. Some people are scared of water or feel sick.

Boy: You're right. Well, maybe going camping is better. They can cook food and sing, and play instruments around the fire.

Girl: I'm not so sure. What about the older people? Will they be comfortable in a tent?

Boy: I don't know. I think having a barbecue is a good idea. Everyone can be comfortable and relax, and it's easier when you're at home.

Girl: I agree. I also think it's a nice idea to watch a film together, with snacks – lots of snacks! What's your opinion?

Boy: I don't agree because then, people aren't talking and that's a bit boring. If it's a celebration, people should be having fun together.

Girl: OK. Do you think a party would be better?

Boy: Yes – with music and dancing and food. Actually, I think a party would be best.

Girl: Me too. OK, we think the party is the best way to celebrate a special occasion.

SPEAKING PART 4

Interlocutor: Which special occasions do you celebrate?

Boy: In my family, we celebrate birthdays and things like good news. We also celebrate weddings and things like that.

Girl: Yes, so do we. And my brother passed his driving test last week, so we went out for pizza to say well done.

Interlocutor: Who do you usually celebrate special occasions with?

Boy: Usually with my family.

Girl: Yes, me too. But I also go to friends' houses if it's their birthday. For example, I go to parties or barbecues.

Boy: Yes, so do I. Sometimes we have a party in our English class, at the end of term.

Interlocutor: Have you celebrated a special occasion in another country?

Girl: Yes, I went to China and we saw the Chinese New Year. It was really exciting – there were dragons and a parade. I really enjoyed it.

Boy: Really? That's great! I haven't been to any celebrations – oh yes, I have! I saw a festival for fishermen in Spain. They had a parade too, and then music and food. It was fun.

Interlocutor: What special celebration have you particularly enjoyed?

Boy: My cousin's twenty-first birthday.

Interlocutor: Why did you enjoy it?

Boy: He had a party on the beach. It was warm enough to swim and we played volleyball, and everyone brought something to eat. All our families were there, and friends, and we stayed till midnight. We had fireworks too.

Girl: That sounds great! I really enjoyed my aunt's wedding. It was similar – there was a delicious meal and dancing. Everyone had a brilliant time.

Interlocutor: Do you think people need to spend a lot of money to have a fun celebration?

Boy: No, of course not. You can just get everyone together and each person can bring games or something to eat and drink.

Girl: Exactly!

Interlocutor: Is it important for people to celebrate special occasions?

Boy: Yes, I think it's very important.

Girl: So do I. It helps to create strong relationships and it's a chance for the family to get together and share news and fun times.

Boy: Right. It helps make special memories. I love celebrations.

Girl: Me too.

Test 6

LISTENING PART 1

71

1 Here's my opinion of the exhibition. The artist who painted the mountain scene is clearly very talented, although those huge peaks were rather depressing and dark. I was more attracted by the paintings with light and water in them, like the waterfall scene and <u>the one of the sea. The way the artist showed the waves, you could almost see them moving. I'd go back to see it again any day</u>. The picture of the waterfall was amazing, but less realistic, so it's not one I'd have on my wall.

2 *Girl:* What shall we do tonight?

Boy: I feel like staying at home and watching a series. There's new one about a group of kids who start a dance group.

Girl: I've heard about that one, but they say the music is old-fashioned. <u>There's a hospital one that's actually a comedy</u>.

Boy: Maybe, or what about the school series with super intelligent teenagers that have adventures?

Girl: I like the sound of that, but <u>I fancy watching something funny this evening. Do you agree?</u>

Boy: OK. <u>Let's watch that then</u>.

3 Visitors to our museum will have a totally new experience with our interactive systems. <u>There will be touch screens giving you all the details of each item on display</u>. These replace the headphones we used to have, but there will still be information in several languages. Our new service is popular with all our visitors and means we no longer need to have an information desk, so no one has to queue any more. We look forward to seeing you soon!

4 *Boy:* What did you buy with your birthday money?

Girl: Video games of course! You know I've been waiting for ages to get City Creation.

Boy: Do you like it?

Girl: I've started playing it and it's alright. It's not as exciting as Car Race 2, which I got last year, and the first stages are a bit too easy. I also had enough to buy Space Star, <u>you can make incredible rockets and the graphics are really special. I've played it more often than the other two</u> because of that. You should try it!

5 *Girl:* Did you get to your football match on time?

Boy: In the end, yes. You know, I usually cycle, but this time it was too far to go by bike and the weather was terrible, so Mum offered to give me a lift. We'd just gone a short way when <u>there was a huge traffic jam, so she turned off and dropped me at the station</u>. Luckily, I just got there ten minutes before the game started.

6 *Girl:* Are you ready for your holiday tomorrow?

Boy: Almost. I just have to pack my suitcase. We went shopping yesterday to get things for the beach. I wanted to get some sunglasses and I needed some sandals. I already have a big towel that I bought last year. <u>I found some cool glasses that weren't too expensive</u>, but they didn't have my size in the shoe shop so I'll have to buy sandals when I get there.

7 Last night, the star of the New Year TV show was the famous Emily Energy. This well-known artist surprised the audience with her strong voice as no one had heard her sing before. Everyone was excited to see <u>her new dance routine and they all agreed it was even better than the style that has made her so popular</u>. This time she also joined the band to play the drums, showing us what a talented performer she is.

LISTENING PART 2

8 *Girl:* The concert was great. I loved the second band that played.

Boy: Yeah, they were pretty good. The singer was amazing, wasn't she?

Girl: She wasn't bad, although I thought the guitarist was more talented. What surprised me was their message. It was so unusual. I'd never heard anything like it before.

Boy: Neither had I. It was interesting.

Girl: But they did look strange in those long coats, a bit like they were from the 80s or something. They reminded me of that other band that you like.

Boy: They are quite similar, but their music is totally different.

9 *Girl:* How was your weekend? Did you go out?

Boy: It was good. We went to that new restaurant on Saturday night. You know, the one that's just by the school so it's really easy for us to walk there rather than taking the car.

Girl: It was your sister's birthday, wasn't it?

Boy: That's right. We were going to go to that expensive place near the cinema, but we tried to book too late so it was full. The new one is pretty big and has plenty of tables, so we chose to go there instead. It didn't cost too much and the meal was delicious.

10 *Boy:* The biology teacher suggested some of us could do a recycling project next term. We'd be organising bins for different types of rubbish and then making sure everything goes in the right place.

Girl: It sounds interesting, but I don't have much time. I'm so busy with the orchestra and football practice.

Boy: I don't think it'd be too much. You wouldn't have to stop doing your usual things. Maybe just an hour or two a week. I'm going to sign up.

Girl: Hmm. Maybe I could.

Boy: It'll be fun. Lots of the others want to take part.

Girl: I'll think about it.

11 *Boy:* It's nearly the holidays. I can't wait!

Girl: Me neither. Did you hear that they want to paint all the classrooms while we're away? Our class teacher sent a message saying we need to clear up next week.

Boy: I suppose that means putting all the chairs and desks somewhere.

Girl: We won't be doing that. It's like taking all the posters down and making sure that all our personal stuff is out because things could get lost when the painters come in. They don't know where everything goes to put it back in its place.

12 *Girl:* Did you see that advertisement for a job in the sports centre?

Boy: No. What are they looking for?

Girl: They need people at the weekend to work on reception.

Boy: Are you going to apply?

Girl: Well, I'd love to have a job and the hours are good so I'd still have some free time, but the money's terrible. I didn't realise they were allowed to pay so little. I suppose they think that students don't need much, but it's awful.

Boy: It doesn't sound great. There must be something better you could do.

Girl: Yeah, I expect there will be other opportunities somewhere.

13 *Girl:* Did you get a photo for our presentation about natural spaces?

Boy: I finally got a good one in the national park, but it wasn't easy.

Girl: Why?

Boy: Well, Dad gave me a lift to the mountain and it wasn't too bad walking up. I'd expected it to be worse. At first, it was really sunny, but by the time I got to the forest, it was so windy that I couldn't get a proper picture of the trees because they were moving so much. In the end I had to wait until it was calmer, so it took a long time.

LISTENING PART 3

Hi everyone. I wanted to tell you about this awesome roller-skating club that I joined last summer. There are classes every day for different levels. I go on Friday afternoons, but if you're just starting, there's a group on Thursdays. I also like to watch the advanced students who train on Wednesdays – they do some amazing tricks!

On Saturdays or Sundays, we do trips to different places in the city, unless it's raining. In that case we go to the skating centre near the football stadium for a couple of hours. The group leaders take us to parks where we're allowed to skate and there we can practise what we've learned.

Of course, you'll need to buy some skates and a helmet. The club recommends you use protection for your knees and elbows as well. On the city trips, they give each of us a yellow jacket so that no one gets lost. Parents are happy about this rule and we look like a real team!

Once we went to watch the National Championships together. When we arrived, we were given seats in the front row. They're normally for more important people than us! We took a lot of photos to remember that day.

Some teams performed dance routines and there was also an amazing jump event. All on skates! We all agreed that we'd like to try that in our next class, but not too high though!

If anyone is interested in coming to train with the club, you'll find it in the secondary school next to the station. They let us use the playground, which is great because it has a roof for when it's very sunny or raining so we don't have to find a sports hall. I hope to see you there!

LISTENING PART 4

Presenter: Good morning James. You've been working as a designer for five years now. When did you first learn about making clothes?

James: In primary school we were encouraged to be creative, so I was always making models and drawing. Then, one day I found an old sewing machine in the attic at home. My mum had no idea how to use it, but I looked online and the videos I saw helped me start. They showed me the basic techniques.

Presenter: What kind of clothes do you design now?

James: The simplest ones, like T-shirts, are often the easiest to make, but I like a challenge. Creating comfortable trousers is my main interest at the moment, although I'd also like to get more into the world of women's fashion, like dresses.

Presenter: Why do you think you are successful?

James: I make clothes that all kinds of people want to wear every day and, more importantly, clothes that they can afford. I like to use traditional materials which are natural and feel better.

Presenter: You showed your designs in the last London Fashion Show. How did you feel about that?

James: I was so lucky to have had this chance. I never expected to be invited but a famous designer asked me to join his team and show a couple of my designs. I hope it'll give me more opportunities in the future as he mentioned my name in his final speech.

Presenter: What do you like most about your work?

James: That's hard to say. I get to know a lot of models and photographers who do a great job, but I'm quite shy really so nothing makes me happier than sitting at my work desk putting my ideas on paper. I'm often away looking for new materials, especially in Asia, and when I am, I miss doing that.

Audioscripts

Presenter: Would you like to try anything new? What's important for you?

James: Apart from designing, I'm interested in the production process, which can be done with a 3D printer. <u>I'm exploring the possibilities of this as it reduces waste and also uses recycled materials, which is essential nowadays.</u> We'll need to train people to work in this area. I know many young people who are interested so I'd like to set up a fashion school to do this.

SPEAKING PART 1

Interlocutor: What did you do last night?

Boy: I didn't do much because it was the weekend and I like to relax the evening before the school week starts again. We had a nice dinner and then watched some programmes on TV.

Interlocutor: What school subject would you like to learn more about?

Girl: I'm interested in ancient history. We've done some at school, but I'd like to know more. I've borrowed books about it from the library.

Interlocutor: And you?

Boy: I don't know. Maybe science. I like to know more about how the world works.

Interlocutor: Tell us about your favourite day of the week.

Boy: I like Thursdays best because in my country, it's the beginning of the weekend. When we finish school, my sister and I go for cake and a drink with our grandma, and in summer we go swimming.

Interlocutor: And you?

Girl: I think Saturday. That's the weekend for me. I go to a hip-hop class and we have a takeaway in the evenings.

Interlocutor: Do you like reading?

Boy: Not really. Well, I like magazines about technology and the future. But I don't like reading books. I get bored.

Interlocutor: What job would you like to do in the future?

Girl: I want to be a vlogger.

Interlocutor: Why?

Girl: I like making funny videos on my phone and it would be great to get paid for them!

Interlocutor: Who makes you laugh the most?

Boy: My sister. She does funny faces and makes lots of jokes. I like comedy films too.

Interlocutor: How long do you study English each week?

Girl: About two hours at school. Sometimes I watch TV in English, but it's quite hard to understand. I listen to lots of American music too.

Interlocutor: Tell us about how you spend time with friends.

Girl: We watch and make videos for our friends. My best friend plays the guitar and I sing, so we sometimes make up songs.

SPEAKING PART 2

A This photo shows three people and a dog in the foreground. It looks like a family because there's a woman and two children. I think the woman is their mother. It looks as though the dog is helping the woman because maybe she can't see or can't see very well. The dog helps her to find her way around. The dog is white or yellow – I'm not sure what kind of dog it is, but it looks patient because it is working. The people are all wearing casual clothes, and the woman's got dark glasses on. Maybe the children have been to school because they've got backpacks, I think. It looks like they might be going for a walk in a park because in the background there's grass and some trees. On the right of the picture there's a seat and there's also some water – maybe it's a lake? There are buildings beyond the park.

B My picture shows people playing music together. There's a girl on the left and a man on the right. He could be the girl's father or uncle, or he might be a music teacher. They're both sitting on a sofa and they're playing guitars. It looks like the man is showing the girl how to play the guitar. The girl's guitar is much smaller than the man's. I'm not sure why. Maybe it's a guitar for learners or children who've got smaller hands. The man looks patient and the girl is concentrating on what she's doing. There's a table in front of the people, which is made from wood. There's a laptop on it. I'm not sure why, but it could have music that they're following. There's another guitar on the wall – it's an electric one.

SPEAKING PART 3

Boy: So, we have to decide which thing would be best for an end-of-term event. I don't think the cinema is a good idea. You have to sit and be quiet.

Girl: I agree. Also, not everyone likes the same films. I think a party in the classroom is a good idea. It's easy and cheap for everyone. The teacher would probably bring the drinks and snacks.

Boy: Yes, and everyone can talk. What about the museum?

Girl: I'm not sure about that. It looks like a science museum, so it depends if you're interested in science. I'm sure it would be difficult to find a museum that everyone likes.

Boy: Yes. A hike in the countryside might be fun. They could take food and see some animals. What's your opinion?

Girl: I don't know about that. It might be difficult for some people to do. And you need to have good weather on the day!

Boy: OK. How about singing songs together? That sounds like a fun thing to do in the classroom. Everyone can join in. I think it's a great idea.

Girl: I think so too. Not everyone can play an instrument and not everyone's a good singer, but it's always fun to do that together. What's left? Playing board games.

Boy: I don't think that's very exciting. Usually, you only need a few people for each game, so people would all be in different groups.

Girl: I agree. I'd prefer it if the teacher did a quiz or something like that – it would be more exciting.

Boy: Exactly! Another thing they could do is play football – or maybe another sport would be better. Like races or something.

Girl: I don't agree. Some people don't like sports and I think it should be something everyone is good at. I think the party in the classroom would be best.

Boy: Well, I like the idea of singing together.

Girl: Well, they're both in the classroom, so we agree about that.

SPEAKING PART 4

Interlocutor: What special occasions does your school celebrate?

Boy: We celebrate the end of term. We've got three terms each year and we do something different at the end of each one.

Girl: We do too. So, in winter, we see a film in the school hall, and in summer, we have a sports day on the field.

Boy: That sounds fun. We have talks by students and the headteacher, but they're fun and interesting.

Interlocutor: Do you go to any clubs at your school?

Girl: I'm sorry, I don't know what you mean.

Interlocutor: Does your school have a sports club or music club?

Girl: Oh, yes. We've got those things, and you can learn to cook after school as well.

Boy: I'd like to do that. Our school has a football team and a music club, but I'm not really interested in those things.

Interlocutor: What kind of club would you like your school to have, for example, an art club?

Boy: Actually, I'd like to learn chess so I can beat my grandad! Some schools have chess clubs. What kind of club would you like?

Girl: I'd like an art club! I like painting, but I'd like to improve.

Boy: Me too.

Interlocutor: Is it important for schools to have sports teams?

Boy: I don't think so, because I'm not into sport. But I think it's important to do exercise. I just think we should have more options. I'd like to do tennis or dance.

Girl: So, would I. My friend's school does dance lessons, but we only do athletics and team sports. But they teach you how to be good in a team and work with other people.

Interlocutor: What kind of activities can bring students closer together at school?

Girl: I suppose anything where students work together in groups. Like when they research a topic or do a project.

Boy: Yes, and social activities too. Like, breaks are a good time to chat and make friends, I think.

Girl: I agree.

Interlocutor: Does school help students to learn useful skills?

Boy: I think so.

Girl: I think so too.

Interlocutor: What skills do you learn at school?

Girl: Well, apart from subjects, you learn how to communicate with other people, you learn to be patient when someone else is talking …

Boy: Yes, and you learn thinking skills too. And you learn how to decide whether what you read is the truth, things like that.

Audioscripts

Exam task type:

three-option multiple choice – reading five real-world texts (e.g. advertisements, emails, messages, notices, signs)

Training focus:

identifying who has written a short text; informal and formal language in different types of notes and messages; leaving words out in signs and notices; using useful phrases to describe amounts; identifying important information

Training

1 Ask students to work in pairs and discuss who they think has written each of the examples 1–5.

Suggested answers: 1 a sports coach (outdoor boots, game, stadium) 2 a friend (Hi, skateboard, have a go)   3 a shop owner/manager (items, store, buy)   4 a museum manager/employee (exhibition, tickets, office, booking)   5 a parent (getting home, We can have pizza)

2 Ask students to think about the emails or texts they might send to different people and whether they use a different style of language with each person. They should then decide which phrases are in formal and which are more formal. Check answers as a class.

Extension

Give students a few minutes to discuss in pairs how they might start and finish an email to a friend or relative, and how they might start and finish a more formal email (e.g. to a teacher).

Suggested answers: 1F   2F   3I   4F   5I   6I   7I   8I   9F   10I 11I   12I   13F   14I   15I   16F

3 Discuss the questions as a class, going over the grammatical names of the kinds of words we can leave out in notices and signs.

Notices and signs often leave out grammatical words such as: articles (a/an/ the), auxiliaries (e.g. am/are/do) and subjects (e.g. I, you, we). Grammatical words can be left out because they aren't always important for the overall meaning of a message. Content words have to remain, however, because they are more important and can carry the meaning of the message on their own.

4 Students work on their own to write complete sentences.

Suggested answers: 1 You must keep this gate closed.   2 (You should) return your books to the shelf when you have finished.   3 Please do not put your bags in front of the door. Access is required at all times.   4 Only students can go past this door.   5 The library staff are currently in a meeting. 6 This area is for quiet study only.

5 Ask students to look at the number phrases in the box and find the one that matches the first item: *nearly 50% off* (answer: 46%) Students then find the matching phrases for the other questions.

1 46%   2 €14.50   3 2.50 pm   4 four novels   5 eight cans of tuna

6 Give students a few minutes to write some example sentences for two or three of the phrases listed. Ask them to share their ideas with the class.

7 Tell the class that when they read a message, they should think about the factual information the message provides. Students can do the activity in pairs and then compare answers as a class.

Suggested answers: 1 written by a sports teacher, to tell students about a cancelled practise session (quite formal)   2 written by a friend, to give information about a game (informal)   3 written by a teacher, to give information about homework (quite informal)   4 written by someone working at a leisure centre, to give information about a closed pool (formal)

8 Ask students to underline any information that will be important in helping them find the right answer.

1 Monday lunchtime
Hockey players! Tonight's practice session is cancelled as your coach is ill. You still have a match on Tuesday, so there's an extra session at Monday lunchtime instead.
2 20%
Jen That game you wanted is on offer today – 5% off, or if you buy two games, the discount's 20%. You have to get them before tomorrow though, so make your mind up fast!
3 a favourite photo
For homework, choose a favourite photo, for example, one of a person or a place you know well. Then, write at least 150 words about it. I can't wait to see your work!
4 1.00
Pool closed until 12.45 today for the rest of the week.
Afternoon lessons start at 1.00 rather than 12.30.

Exam Practice

Before students complete this Reading Part 1 test, ask them to think about the kinds of messages and notes they see every day at school and in their local area. Ask them who they last wrote a message to, and who they last received a message from.

Remind students to look at each text to see if it is an email, a text message, a sign, etc. Ask them to suggest features they would expect to find in an email (*From: / Subject:*) and the sorts of greetings and sign-offs they might expect to see in different sorts of messages (messages from a friend: *Bye! / Can't wait to see you!*, more formal email: *Please ask if you have any questions.*).

Students should compare answers. They can also discuss why the other two options were incorrect.

1 C (Your swimming coach called … The race now starts at 4 pm, not 3 pm)
2 B (it's up to you)
3 A (Many items half price … One week only)
4 B (Make sure your picture … shows a group of two or more people)
5 A (my bus is delayed … can't meet you at the ice cream shop)

Exam task type:
matching – descriptions of five people and eight texts

Training focus:
identifying text types; understanding how things can be paraphrased using the opposite kind of language; identifying what people require; paraphrasing what people require

Training

1   Tell students that in Part 2 of the test, they will read eight short texts which may be advertisements or reviews. Elicit the differences between reviews and adverts (e.g. reviews can mention things the writer liked about something they paid for, as well as problems they had; advertisements are about selling something to someone, focusing mainly on positive things). Ask students to read the examples of short texts to familiarise them with typical Part 2 text types. Discuss the answers with the class.

A review (while the information might not be particularly easy for younger children to follow …)   *B advertisement* (we recently won a prize …)
C review (Those hoping to find out lots of details about future space plans may find the information rather basic …)

2   Ask the class to look at sentence 1 and elicit that the sentence contains a negative structure. Ask them to find the correct match (sentence c) and point out that this sentence contains a positive structure. Ask students to complete the rest of the exercise individually and then check their answers in pairs.

1c   2e   3b   4a   5d

3   Ask students to complete the underlining task individually and compare answers with a partner.

1 Ali hopes to do a writing course with <u>other young people</u>. He needs <u>tips on writing funny stories</u> and wants to <u>read some of his stories to the group to see what they think.</u>   2 Jane would love to <u>learn from a successful writer</u> and to <u>find out about how to add pictures</u> to her stories. She's interested in learning <u>how to put her stories online</u>.

4   Ask students to look back at the people's requirements in Exercise 3 and decide which words might appear in a text which matches what they want. They should then compare their ideas in pairs.

Suggested answers:
Ali: advice; comedy; for children and teenagers; get opinions; share your stories
Jane: advice; drawings and cartoons; publish on a website; well-known author

Extension

Ask students to think of more words and phrases that might be found in a text that matches each person's requirements.

Exam Practice

Ask students to look at the people and read the descriptions of what they want. Look at Amal together, and encourage students to underline the three requirements (*have a day out at a museum, see inside an old ship, somewhere for Amal's small brother to play*).

Ask students to look through the eight texts and find ones that could match the first of Amal's requirements, *have a day out*. Texts B (*entertain for the whole day*) and G (*spend several hours*) would both be suitable.

Ask students to do the same for the second requirement (*see inside an old ship*), which should lead them to B (*18th-century boat*). They will also see other references to ships in G (*cruise ship captains*) and H (*in charge of a spaceship*). Point out that while G mentions ships, there is no reference to *seeing inside*. H mentions the wrong kind of ship.

Do the same for the final requirement (*somewhere for Amal's small brother to play*). Point out that as text B has so far matched two of the three requirements, it might be a good idea to check this first. Here they will find *garden where little ones can run around*, giving them the answer.

6 B
7 A (Niall wants to watch a film about transport methods around the world and in A we learn that the exhibition includes videos about transport used in other countries. He also wants to learn how transport might change, and A says that the Next Steps exhibition tells us how we could be travelling in the years ahead. Finally, Niall would like to buy something to remind him of his trip. A describes how the cards in the shop make fantastic souvenirs.)
8 E (Kazue would like to find out about the history of trains. Text E has an exhibition about the start of the rail industry. She also wants to know more about the people who work on important transport projects. Text E has displays about those who design, build and run international city transport centres, like airports or ports. Finally, her family hope to have a picnic during the visit. E describes tables outside if you're bringing food.)
9 G (Dariusz wants to know about early space travel and in text G we can see plans for the first space rockets. Text E mentions 'space', although it's a different use of the word. Dariusz wants to find out about working in the airline industry, which matches with Listen to interviews with people talking about transport-related jobs: everything from pilots … in G. Finally, his family don't have a car so need to visit a city centre museum, so being in a convenient location not far from the heart of the city makes G the correct option.)
10 F (Esme and her dad want to go round a museum with a guide, which matches with go round with an expert. They both want to see some old racing cars, which fits with early record-breaking vehicles on display. Esme can experience what it's like to drive a train, as she can operate the controls of a real train.)

Exam task type:
four-option multiple choice – a long text and five questions

Training focus:
ordering events; using narrative tenses; using adjectives to describe opinions and feelings; dealing with Question 15

Training

1 Ask students if they can think of a young person from their country who has done something interesting. Discuss this person's life and achievements and point out any past tenses that students use to tell their story. Elicit the idea of narrative tenses and revise their structures if needed before completing the matching task.

1b 2d 3c 4a

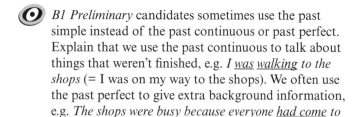 *B1 Preliminary* candidates sometimes use the past simple instead of the past continuous or past perfect. Explain that we use the past continuous to talk about things that weren't finished, e.g. *I was walking to the shops* (= I was on my way to the shops). We often use the past perfect to give extra background information, e.g. *The shops were busy because everyone had come to buy new clothes* (= people had come before I got there).

2 Read through the first example with students to help them understand the task.

2 *A friend recommended a sailing documentary. Juan watched the documentary. Juan decided he wanted to sail around the world.*
3 *Emilie applied to go on the trip to Antarctica. She started her final year at university. She finished her degree. She got on a plane to South America. She caught a flight from Chile. She arrived in Antarctica.*
4 *Someone dropped a necklace in the sand. Gavin was walking along the beach. He noticed something shiny. He stopped. He picked up the necklace.*

Extension

Students work in pairs to name the tenses used in Exercise 2 and discuss why they have been used.

Sally took climbing lessons. By the time she had her fifteenth birthday … (past simple: completed actions in the past).

… she had climbed three mountains (past perfect: action that took place before another completed action in the past).

3 Do the first sentence as a class. Students should discuss their answers with a partner.

Suggested answers: 1 I had never been close to an elephant before I did a safari. 2 I knew I had done enough training, but I was still worried about completing a long bike race. 3 Shelly was cycling in the mountains when she got a flat tyre. Luckily, her mum had packed a repair kit.

4 Ask when we use *-ed* adjectives (e.g. *exhausted*) and when we use *-ing* adjectives (e.g. *confusing*). Elicit that we use *-ed* adjectives to say how something makes us feel and we use *-ing* adjectives to say how something else is. Ask students to match an adjective to an extract. They should discuss their choices with a partner.

Possible answers: 1 surprised / confusing / unexpected 2 amusing / enjoyable 3 surprised / unexpected 4 efficient 5 exhausted 6 enjoyable 7 rude 8 afraid / anxious / nervous

5 Ask students to read the extracts. Explain that they come from different parts of the same long text. Students should then decide which of the comments (A–D) is correct.

B is correct because this matches extract 1. This extract explains that although Sam spends so long practising, his coach encourages him to have a social life, and that when he sees his friends, he always plans special activities.
Option A is incorrect because in 2, we discover that Sam does still play games against his friends. Option C is incorrect because in 4, we read that Sam doesn't get nervous – he feels excited. Option D is incorrect because in 3, we learn that Sam's parents were good at tennis, but not professional players, as they made time for tennis when they weren't working.

Exam Practice

Read through question 11 and get students to look for the answer in the first paragraph. Discuss the options as a class and ask students to underline the part of the text that gives the correct answer (*I had accompanied a school friend*). Discuss why the other three options are wrong. Ask students to answer the remaining questions individually.

11 D
A is wrong because his teacher thought he was talented, but she hadn't recommended the club to him. B is wrong because Toby's aunt had been involved in a drama club, but she didn't run it. C is wrong because Toby went to watch plays when he was a child, but there is no mention of him watching other children perform.
12 B (I was really calm during the whole thing though, which I hadn't expected)
A is wrong because she relates the idea of a famous actor relates to someone who famous at a later date. C is wrong because Toby didn't have that much to do. Option D is wrong because the idea of success relates to the success of other films, not the one Toby was in.
13 D (accept as much work as you can! Even two minutes on camera is useful.)
A is wrong because Toby says to ignore reviews and comments. B is wrong because the reference to directors simply says that lots of them are looking for actors for new projects. C is wrong because Toby says that people think who you know is important, but he doesn't agree.
14 A (I'm taking advantage of a break to do some horse riding.)
B is wrong because Toby didn't get the part in the series. C is wrong because he only mentions action films in relation to his CV. D is wrong because he talks about being taught things, not teaching.
15 C (A while later, a film director saw me in one of the club's plays and asked me to be in her film. I said yes, and for me, that was the start of everything.)
A is wrong because Toby isn't upset about not getting a part. B is wrong because he finds comedy films hard to do and was pleased when the one he worked on was completed. D is wrong because he signed up to the drama club that same evening – he didn't waste time deciding whether or not to do it.

Test 1 Reading Part 4

Training

1 Ask students to match the pairs of sentences. Students should underline the words and phrases which helped them decide and discuss their ideas with a partner.

> 1 c (it *matches* This creature; make a safe home ... *is an example of being* clever) 2 d (they *matches* They; run incredibly fast *extends the idea of being* fantastic swimmers) 3 e (they *matches* Students; look online or go to the library ... *are different ways to find out*) 4 f (they *matches* Butterflies; fly over 1,000 km ... *is an example of* amazing abilities) 5 a (it *matches* The route; very steep and takes ten hours ... *is an example of being hard*) 6 b (Getting to the top *is an example of* all sorts of challenges)

Extension

Students can write more sentences to follow on from sentences a–f, taking care to match the pronouns and tenses.

2 Point out that in Reading Part 4, students should look for paraphrases of words or ideas that link the sentences that come before or after a gapped sentence in the text.

Students complete the activity in Exercise 2, finding the paraphrases in the sentences. They might want to use different colours or underlining styles, as there will be more than one paraphrase pair in each example.

> 1 The building = the home
> allow ... into = lets in
> light = the sun
> room = The kitchen
> 2 holidaymakers = tourists
> very busy = no time for lying around the pool
> a problem = an issue
> 3 scientists = The experts
> experiments = further study
> fish = the creatures
> different conditions = In warmer water

Extension

Ask students to find an article on something that interests them. It could be about a place, a person, etc. Ask them to look at a short part of it and highlight the reference words and how the same ideas are expressed in different words. Students can share what they found with the class.

3 Ask students to note the linkers of addition in extracts 1 and 2 in Exercise 2.

> 1 also 2 Another thing is

4 Do the first one together. Remember that there are different ways to join the ideas, so monitor as students are doing the activity and give support where needed.

> *Possible answers:* 1 *There is a football pitch on the campsite. There is also a swimming pool. / There is a football pitch on the campsite. As well as that, there is also a swimming pool.* 2 *We saw a huge range of animals on our trip. We saw lots of interesting buildings, too. / We saw a huge range of animals on our trip. As well as that, we saw lots of interesting buildings.* 3 *The musicians played all their hit songs. Apart from those, they played songs from their new album. / The musicians played all their hit songs. In addition to that, they played songs from their new album.* 4 *There are ski lessons available. There is also a place where you can hire equipment. / There are ski lessons available. There is a place where you can hire equipment as well.*

Exam Practice

Read the title of the article with students. What do they know about bees? Ask students to quickly read through the text without looking at the options, to get an idea of what it's about. Get them to share ideas with a partner.

Ask students to read the first paragraph carefully, and then read through the options to find the correct gapped sentence (E). Remind them that they need to read both the sentence before the gap and the one after the gap. As a class, talk about why E is the right answer. Point out the following matches: *scientists = they; experiments = results; the insects = bees.* Point out that *also* in the gapped sentence adds additional information to the first sentence.

Students complete the remaining gaps individually and compare their answers with a partner. Do they agree? If not, ask them to look again at what they've chosen.

> 16 E
> 17 B (In the other *contrasts with* One area *in the sentence before. There is also a contrast with the balls which were stuck and the ones which could be moved. In the following sentence, there is reference to* this second room *and the balls the bees could move.)*
> 18 H (The link here is that the bees were stopping to play with the wooden balls and there was no reason related to the food, *as both ways led to a reward. The following sentence refers to the decision – the reason for choosing one of the ways over the other.)*
> 19 F (The option contains the idea of allowing time for the bees to explore, which is referred to in the preceding sentence. Also, there is repetition of the idea of the bees and the balls being in the areas. The following sentence tells us the bees were put back again, which links to the fact that they were removed in F.)
> 20 C (There is one difference mentioned in the preceding sentence and another example in the following sentence, which links with the idea that this is not the only difference seen.)

Extension

Students can use a computer to make simple versions of this type of task for other people in the class, using a short factual text from a website. This will help them think about the way information is ordered in a paragraph, and better understand how reference words and linking expressions work across sentences.

Exam task type:
four-option multiple-choice cloze with six spaces

Training focus:
predicting what type of word is missing in each gap; making verb–noun collocations; word beginnings and endings

Training

1   Ask students to look at sentences 1–5 and work with a partner to decide what type of word is needed and how they know, and to suggest a word for the gap. If needed, revise word types and give examples (e.g. nouns, verbs, adjectives, adverbs, prepositions, articles).

> *Possible answers: 1 found / discovered (verb)   2 very / extremely / really (adverb)   3 wide / exciting (adjective)   4 ran / walked / crept (verb)   5 useful / important / helpful (adjective)*

2   On the board, write *make mistakes*. Elicit that this is a verb-noun collocation (two or more words that commonly go together). Tell students that there are lots of verb–noun collocations in English. Students read through the two lists and match verbs and nouns to make common collocations.

> *Possible answers:* **accept** *a decision / a reason / an offer* **begin** *a journey* **enter** *a competition* **give** *some help / a reason / a decision* **have** *a break / a reason* **make** *a decision / a mistake / an offer* **offer** *some help / a reason* **regret** *a decision / a mistake* **tell** *the truth*

3   Point out that in this part of the exam, each of the options (A–D) will be the same type of word (a noun, a verb, an adjective, etc.). The words may have similar meanings, but only one can be correct in the gap.

Elicit which kind of words usually end in the suffix *-tion* (nouns) and which end in *-ity* (nouns). Elicit what the prefix *un-* does to a word (makes it negative). Ask students to think of examples of other adjectives that use the prefix *un-*. If they need support, give them the word *unhappy* and see how many more they can think of, e.g. *unkind, unpleasant, unfriendly, unfair, unlucky, untidy.*

Ask students to read the text first before looking at the options and think about what kind of word is needed in each gap. Then, they should choose the correct options A–D. Students compare their answers with a partner. Ask them to check again if they disagree.

> *1 D (ambition refers to a plan, which fits the meaning of the sentence. A imagination refers to a characteristic someone has – we'd say 'a good imagination' for example, rather than using it to refer to a plan. B situation refers to something that is happening at a particular time. C invention refers to an object that someone has created, so doesn't fit the meaning here.)*
> *2 A (unlikely tells us what the writer thought about her low chances of earning enough money for her trip. B unlucky doesn't fit the context. If the option was 'lucky' then a sentence such as 'I'd be very lucky to earn enough money …' could work. C unusual doesn't fit the rest of the sentence. It could work if the sentence continued '… unusual for me to have enough money available'. D unimportant doesn't fit the meaning of the sentence.)*

> *3 B (opportunity means 'have a good chance' and it also collocates well with wonderful. A ability would refer to something the person possessed already, rather than something that was being given to them. C reality describes something that exists or happens, so does not fit the context of a future possibility.)*

Extension

Give students two or three short texts on an interesting topic. The passages should be ones that stand alone and are easy to understand. They should contain a range of collocations. Students can choose one and highlight the collocations. They can make their own sentences using these collocations to illustrate the meanings.

Exam Practice

Ask students to look at the photograph and the title. Talk about what they already know about octopuses. Ask them to quickly read the text (ignoring the gaps for now) and ask if it contains any information they already know.

Ask students to read the first two sentences of the text and look carefully at the four options and choose the correct one for gap 21 (C). They check with a partner and discuss why the other options are not correct (*positions* is wrong as it describes where one item or object is, rather than where the creatures are found around the world; *situations* is wrong as this word refers to things that are happening; *locations* is correct because this word describes the different places where things are found; *directions* is wrong as this word describes movement, not where something is found).

Ask students to complete gaps 22–26 individually. When they have finished, they compare answers with a partner and check the options again if they disagree. Conduct class feedback.

> *22 C (Typically is the only adverb which describes a habit, which is what is needed here.)*
> *23 D (Achieving is the only verb which has the meaning of 'managing to do' or 'reaching' which is needed here. Completing refers to a step-by-step task and succeeding doesn't fit grammatically, as it would need to be followed by an -ing form. Aiming is used to talk about a goal or plan.)*
> *24 A (To prevent is to stop something happening, in this case, to prevent other animals from seeing the octopus. To avoid is to not go near something so this does not fit the context. Escape describes what the octopus eventually does, not the process of hiding in the ink. Because of the position of the gap in the sentence, protect would refer to other animals, not the octopus. It therefore can't fit the context as the ink does not protect other animals.)*
> *25 C (This option collocates with both high and intelligence, whereas the other options do not. While we can say 'high numbers', we don't use the phrase 'numbers of intelligence'. Values and quantities also do not collocate with intelligence and would not be commonly used with high.)*
> *26 A (This is part of the phrase in order to do something, whereas the other options are part of different phrases. In case is used to describe something we do to prepare for a possible situation. In fact is used to give extra information, or to say that something is true. In full means without any part missing.)*

Extension

Students can identify the type of word used in each set of options and try to add one or two more to each, using a thesaurus if necessary. Examples for Question 22 could be the adverbs *generally, totally*, etc. The aim here is to build lexical sets.

Exam task type:
reading a text with six gaps and filling each space with one word

Training focus:
reading further in the text; using pronouns and possessive adjectives; identifying short phrases

Training

1 Demonstrate by writing the first part of sentence 1 on the board: *I _____ never been on a boat ride …* Ask students what could come in the gap and elicit the auxiliary verbs *have* or *had*. Next, write the second part of the sentence on the board: *… until my cousins came to stay.* Discuss why the answer needs to be *had*. Tell students they can complete the gap with the contracted form *'d*.

   Ask students to think about the gap for sentences 2–4 and discuss their choices as a class.

> *1 had   2 gets (The first part of the sentence forces the present tense and makes* got *incorrect.)   3 was (The second part of the sentence forces the past tense and makes* am *incorrect.)   4 How (The question needs* How, *as it is answered with* by car.*)*

Extension

Tell students to look again at sentence 3 in Exercise 1. Underline the different pronouns and possessive adjectives, and ask students to explain why the forms are used.

Before I was able to take the bus on my own, my mum made me practise a few times with my older sister.

I = subject pronoun used to refer to the person doing the action.

my = possessive adjective used to describe ownership or possession. In this example, this refers to possession of 'own self', 'mum' and 'older sister'.

me = object pronoun, used to refer to the person affected by an action, which in this example is the person being 'made' to practise.

2 Students complete Exercise 2 individually, then check with a partner. Ask students to underline the words which helped them decide, before conducting a class feedback session.

> *1 our   2 us   3 We   4 They   5 it   6 them*

3 Point out that sometimes, the missing word is part of a short phrase. On the board, write: *All of them were wearing warm coats.* Draw students' attention to the phrase *all of them*. Ask students to work together to decide which words complete gaps 1–4 and underline the phrases. They then check with a partner. Elicit the phrase that each gap is part of.

> *1 my (one of my own)   2 one (one of the best)   3 myself (go by myself)   4 as (as soon as)*

Extension

Students can make a list of useful short phrases and make a poster for the classroom wall. Alternatively, they could write a short email to a partner, using some phrases they have learned recently. If the email has a request for information, then partners can write replies.

Exam Practice

Talk to students about going to the theatre. Have they ever been? Why/Why not?

Remind students that in this part of the test, they don't have words to choose from, and they have to think of the words by themselves. Ask students to read the title of the text and establish that they're going to read a review. Ask them to read the whole text first without filling in any gaps. Ask them to briefly talk with their partner about the text and say what they remember from it. Ask them to work individually to complete the gaps.

> *27 one (completes the structure* one of the *+ noun to describe one example of a group)*
> *28 had / 'd (the auxiliary verb needed to complete a past perfect tense needed here to talk about a time before the class trip event)*
> *29 of / over (both these prepositions can follow the noun* view *to describe what could be seen from the seats)*
> *30 to (forms the phrase* be able to*)*
> *31 we (needed to describe who was talking; the plural is the correct choice as it comes before* all*)*
> *32 a (this is used to refer to live performances in general, not a specific one)*

Exam task type:
writing a reply to an email with notes

Training focus:
understanding the task; using vocabulary related to the environment; understanding word building; making suggestions

Training

1 Focus students on the email on page 30. Give them a minute or two to read it. Ask students to imagine they have received the email from Jessie. Students should also imagine that they have written the four notes in response to Jessie's email. Point out that students must base their reply on the notes.

Give students time to look at sentences 1–6 on page 28 and decide which ones are true.

> 1F 2T 3F 4F 5T 6T

2 Ask students to match each note with two possible responses. This could be done in pairs.

> 1d,g 2c,e 3b,h 4a,f

3 Tell students they can make brief notes if they wish, but as this is the ideas stage, they don't need to write full sentences yet. They can do that when they start drafting their emails for the Exam Practice task. Write down some of their ideas so that students can see a range of responses for each of the notes.

> Possible answers   (Me too!) I can't wait, looking forward to   (Tell Jessie) How about, Why don't we ...?   (Yes, because ...) it's a great way to ..., lots of people will see them   (Suggest ...) Let's go to ..., We could always ...

4 Write *the environment* on the board and ask students what they think of when they see this word (e.g. the world around us, the air we breathe, all the things that live and grow). Ask students to look at the matching task. Ask them to think of any vocabulary related to this topic and record their ideas. Then ask students, in pairs, to match the vocabulary with the correct images. Quickly check answers.

> A litter B wildlife C recycling D the coast E pollution

5 Ask students to complete the table in pairs or small groups. Remind them that they should try to use a range of vocabulary in the Writing exam, and word-building exercises can help them to remember words with a similar meaning. Check everyone has the correct answers.

> 1 environmental 2 pollution 3 to pollute 4 coastal 5 recycled
> 6 to recycle 7 damage 8 damaged / damaging

(⊙) *B1 Preliminary* candidates often make verb choice errors with *should* for advice. Remind them that we never use *don't* before *should* to make it negative.

6 Explain that the email task in Writing Part 1 will often ask candidates to make suggestions or recommendations. The exercise will help students practise language commonly used to say whether something is a good or bad idea. Point out the grammatical structure for sentences 1–6 (*should/shouldn't* + infinitive).

> Suggested answers: 1 shouldn't 2 should 3 shouldn't 4 should
> 5 should 6 shouldn't

Extension

Pair students with people they don't usually work with. Ask them to discuss things they think we should and shouldn't do in order to protect the environment. Ask groups to present their ideas to the class.

Exam Practice

Remind students to read the email carefully and pay particular attention to the four notes. The notes tell students what information they need to include in their reply email, which they can address in any order. Point out that the notes will test a range of functions. Ask students to look at each note on Jessie's email and say what they have to do *(Me too!* – agree with Jessie; *Tell Jessie* – let Jessie know something; *Yes, because ...* – give a reason for an opinion; *Suggest ...* – make a suggestion).

Ask students to draft some ideas for the four notes using their ideas from Exercise 3, then write a full response to Jessie's email. Remind students to use an appropriate email format. This includes an appropriate greeting (e.g. *Hi/Hello Jessie*), the message which covers the four notes, and then an appropriate ending (e.g. *Bye, See you soon*), followed by the student's name in the final line of the email.

> **Sample answer**
> *Hi Jessie*
> *I can't wait to go to this year's Beach Clean. I went last year and couldn't believe how much rubbish we collected in an afternoon!*
> *How about we cycle there? It's supposed to be nice weather, and it'll only take about half an hour to get there.*
> *I think we should post lots of photos on social media, so everyone can see how much litter is left on the beach. Hopefully, our posts will encourage more people to look after our beach so that everyone can enjoy it.*
> *My dad said he can make some sandwiches to take with us. Let me know what you think.*
> *Bye*
> *Dani*
>
> **Comment**
> *This response contains appropriate functional language in reply to Jessie's email. Dani has included all four content points, and the word length is suitable (110 words). This is a clear and well-written answer with a range of vocabulary and structures.*

Test 1 Writing Part 2

Exam task type:
writing an article or a story in about 100 words

Training focus:
understanding the task, studying an example answer; linking ideas together; using prepositions of time (*during*, *for* and *since*)

Training

1 Ask pairs to study the task and, if necessary, check that they understand it. Students should focus on looking at sentences 1–5 and deciding if they are true or false. They do not actually write the article.

> 1 T 2 T 3 F 4 T 5 T

2 Make sure students understand all the expressions in the box before they begin the exercise. Give pairs plenty of time to decide which expressions belong in the sample answer. Tell students that three questions have more than one answer.

> 1 Firstly 2 For example / For instance 3 Above all 4 For example / For instance 5 especially 6 Another thing 7 In particular / Above all

3 Ask students to study the sample answer in Exercise 2 and then complete questions 1–4.

> 1 yes (I'm not interested in wearing the latest trends; I always give my old clothes to charity shops) 2 I love learning how to sew some of the things I wear; I recently made a long black dress 3 I'm not interested in; that doesn't mean I'm not into fashion; I love learning how to; I like knowing that 4 yes (It's just over 100 words long.)

4 Explain to students that their writing will be stronger if they use linking expressions to connect their ideas across sentences. Ask students to decide which words and phrases from Exercise 2 belong in each category.

> ordering information: firstly, another thing, finally
> stressing a point: in particular, above all, especially
> giving an example: for instance, such as, for example

Extension

Ask students to write an article for the *Staying in fashion* task in Exercise 1, using the linking expressions in Exercise 4 in their article. Have students check each other's work and provide feedback on ways to improve their articles.

5 Explain that students sometimes confuse *during, for* and *since*, which are prepositions related to time. Ask students to complete the task. Have students compare their answers before checking as a whole class.

> 1 since 2 for 3 during 4 for 5 since 6 during

6 Ask students to complete the task and then go over the answers.

> 1 since 2 for 3 during

Exam Practice

Remind students that they get to choose whether they want to write an article or a story. Look at the tasks as a class and review the Advice box. Have students study the tasks to see which they would like to write. Encourage students to choose the task they think would demonstrate their writing skills most confidently.

> **Question 2 Sample answer**
> *It's easy to be on social media for hours, so it's important that I don't waste too much time on there. That's why I only go on social media for a short time after finishing everything I need to achieve, such as my homework.*
> *In my opinion, there are good and bad things about social media. For instance, it's an especially good way to keep in touch with people with similar interests. I've made a lot of friends since I started using social media. However, I really don't like it when people post things just to get lots of followers.*
>
> **Comment**
> *This article is an appropriate length (100 words). The article is organised into two paragraphs to include the two content points. It also uses expressions* (such as, For instance, However) *to link the main ideas together.*

> **Question 3 Sample answer**
> They jumped up and down with excitement when they heard the news. *The friends had just won first prize at the science competition! To begin with, they didn't know what to enter when they heard about the competition. Then one day, Brian took a really long shower and thought of an invention to help save water. His friends loved his idea, and after months of hard work, they created a smart device that measures how much water someone uses and makes a warning sound when they've been in a shower for too long. The friends hope that one day everyone will have this invention in their homes.*
>
> **Comment**
> *The story begins with the sentence provided to set the context and it is 107 words, which is an appropriate length. The story has a good range of tenses* (had just won, didn't know, will have) *and time phrases* (To begin with, when, one day, after months) *to explain the sequence of events. The vocabulary and sentence structures are appropriate for the level.*

Exam task type:
three-option multiple choice with seven picture-based questions

Training focus:
vocabulary related to places and activities; time expressions and verb forms

Training

In this part of the test, candidates will hear recordings on a variety of topics. They have to choose from three pictures. They should aim to build their vocabulary on common topics and also identify functions and grammar, including time expressions and verb forms.

1 Focus on the five headings in the table and make sure students understand their meanings. Ask the whole class to find a word from the box for the first category, *furniture*. Students then complete the exercise in groups and discuss their answers. Explain any words the students are not sure about.

furniture	clothes	sport	music	buildings
cupboard	coat	diving	band	café
shelf	glove	fishing	DJ	cottage
sink	scarf	football	keyboard	railway station
wardrobe	tie	surfing	recording	shopping centre

2 Focus students on sentence 1. Ask students what things they might see in a museum, on a farm or at a beach. Then, students do the exercise individually and check their answers with a partner. Check answers as a class. Check understanding of the incorrect options.

1 beach   2 fountain   3 earrings   4 record music

Extension

Students can practise more vocabulary sets by playing the game *Stop*. Students make a table like the one in Exercise 1 with five columns. Each column should have a heading for a topic area, either the ones in Exercise 1 or others such as *Food and drink, Jobs, Transport or Animals*. Call out a letter of the alphabet. Students work in pairs to write a word for each category that begins with that letter. The first pair that completes all the categories says 'Stop' and everyone stops writing. Check the words that each pair has written, awarding a point for each correct word and five extra points for the first pair. Continue with other letters of the alphabet. At the end, add up all the points to find an overall winner.

3 Focus on the six pictures. Ask students to describe the pictures, saying what they can see. Write the words that they suggest on the board, e.g. *cottage, microphone, recording*. Play the recording, pausing after each item to give students time to think.

1 F   2 D   3 E   4 B   5 A   6 C

 B1 Preliminary candidates often confuse *used to* with *usually*. Remind students that *used to + infinitive* is for past habits, and never for things happening now.

4 The aim of this activity is to focus on different verb forms and whether they refer to the past, present or future. Point out that questions in Listening Part 1 may ask about whether something happened, is happening or is going to happen, using a verb form and/or a time expression. Ask students to underline the verb in each of the sentences before they work in pairs to decide the answer.

1 future   2 present   3 future   4 past   5 future   6 past
7 future   8 future

5 Before listening, ask students to look at the pictures and describe what each one shows. Write the important vocabulary on the board. Pause after each question and discuss what verb form the speaker used in each case for the action in each picture.

1 future   2 past   3 present   4 present   5 future   6 past

6 The aim of this activity is to draw students' attention to other clues that help them identify the time of an action. Play the recording, pausing after each part to give students time to write the answers and discuss any other language that helped them get the answer.

1 as soon as possible   2 won, scored   3 all morning   4 right now
5 'm looking forward to, at the end of term   6 nearly missed

Exam Practice

Remind students that they will hear each of the seven recordings twice. On the first listening, they should choose and answer. They should use the second listening to confirm their answer, or to choose a different option if necessary.

Remind students that the information which answers the question correctly may be in any part of the recording: the beginning, the middle or at the end, so they shouldn't make a decision until they have heard the complete dialogue.

Play the recording for students to complete the task. Go through the answers, making sure that all students understand why each answer is correct. If necessary, play each recording again, one question at a time, analysing the language used.

1 C   2 A   3 B   4 C   5 A   6 B   7 C

Extension

Ask students to focus on the incorrect options and identify why they are wrong. Play the recording again and elicit feedback.

Exam task type:
three-option multiple choice with six questions

Training focus:
using adjectives; explaining why

Training

In this part of the test candidates will hear six dialogues or short monologues on a variety of topics. The focus of the task is understanding the gist of the situation, particularly the speakers' feelings, opinions, attitudes or reasons for doing something.

1   Write some adjectives on the board, e.g. *exciting, lucky, confident, noisy, old-fashioned, sweet*. For each one, ask students to give you examples of objects, people or things that these words could describe to check the meanings. Ask students to do the same in pairs with the adjectives in sentences 1–6. Monitor any difficulties they might have and if necessary, explain the meaning of any unknown words. Play the recording, pausing after each speaker to check the answer with the class.

> 1 *anxious*   2 *cute*   3 *quick*   4 *tall*   5 *amusing*   6 *enormous*

2   Explain that in Listening Part 2, the words in the questions will not generally be exactly the same as the words heard in the recording. Therefore, it is important to know different words with similar meanings (synonyms) and also words with the opposite meanings (antonyms).

> 1 *nervous*   2 *sweet*   3 *fast*   4 *high*   5 *funny*   6 *huge*

Point out that *fun* means that something is enjoyable. *Funny* means that something is amusing and makes you smile or laugh. Ask students to give you examples of situation or things that can be *fun* or *funny* to clarify the difference between them.

Extension

Ask students to prepare small pieces of paper, and to write an adjective on each one. Put all the pieces of paper together face down in two piles. Divide the class into two teams. One person from each team comes to the front of the class, takes a piece of paper and mimes its adjective. As soon as the team guesses it, another person from the team goes to the front and takes another adjective. Set a time limit. The winning team is the one that guessed the most words within that time.

3   Explain that there are different ways of answering the question *Why?* Write these sentence stems on the board:

1   *The boy wore a helmet because …*
2   *The boy wore a helmet so that …*
3   *The boy wore a helmet to …*
4   *The boy wore a helmet so …*

Ask students to give you ideas for completing the sentences. (Suggested ideas: 1 he was going to ride his bike; 2 he could cycle safely; 3 protect his head; 4 his parents weren't worried.)

Students do Exercise 3 in pairs. Check answers with the whole class.

> 1 *d*   2 *c*   3 *a*   4 *f*   5 *g*   6 *b*   7 *e*

4   The aim here is to raise awareness of the kind of dialogue students might hear in Part 2 and to identify why an answer is correct or incorrect. Play the recording and ask students to explain why options A and B are incorrect.

> C (there was an important game and I had to be there for the team, so I came back)
> A is wrong because the boy says I was feeling fit.
> B is wrong because the boy says I'd just finished all my exams.

Exam Practice

Tell students to read the questions and options carefully to predict who is speaking and what they are talking about. Remind students that they will hear the recordings twice. As with Part 1, suggest that students choose an answer during the first listening and check that it is correct during the second, adjusting their response if necessary.

Explain that the information required to answer the questions correctly may be in any part of the text and may come from several sections of the text. This is because Part 2 questions often test students' understanding of overall gist.

Students complete the task. Go through the answers. Make sure that students understand why each answer is correct. If necessary, play the recordings one at a time, or use the audioscript, analysing the language used.

> 8 C   9 A   10 A   11 B   12 C   13 B

Exam task type:
monologue with notes to complete

Training focus:
predicting answers; understanding contrasting information

Training

1   Explain that in Listening Part 3, students will listen to one speaker talking about a topic and have to complete some sentences or notes with words they hear. They need to develop awareness of the language that they are likely to hear using their knowledge of topic vocabulary and prediction skills.

The aim of Exercise 1 is to help students think about the type of words they might read and hear according to the topic of the task. Focus students on sentence 1 and ask students what kind of word could go in the gap (e.g. a noun, a classroom object). Repeat for the other questions. Students work in pairs to complete the task.

Students' own answers.

2   Tell students that they can complete the gaps with a word or a number. If they write a number as a figure, they are less likely to make spelling mistakes. Check they know how to write dates and times in figures (e.g. *24th*).

1   calculator
2   café
3   fourth (4th)
4   shop window
5   presentation
6   tired
7   documentary
8   two (2) days

Extension

Go through the Remember box and ask students how each number is spoken. Give students practice by saying some different types of numbers (including times, dates, monetary units and measurements) and asking students to write them down (in number form). Where possible, include the information to be written in a sentence.

3   The aim of this activity is to raise awareness of words that show a contrast in order to help students identify the correct option when they hear more than one possibility. Explain that the words in the box are used to link two ideas that show a contrast, but they can come in different places in a sentence. Students complete the activity in pairs. Point out how the words are used in each case, e.g. note that *However* in sentence 1 begins a new sentence.

1   However
2   actually
3   otherwise
4   although
5   instead
6   despite

4   Tell students that often, they will hear more than one word that could logically fit a gap, so they need to listen to the context as well and not just write the first possible answer they hear. Students listen and check their answers together.

1   cinema
2   backpack
3   go running
4   clean his bike
5   £10

Exam Practice

Tell students to carefully read the rubric and the information given about the recording before it starts. This will tell them who is speaking, what they are going to talk about and what kind of information they need to listen for. Ask students not to write anything yet.

Explain that the information is in the same order as in the recording and there should be enough time to write answers while listening. Remind students they will hear the recording twice, so they can check their answers and fill in any missing information during the second listening.

Draw students' attention to the Tip box. Students read through the task and predict the kind of information that is missing in pairs (e.g. the answer to Question 18 needs to be a number). Students then listen and complete the task.

14   cousin
15   caves
16   sweater
17   sunny
18   15.50
19   hands

Test 1 Listening Part 4

Exam task type:
an interview with six multiple-choice questions

Training focus:
identifying a speaker's intention, opinion or attitude; identifying how information is paraphrased

Training

1   In Listening Part 4, students listen to a longer text, which will be an interview. The texts are from a range of contexts and are largely informational. The information required to answer the questions may be about places and events or people's lives, interests and experiences. Students need to focus on detailed understanding of the meaning of the text.

The aim of Exercise 1 is to help students understand the questions in Part 4. Encourage students to focus on the meaning of each verb and the choose the one that fits the meaning of each sentence best.

> 1 explained   2 persuade   3 encouraged   4 think   5 promoting
> 6 suggested   7 advised   8 warned

Extension

Ask students to create their own short dialogues to illustrate the sentences in Exercise 1. Point out the typical language they can use for suggesting (*Shall we…? Why don't you …?*), warning (*you should be careful …*), encouraging (*I'm sure you can do it!*), etc.

2   Give students an example of information that is paraphrased (expressed in a different way), e.g. *I wouldn't like to go to the beach today* is another way of expressing *I don't fancy going to the beach today*. Ask them if they can think of other ways to express the same idea. Read out sentence 1 and ask students to match it to a similar phrase in a–f (f). Students match the other sentences. In each case, ask students to identify the paraphrase that helped them decide the answer.

> 1 f   2 e   3 a   4 c   5 b   6 d

3   Ask students to read the question and underline the key words (*main reason, decision, go to India*). Point out that the word *main* is very important as the other options may also be reasons, but not the most important ones. Play the recording twice and ask students what helped them decide that B was the main reason.

> *B – (it was the chance to find out about the wildlife there that made up my mind for me)*

Exam Practice

Tell students that they should read the introductory rubric carefully before they listen. This will give them information about who is speaking and what that person is talking about. Remind students that this part of the test is an interview, so they will hear one person asking questions and another answering them.

Explain that in the test, students will have time to read through the questions before they hear the recording. Tell them not to worry if they don't understand some of the words: they should focus on the meanings of the questions as whole, and the corresponding answers. This will help them prepare for what they are about to hear.

Point out that the interview in the recording follows the same order as the questions on the page, and that the interviewer's questions are often very similar to the students' questions. This will help students work out where they are in the tasks as whole as the recording plays.

Students listen to the interview and answer the questions. Check the answers and discuss with the students why the other options are incorrect.

> 20 A   21 A   22 B   23 C   24 B   25 A

Exam task type:
conversation with interlocutor

Training focus:
answering personal questions; understanding the interlocutor

Training

Explain that in Part 1 of the Speaking test, students will talk about themselves in two phases. They will be asked questions about their lives, which may include personal details, hobbies and school. Explain that students should try to practise talking about themselves before they take the test. They could also ask a friend or family member to ask them questions, to prepare in a more realistic way.

Explain that in the test, one student is Candidate A and the other is Candidate B. Sometimes, there may be three candidates. If this is the case, the test will be a little longer, but they will not have to say more individually because of this.

1   During Phase 1 of Part 1, the interlocutor will ask each candidate two questions. These will be about where they live and how old they are. In Exercise 1, students should answer the questions truthfully in the spaces provided. Then they practise asking and answering the questions with a partner.

> Students' own answers.

2   During Phase 2, the interlocutor's questions will widen to include current interests and activities, past experiences and future plans. In Exercise 2, students match the questions and answers before checking them with a partner.

> 1 b   2 c   3 f   4 a   5 d   6 e

3   Students take turns to ask and answer the questions from Exercise 2 in pairs.

4   Students listen and complete what was said. Ask them to check their answers with a partner. Then play the recording again for students to check their answers.

> 1 do you like doing in your free time
> 2 often do you exercise
> 3 us about a teacher you like
> 4 going to the cinema or watching a film at home
> 5 long have you studied English for
> 6 do you practise speaking English

5   Students ask and answer the questions in Exercise 4 with a partner.

Extension

Ask students to think of two more questions about their current interests and activities, past experiences and future plans. They then give their answers to the questions for their partner to work out what the questions are. They then practise asking and answering the questions together.

Exam Practice

Students read the Phase 1 questions. Then they take turns to ask and answer them with a partner. Encourage them to give as much information as possible.

Students then look at the Phase 2 questions. Ask different students to answer them in turn. Remind them to avoid giving one-word answers and to give extra details where possible. For example:

How long do you spend on a mobile phone every day?

Possible response: *I use my mobile phone for about three hours, but I don't use social media because I don't like it. I use my phone to watch movies or look up information.*

Tell us about your best friend.

Possible response: *I don't really have one best friend. I have three friends who I'm really close to. One of them is called Naoki. He's really intelligent and funny, and he plays the guitar really well. We often hang out together at the weekend.*

How often do you listen to music?

Possible response: *Not very often. I usually watch films or read books instead. I'm not sure why because I do like music, especially pop and rock.*

Explain that during the test, students can ask the interlocutor to repeat a question if they don't understand it. The interlocutor may ask the question again using different words to help. For example, the three questions above could be rephrased as:

Do you use your mobile phone every day? (Why? / Why not?)

Which friend do you really like? (Why?)

Do you listen to music sometimes?

Now tell students that they are going to listen to other students answering some Part 1 Phase 2 questions. Play the recording. They should listen and compare their own answers with the responses they hear.

Exam task type:
extended turn: talking about a photograph

Training focus:
describing people, things and places

Training

In Part 2, students take turns to talk about photographs they are shown. Tell the students that they will each have a different photograph to talk about. They should describe what they can see in the photograph in as much detail as possible. Before the test, they should practise describing people and what they are doing. They could also build a list of vocabulary for different situations, such as the home and things in it, for example, furniture or appliances.

 B1 Preliminary candidates often use the present simple instead of the present continuous when describing things in progress around now. Remind students that we often use the present continuous to describe what we can see in pictures (*They are eating ... She is wearing ...*, etc.).

1   Students look at the photograph also on page C10 and think about what they can see. Give them two minutes to write down as many of the objects in the photo as they can. They then compare their ideas with a partner. Elicit the vocabulary and create a list on the board. Ask whether there are any objects they don't know the names for and ask them to think about how they could describe them using other words. Draw their attention to the first Remember box. They could say, for example, *There are some things behind the girl on the left, but I'm not sure what they're called. They're for putting things in and carrying them.*

Ask students to look at the people in the photograph. Ask questions about them: *Where are they? Are they family or friends? Do they have a good relationship? Are they having a good time? What do they look like? What's the girl on the left doing? What's the girl on the right doing? What are they wearing?* Elicit answers from students and encourage them to say anything else they would like to about the people. Remind students to use the present continuous to describe what the people are doing or wearing.

2   Students look at the words in the boxes. They work with a partner to match the adjectives with the items. Explain that they may be able to use the same adjective with more than one item.

> *Possible answers:*
> *amusing conversation/joke, close relationship, comfortable clothes, interesting conversation/joke, small kitchen/space, tasty meal, tidy kitchen/space*

Extension

Ask students to work with a partner. They should take it in turns to say one sentence about the classroom they are in and the people in it. They should try to keep talking for about one minute.

3   Explain to students that they will hear a candidate describing the photograph they have just talked about. Ask them to listen for anything the candidate says about the photograph which was different from their own descriptions.

Exam Practice

Students each talk about the photograph they are given for one minute, describing what they can see. (See pages C1 and C2 for photographs. There are photographs for a third candidate on page C7 if required.)

Remind students that they should say as much as they can about the photograph, including what the people are like and what their relationships is, what they are doing, what they are wearing, what the weather's like and what else they can see.

Explain that they should also try to describe things they may not know the words for, using the phrases they have learned. This will help them gain more points than ignoring an object they don't know the word for, especially if it is an important part of the photograph.

When they have finished, play the recordings relating to photographs A, B and C so students can listen and compare the candidates' responses with what they said themselves.

Exam task type:
discussion between candidates

Training focus:
making suggestions, agreeing and disagreeing

Training

In Part 3, students discuss a situation which the interlocutor gives them. This is a hypothetical situation, which the students will discuss with their partner. Explain that they will be given a set of picture prompts to guide their conversation. Before the test, it is a good idea for students to learn and practise phrases for agreeing and disagreeing, asking for and making suggestions, and responding to their partner.

Write three headings on the board: *Suggestions*, *Agreeing* and *Disagreeing*. Ask students to come to the board in turn and write a phrase they know for suggesting, agreeing and disagreeing. Prompt them where necessary, for example: *I don't … (agree)*.

1   Students say what they can see in the pictures and guess who these gifts might be for and why.

> They are for someone in hospital.

2   Students read the scenario. Ask them to predict what the students will say in the recording. Then play the recording for them to listen and check which gift the students think is best and why.

> They agree that the tablet would be the best gift because the person in hospital can keep in touch with friends and family.

3   Ask students to close their books. Play the recording again and ask them to make a note of any phrases they hear for making suggestions, agreeing and disagreeing. Elicit the phrases and ask them to check whether they are the same or different from the ones on the board.

Students open their books again and look at the list of phrases in Exercise 3. Ask them to compare their notes from Exercise 2 with the phrases they can see.

Students work with a partner to decide whether the phrases are for making suggestions, agreeing or disagreeing.

> 1D   2S   3A   4A   5D   6S/D   7S   8S   9A   10S

4   Students decide individually which of the gifts they think would be best for someone in hospital and why. They then discuss this with a partner, giving reasons for their opinion.

5   Students read the scenario and look at the ideas for a gift. Explain that they have to decide which of the ideas they think will make the best present for their aunt and

her new baby. Ask students to give other possible ideas for presents and write their ideas on the board.

Elicit some of the phrases students have learned for making suggestions. Students then discuss the scenario with a partner. Remind them to respond politely to what their partner says and to offer reasons for their own answers. Monitor as they are working and help if necessary.

Exam Practice

Remind students that in Speaking Part 3, they will talk together with their partner and not with the interlocutor. The interlocutor will read out the scenario that the candidates will discuss and show them some pictures to aid the conversation. Candidates should look at each other as they speak.

Students work in pairs. Read the scenario to them and ask them to talk together, using the pictures for Exam Practice Speaking Part 3 (page C11 and below).

Write the following steps on the board:

1   *Talk about all the pictures first, saying why they would be good places for a group of friends to visit or not, and give reasons.*

2   *Decide together which would be the best place to visit.*

Students should talk together for two to three minutes, using the phrases they have learned for making suggestions, agreeing and disagreeing. Remind them to ask their partner for their partner's opinions and make sure to allow them time to speak.

When they have finished discussing the scenario, students listen to the sample conversation and compare it with their own. Ask them whether the candidates they listened to did anything better than they did themselves and why.

Exam task type:
discussion related to Part 3

Training focus:
talking about likes, dislikes and preferences

Training

In Part 4, students discuss questions that the interlocutor will ask that are related to the topic in Part 3. Candidates may be asked different questions, or they may be asked to discuss their answers with their partner.

1 Elicit the kinds of gifts that students like to receive. Then ask them to read through the conversation and think about the words that might be missing from the gaps. Next, play the recording for the students to listen and complete the conversation. Students check their answers with a partner. Play the recording again, if necessary, for them to check their ideas.

   Ask students to look at the completed phrases and ask them what kind of phrases they are (they express likes, dislikes and preferences).

   1 lovely   2 brilliant   3 would   4 too   5 What about you   6 really
   7 like   8 love   9 favourite   10 prefer

2 Students work individually to read the conversation and underline the relevant phrases. They then check their answers with a partner.

   Elicit any further phrases that the students may know for expressing likes, dislikes and preferences, for example, *I hate … I prefer … .*

   Me too.   Exactly.   I think it's good to …   Right!   I'd rather (not) …
   I'm not so sure.   I guess so.   Right, but …

Extension

Elicit different occasions when people give each other gifts (for example, a wedding, a birthday or passing an important test) and write them on the board. Then elicit the kinds of gifts people might give on these occasions in their country.

Students discuss the ideas on the board with a partner, explaining what kind of gift they would give for the different occasions and why. Remind them to use phrases for expressing likes, dislikes and preferences.

3 Go through the responses and check that students understand how to use them. They then take turns to read out the statements and select an appropriate response for each one. They could respond positively or negatively.

Possible answers:
1 Really? / Me neither! / I am! / Is that true?
2 So do I! / Really? / Exactly! / I don't!
3 I don't! / Really? / So do I!
4 Really? / Me too! / I wouldn't!
5 Me neither! / Really? / Is that true?
6 Exactly! / So do I! / Me too! / Is that true? / Really? / I don't!

Exam Practice

Ask students what the task and pictures in Part 3 were about (choosing a place to visit with friends). Get them to predict what the Part 4 questions could be about (visiting new places).

Divide students into groups of three. One student is the interlocutor and the other two are the candidates. The interlocutor asks some of the questions in the list to individual students and other questions for both students to discuss. Time the students as they are working and encourage them to keep going for at least three minutes. Remind students that if they can't think of anything to say, they could ask their partner a question. This may give them something new to talk about. Explain that the interlocutor will ask another question if they run out of things to say, and that they should not worry if this happens.

Remind students that if they are asked a question to discuss together, they should make sure that they give their partner a chance to speak, and that the conversation should be as equal as possible.

After they have completed their conversations, ask students to each think of two more questions they could ask on the topic. For example, *What is one place that you think everyone should visit in their lifetime? Do you think people like different kinds of places at different ages? Why?* Monitor as they are working and help if necessary. When they have written their questions, students then work with a new partner to take turns asking and answering them.

When they have finished, play the recording and ask students to assess the candidates' performance and compare it to their own.

Test 2 Reading Part 1

Exam task type:
three-option multiple choice – reading five real-world texts (e.g. signs, notices, emails, messages, advertisements)

Training focus:
understanding what you have to find in a short text; the passive in notices and signs; identifying examples

Training

Students read the bullet points about this part of the test and answer the questions. They check their answers in pairs.

- *how well you can understand a short text*
- *signs, notices, short personal messages (e.g. emails, texts, notes)*

1 Ask students to work in pairs and to look at the texts and questions 1–4. Ask them to underline the important words in the questions that tell them what they need to look for. They do not answer the questions yet.

1 *When will the* shop shut today?
2 *What* transport problem *has Nate had?*
3 *What are students* not required to bring?
4 *Why* is Sandra writing this text message?

2 Check students understand the idea of paraphrasing, and read through the example with them. Students look back at the short texts in Exercise 1 and in pairs, identify the words which give them the right information.

1 *Shop* closing *early* this afternoon at 2.30 *due to staff* illness
Usual closing time of 5 from tomorrow.
2 *Hi Nate,*
I'm sorry, my bus was cancelled! *I'll get the next one, but I'll be really late.*
I'll get there as soon as I can, but it won't be before 3 at the earliest.
3 *Bring your coats as it will be cold on the river. You'll also need a pen and notebook, but* don't worry about snacks.
4 Don't forget to bring the book *to school tomorrow! I can't wait to read it!*
Sandra

3 Encourage students to use the information they found in Exercise 2 to answer the questions in Exercise 1.

1 *at 2.30*   2 *His bus was cancelled.*   3 *snacks*
4 *to remind someone to bring a book tomorrow*

4 Ask students to look again at short text 4 in Exercise 1. Elicit that Sandra is writing to *remind* someone to do something. Read through the information in Exercise 4 together, before asking students to match the phrases with the verbs. Point out that more than one answer might be possible. Go through students' answers with the class.

Suggested answers: *2 apologising* *3 admitting* *4 warning* *5 explaining*
6 suggesting *7 requesting* *8 confirming* *9 choosing* *10 promising*

Extension

Students can write more example sentences to illustrate the verbs in Exercise 4 and add them to their vocabulary notebooks, or even use them to create a poster for the classroom wall.

 B1 Preliminary candidates often make errors with the passive. Remind them of the form (*be* + past participle verb). Also remind them that the passive is used when we don't know or are not interested in the person doing the action – we are more interested in the action or instruction itself.

5 Remind students of the structure of active and passive sentences by putting an example of each on the board, e.g. (active) *My friend gave me a present.* (passive) *I was given a present.* Students should work in pairs to decide which sentences are written using passive forms.

2 *Cups* must be returned *to the kitchen.*
4 *Access* is required *at all times.*
5 *You* will be taken *to your seat.*

6 Students work in pairs or small groups to change sentences 1 and 3 using passive forms.

1 *Books must/should be left on the shelf.*
3 *Tickets must be bought from reception.*

7 Students complete the second of each pair of sentences with the correct word from the box. Explain that they should not use all the words in the box. Check answers as a class, discussing the reasons for each choice.

1 *rain*   2 *ice cream*   3 *trainers*   4 *mountains*

Extension

Students could choose the extra words from the box and make similar sentence pairs.

Exam Practice

Elicit the different text types that students might see in this part. Remind them that when they do the task, they should look for facts and details that will answer the question. Ask students to read the texts and choose the correct answer. Monitor how long it takes until everyone has finished – they should be getting a little faster each time they do a practice test.

Students compare answers with a partner before you check answers as a class. They can also work together to discuss why the other two options were incorrect.

1 *B (We've tried booking tickets … the website isn't working)*   2 *B (Use hall lockers provided.)*   3 *C (I'd better collect you after school …)*
4 *A (Volunteers also required to run the event …)*   5 *C (Please come to school in sports kit – no uniforms!)*

Extension

Students can discuss how formal each text is, and how the language reflects this.

Test 2 Reading Part 2

Exam task type:
matching – descriptions of five people and eight texts

Training focus:
predicting what might appear in the eight short texts; understanding requirements; conditional structures

Training

Students read the bullet points about this part of the test and answer the questions. They then check their answers with a partner.

- You have to read five short descriptions of what people need and want, and eight short texts on a particular topic.
- Each person is matched with one short text.

1 Students can complete this exercise individually before checking their ideas in pairs.

Possible answers:
1 level of course (beginners/advanced), qualifications, length of course, equipment hire
2 topics covered, e.g. wildlife, people, landscapes; exhibitions and displays; dates and times of courses
3 details about the course teacher; age of group of students; information about different types of writing
4 where walks take place; length and difficulty of routes; facilities available on the walks

2 Read through the descriptions with students and point out that there is no single right answer – they have to think of things that will match the requirements for the two people. Go through the example in the first gap as a class and discuss other words that could go here (e.g. *machines*). Then ask students to discuss the remaining gaps in pairs. Remind them that they shouldn't use the same words as those which are underlined in Frank and Simone's requirements. Get feedback from the whole class.

Possible answers: 2 open at 8   3 soup / pizza / fish and chips / cakes and toasted sandwiches   4 quiet paths / routes with no cars   5 five people
6 deer / horses

3 Read through the sentence beginnings and elicit a suitable ending for 1. Students can complete 2–4 in pairs and then discuss their suggestions with the group.

Possible answers: 1 If you love watching films, then you'll love Blue Monday.   2 If you're the sort of person who likes exercise, then this holiday on the beach might not be the one for you!   3 This restaurant is perfect if you like spicy food.   4 The campsite is a good choice if you don't want to spend too much money.

Extension

Students can extend their descriptions to form short reviews in a range of scenarios. They could use websites of holiday companies for ideas about different reviews to write. This will also help them increase their vocabulary.

Exam Practice

Ask students to talk about any festivals they know about – music, literature, drama, sport, etc. Highlight any new vocabulary that comes from this discussion and pre-teach any vocabulary that you think will be helpful when students come to do the task. Examples could include *traditional, century, consist of, decade, ancient, aimed at.*

Ask students to look at the people and the descriptions of what they want. Look at the first person together (Eleanor). Students should underline Eleanor's three requirements (*learn about important historical people from the local area, discover how people entertained themselves, buy a history book*).

Ask students to look through the eight texts and find ones that could match Eleanor's first requirement. Text E has *region … also produced people who changed the world*; C mentions *two important 14th-century families* and H says *powerful kings,* so all might be suitable.

Now ask them to do the same for Eleanor's second requirement. This should lead them to E (*games and puzzles they enjoyed*) and D (*imagine them having fun after school or work*).

Do the same for her final requirement. Text E says *to read at home, there's selection from various history experts on sale*; F mentions a *local author*; G has *books and posters*. However, only E matches all three requirements.

Ask students to complete the other questions in the task individually. Remind them to underline the key information for the other four people before they begin.

6 E
7 A
Arjun wants information for a school project on old houses (discover fascinating details about the past, including how the places people called home) and tips on making sure information he uses is accurate (Guides also explain how using the internet helps check facts for your research). He'd like to learn about clothes in the past (Have fun working in groups to design an 18th-century costume).
8 G
Cassie is interested in food people ate hundreds of years ago (preparing centuries-old recipes) and wants to do a history quiz (Pay attention – there will be questions). She'd love information about a local history group for other young people (holds regular meetings for a club aimed at history-loving teens).
9 C
Zander thinks hearing some traditional music would be fun (finish with a concert) and he hopes to learn about jobs people used to have (try some of the things people did for work). He'd also like to attend a history talk on battles (Start with a lecture on a decades-long fight).
10 H
Cindy loves art and hopes to see important old paintings (examining valuable and rare pictures). She'd like to make something to take home (decorate a box to keep) and thinks watching a show about a historical period is a good way to learn (watching a play describing a 50-year-long local 15th-century battle).

Exam task type:

four-option multiple choice – a long test and five questions

Training focus:

phrases that describe opinions and attitudes; expressing comparative and superlative ideas; deciding why an option is wrong

Training

Students read the bullet points about this part of the test and answer the questions. They then check their answers with a partner.

- *One long text, often about or by a young person and their achievements or experiences.*
- *Question 15 focuses on how well you understand the whole text, not just a part of it. The answer can be found anywhere in the text.*

1 Remind students that there will be some questions about opinions or feelings in Reading Part 3, not just details. Read through the instructions together and ask students to underline the opinions in the text.

Opinions (from most positive to most negative): absolutely fantastic – pretty good – wasn't too bad – really disappointed

2 Ask students to give you an example of something they find very difficult to do, and something they find very easy to do. Then ask them to read through the list of expressions and put them in order. Point out that some are very similar in meaning.

very simple / pretty easy   not too difficult   quite hard
extremely challenging   almost impossible   totally impossible

3 Ask students to write some sentences using two of the expressions in each sentence. They can discuss these with a partner before presenting them to the class.

Extension

Students can write expressions using three of the phrases.

4 Explain that the text might use a range of phrases to indicate what someone likes the best/most/least.

1 At the leisure centre open day, I got to try different sports. The badminton courts were <u>pretty good</u> and the gym was <u>fantastic</u>. <u>Above all</u>, it was the fact that the staff <u>were so welcoming</u> that made our visit worth it. (The phrase Above all is used to indicate the superlative idea.)
2 The lecture on how wind power will change the way we heat and light our homes was <u>better than I had expected</u>. I also thought the film we saw on new environmentally friendly methods of growing food was <u>extraordinary</u>. But <u>what has really changed how I think</u> about the planet was watching a documentary about ice levels in the Arctic. (The phrase But what has really changed … is used to indicate the superlative idea.)

5 Ask students to compare their sentences with a partner.

Possible answers: 2 I'm not too bad at remembering what notes to play on the piano, but my biggest problem is finding time to practise.   3 The centre has a great swimming pool, but what I love most of all is the gym.

6 Pre-teach any vocabulary, depending on your group, e.g. *nervous, persuade, worth it.* Students then complete the activity individually.

A (The region she would fly over was known for having wildlife that was almost impossible to get close to on the ground. She therefore realised this flight might give her the only opportunity to see it.)
B is wrong because Gemma's friend was hard to persuade.
C is wrong because the company charged quite a bit.
D is wrong because Gemma had done previous helicopter trips.

7 Explain that students now have to work out the question from the paragraph.

Suggested answer: What did the writer like best about the film?

Exam Practice

Ask students if they have a favourite band – what do they like about them? What do they think it would be like to be in a band?

Ask students to read through the whole text first and then summarise the key points they remember to a partner. If you think students need support, ask them to read question 11, and look for the answer in the first paragraph. Discuss which option is correct (A), and then get students to underline the part of the text that gives the answer (*I messaged the drummer and the keyboard player*).

Ask students to answer the remaining questions individually. Go through the answers as a class.

11 A
(B – His music teacher knew Jacob wanted to be in band but didn't suggest one. C – Jacob's classmates didn't like rock music, so this wasn't how he found band members. D – Jacob and the new band members only became friends later.)
12 C (being in front of an audience improves our performance)
A is wrong because he says he still feels nervous before a concert. B is wrong because he doesn't mind that things go wrong. D is wrong because he says the atmosphere's incredible, with everyone videoing their favourite songs.
13 A (And he's put a link to us on his on his social media. More than anything, that's what's got even more people talking about us.) The others are wrong because of the phrase More than anything … really changes things).
14 B (Giving away tickets to shows is a good way to do this.)
A is wrong because because there is no reference to websites. C is wrong because he says not to rush into getting a manager. D is wrong because he says it's important to develop your own style and be original.
15 D (And we're very happy to be in photos and chat with people)
A is wrong because the band members have different roles. B is wrong because the band play concerts at home when they tour. C is wrong because the lead singer of The 45s didn't sing the song with the band in the recording studio.

Exam task type:
A text from which five sentences have been taken out and jumbled with three other sentences. The five missing sentences must be replaced in the text.

Training focus:
linkers of contrast; identifying topic connections; pronouns and determiners

Training

Students read the bullet points about this part of the test and answer the questions. They then check their answers with a partner.

- One long text, about a particular topic.
- five

1   Explain the idea of contrast, giving examples with linkers of contrast as needed, e.g.
   I thought the film would be terrible. <u>However</u>, I really enjoyed it!
   The queue for the café was very long. <u>Despite this</u>, we decided to wait.
   <u>Although</u> he had never surfed before, he managed to stand up for ages on the board!
   Read through the instructions and ask students to complete the task. Students can then discuss their choices as a group.

1c   2d   3a   4b

2   Students work in pairs to write a second sentence for each of the prompts using the linkers from Exercise 1, or any others that they wish to use. Monitor and support as needed.

Possible answers: 1 The weather forecast was for sun and showers. However, it actually started snowing!   2 The friends thought they would never be able to climb the steep hill, although they managed without any problems.   3 We hardly had any time to work on our presentations. Despite this, the teacher was really pleased with what we did.

3   Explain to students that they might see words of the same topic in both the main text and the missing sentences, and in Part 4, this will help them identify the right option for a gap.

hot and dry – no rain
results – scientists; they – do experiments
make a living – been successful; painting – artist
competition – judges – second prize

4   Ask students to work in teams to brainstorm vocabulary related to each topic area and build up the answers on the board.

Possible answers:
animals: creatures, wildlife, bear, donkey, insects
education: learning, study, students, lessons
fitness: exercise, sport, healthy eating
the environment: climate change, global warming, pollution, rubbish

5   Remind students that in sentence 2 in Exercise 1, *scientists* were referred to using the pronoun *they*.

   They should first read through the text quickly to get an idea of what it's about. They should then read it again and decide which word goes in each gap. Point out to students that they can use words more than once. Check answers as a class, and as you do so, get students to underline the words in the sentences before or after each gap which helped them decide what words to use (see underlined words in the answers below).

*People go to the beach for <u>windsurfing and sailing</u>. **(1) These** sorts of activities have been popular for many years. Particularly in the summer months, there are lots of <u>visitors</u> to the area. Local business owners are always very happy to see **(2) them**. One of the most popular places **(3) they** stay in is the <u>Grand Hotel</u>. **(4) Its** central location is perfect for visiting all the major sites of the city <u>and also</u> the <u>beaches</u>. With **(5) their** beautiful sand and warm water, **(6) they** / **these** are very popular with hotel guests and easy to reach on foot.*

Extension

Give students a selection of short texts – factual ones work well – and ask them to underline any pronouns and determiners (*it, they, this*, etc.) and what they refer to.

Exam Practice

Focus students on the title of the article and the photo. What do they know about oceans? What do they think the article will be about? Pre-teach any vocabulary as needed: *kit, technology, waves, signal*, etc.

Ask students to quickly read through the text (ignoring the gaps for now), to get an idea of what it's about. Get them to summarise the text in pairs.

If you think students would benefit from doing one question together, ask them to read the first paragraph carefully and then read through the options to find the correct gapped sentence (F). Remind them that they need to read both the sentence before and the sentence after the gap to fully understand what's missing. As a class, discuss why F is the correct answer. Students should underline the words that tell them this is the right answer in the gapped sentence and the preceding and subsequent sentences.

16 F (At the same time points to the fact that another point has been made, and the use of their refers back to children's.)
17 C (items is repeated in These included. The following sentence has things like these to refer to the photos and coins.)
18 D (Some believed … links with Others, however …. They also refers to the students and others in the preceding sentences.)
19 H (They refers to the students; these refers to the huge waves; but this wasn't what happened refers to the destruction of the boat.)
20 A (It refers to the boat and Luckily, though, is a contrast linker referring to the badly damaged boat.)

Exam task type:
four-option multiple-choice cloze with six gaps

Training focus:
phrasal verbs; fixed phrases; dependent prepositions

Training

Students read the bullet points about this part of the test and answer the questions.

- One short text, with six words missing.
- Complete the text, choosing from four options for each missing word.

1   Ask students for examples of phrasal verbs. Give them some examples to help if needed, e.g. *set up a business, set off on a journey.*

   Students should work in pairs to make phrasal verbs from the options. Point out that they will be able to make various phrasal verbs using combinations from the lists, but they should form ones that fit the sentences.

   Remind them that the grammar of the sentence needs to be correct (e.g. they might need to change the form of the main verb).

1 *run out*   2 *taken up*   3 *stay behind*   4 *thrown away*
5 *go for*   6 *broke up, based on*   7 *put off*

2   Point out to students that they might have to complete part of a fixed phrase in Reading Part 5. Ask students if they understand what a fixed phrase is. Write some examples on the board to help: *believe it or not, to begin with*, etc. Students should then complete sentences 1–8 using one word in each gap.

1 *got*   2 *have*   3 *doubt*   4 *believe*   5 *miss*   6 *feel*   7 *changed*   8 *do*

Extension

Students can make posters of common phrasal verbs and fixed phrases (with example sentences) to go on the classroom wall.

3   Write this gapped sentence on the board: *I am very similar ___ my sister.* Elicit the missing preposition (*to*).

   Explain that dependent prepositions (prepositions which always go after a particular adjective, noun or verb) are another area of language that they might be required to know to complete a gap in Reading Part 5.

   Students should complete the sentences in pairs. If necessary, do the first sentence together.

1 *of*   2 *about*   3 *between*   4 *about*   5 *of*

Extension

For extra practice, write the following list of words and their dependent preposition on the board. Nominate students to choose a word + preposition and use it in an example sentence.

- adjectives: *available to, brilliant at, famous for, similar to*
- nouns: *collection of, decrease in, information about, interest in, reason for, solution to*
- verbs: *argue with, apologise for, consist of, depend on, inspired by, rely on*

Exam Practice

Ask students to look at the picture and the title. Talk about what they already know about this style of art. Is there anything they'd like to know from the text?

Ask them to quickly read the text and talk to each other about what they can remember about it.

If you think students need support, ask them to look at just the first two sentences, and look carefully at the four options, before choosing the correct word for gap 21 (C – This is the only option that creates the fixed phrase *it is perhaps no surprise that …*). Point out the none of the other options can complete this fixed phrase.

Ask students to complete gaps 22–26 individually. When they have finished, they can check their answers with a partner, checking the options again if they disagree.

21 C
22 B (take *is the only option that goes with* up *to describe starting an activity such as calligraphy*)
23 D (accurate *is the only option that collocates with* completely *to mean that a process is carried out correctly*)
24 C (consisted *is the only option which is found before the dependent preposition* of)
25 A (range *is part of the fixed phrase* a wide range of)
26 C (cover *is the only option that fits the meaning needed here, that the wall is completely painted*)

Extension

Students identify the types of words in each set of options and try to add two or three more to each set. Doing this helps build their knowledge of lexical sets.

Test 2 Reading Part 6

Exam task type:
reading a text with six gaps and filling each gap with one word

Training focus:
auxiliary verbs; using definite and indefinite articles

Training

Students read the bullet points about this part of the test and answer the questions. They then check their answers with a partner.

- One short text, with six words missing.
- Students have to think of the correct word to complete each gap. No options are given.

1 Ask students if they can explain what auxiliary verbs are, and give support as needed. Students can complete the task individually before checking in pairs.

1 Where <u>do</u> you live?   2 I <u>didn't</u> see you at school yesterday.   3 They <u>are</u> taking photos in the park.   4 She <u>wasn't</u> waiting at the bus stop when I got there.   5 She <u>has</u> been my best friend for five years.   6 By the time we arrived, the film <u>had</u> started.

2 Read through the instruction with students and do the first sentence together. Students should then work individually to write sentences, before comparing with a partner and checking as a class activity.

Possible answers: 2 Are you applying for a summer job in the holidays?   3 She has visited many different countries.   4 Did you forget your keys?   5 I wasn't listening to what you said – sorry!   6 I wasn't hungry as I had eaten a big lunch.

3 Ask for examples of definite and indefinite articles, and give a brief explanation if needed (e.g. the indefinite articles *a/an* are used the first time you refer to something; the definite article *the* is used to refer to an item a second time).

Explain that this task focuses on the different uses of the definite article. Ask students to discuss why the definite article is used in each case and get feedback from the class.

1 a noun that is repeated
2 part of the phrase one of the best / most expensive, etc.
3 names of oceans and used with superlatives
4 unique objects – the sky / the moon, etc.
5 used when a word is first mentioned but is immediately defined; used with superlatives
6 nationalities as a group
7 only one of something in a particular context
8 talking about something as a general fact
9 used with services and systems like transport

4 Students can do this activity individually or in small groups before feeding back to the class. Remind them that they also need to use indefinite articles in this activity.

1 a   2 the   3 the   4 the   5 a   6 the   7 the   8 the   9 The

Exam Practice

Talk to students about how they contact their friends. Do they use emails or texts? If they want to make an arrangement with a friend, how would they do it?

Now ask students to look at the text, and establish that it's an email. Ask them to guess the relationship between the two people (e.g. they're friends or classmates). Ask them to read the whole text first without filling in any gaps, to get a sense of what it's about. Then, they should work individually to complete the gaps.

Monitor how long it takes until everyone has finished – they should be getting a little faster by now. Students check their answers in pairs. Do they agree? If not, they should check again and try to reach a decision before you conduct a class feedback session.

27 a (part of the phrase a few days ago)
28 have / 've (auxiliary verb forming the present perfect)
29 do (question word followed by the auxiliary do)
30 if (part of a conditional sentence)
31 As (part of the fixed phrase As you know)
32 the (referring to one specific thing)

Extension

Give students further exam practice by giving them sentences of your own, or sentences from a short text, and asking them to remove a grammar word from each one (e.g. an auxiliary verb or an article) or to remove one word from a fixed phrase. Then ask them to exchange their sentences, in pairs, for their partners to guess what the missing words are.

Exam task type:
writing an email with notes

Training focus:
understanding the task; understanding the notes; studying a sample answer; informal and formal style; gradable modifiers

Training

Students read the bullet points about this part of the test and answer the questions. They then check their answers with a partner.

- *an email*
- *You are given four notes, or instructions.*

1   Tell students to study the email carefully. Encourage them to always read the instructions, email and the four notes very carefully so they know who they need to write to and what register (formal or informal) their email should use.

1 your English teacher Ms Shipton   2 helping a charity   3 four
4 around 100 words

2   Use this exercise to help students identify what the notes are asking them to do. Encourage students to think of ways to complete each sentence. Get feedback from the whole class.

Suggested answers: 1 d – I think this idea is wonderful.   2 c – Perhaps we should support one that helps young children who have health problems.   3 a – Some kind of contest would be a good idea because that would give people a reason to take part.   4 b – I'd be very happy to help design posters and put them around the school.

3   Studying this sample answer could be done in pairs or small groups. Ask students to underline the information in Kerry's email that answers the questions. Ask students to pay particular attention to question 3. Explain that Kerry is responding incorrectly to one of the content points. Instead of offering to do something, Kerry suggests that Ms Shipton do something.

1 Only the first three points are covered: (Great!) a charity this term is a very good idea; (Tell Ms Shipton) we should support one that is extremely good at helping animals; (Explain) having a disco is the best idea …
2 yes, 102 words
3 Kerry suggests Ms Shipton could design some cool really posters to put around town. Instead, Kerry should offer to do this.
4 formal – Dear, Best wishes, no contracted forms are used

Extension

As a class, brainstorm different ideas to improve Kerry's response to the fourth content point (*Offer to …*), e.g. *I could text everyone I know. / How about if I design some adverts to put around town?*

4   It is important that students identify the register in this part of the exam, as their reply should be in the same style. In pairs, ask students to decide whether Ms Shipton uses formal or informal language in her email.

It's more formal than informal: Dear Students, Kind regards, no contracted forms are used.

5   You could point out to students that Ms Shipton is a person that the writer is supposed to already know quite well. For that reason, we wouldn't expect to see *Yours sincerely* or *Yours faithfully* in an email to her.

2, 5

6   In pairs, ask students to identify which sentences would be appropriate for a formal email. If they need additional support, ask them to underline any informal language in the options (*1 cool, 4 it'd be awesome, 5 amazing, don't you think?*).

2, 3, 6, 7, 8

7   Tell students that most adjectives are gradable, and we can make them weaker and stronger with modifiers. They can also add more variety to students' writing. Ask students to order the words in the list (1–4).

1 a bit   2 fairly / pretty   3 really / very   4 extremely

Exam Practice

This email task helps students to identify when it is appropriate to write a formal email rather than an informal one. Give time for students to read the email and the notes, and then encourage them to discuss what they should and should not include when replying to Mr Anderson's email.

Sample answer
Dear Mr Anderson,
I would really love to study abroad for six months as this would be an incredible opportunity. I have always wanted to visit Japan because I am a huge fan of Japanese films such as Princess Mononoke *or* My Neighbour Totoro.
I think it would be an amazing experience to learn about another culture by living and studying there. As well, I am pretty good at learning new languages. Could you please let me know how much it will cost to study abroad? I would also like to know when you will announce who is taking part in the programme.
All the best
Sam

Comments
This task contains appropriate functional language in reply to Mr Anderson's email. It is a correct length (106 words). Sam has included all four content points in the reply email. The email has an appropriate beginning and ending in the correct formal register. This is a clear, well-written answer that uses various structures and a range of vocabulary.

Exam task type:
writing an article or a story in about 100 words

Training focus:
linking expressions; past tenses, contrasting ideas; understanding the task; studying a sample answer

Training

Students read the bullet points about this part of the test and answer the questions. They then check their answers with a partner.

- one
- *Students will have the choice of writing an article or a story.*

1 Ask students to complete the sentences. In some instances, there is more than one answer is possible.

1 as / because   2 so   3 As / Because   4 and / so   5 When

2 Point out that two of the expressions have the same function.

1 when   2 and   3 as / because   4 so

⊙ *B1 Preliminary* candidates often make mistakes with past forms, using present forms instead. Encourage students to check their work to make sure they haven't used the present simple or present perfect when they should be using the past simple.

3 Go through the sentences in Exercise 1 as a class. Point out that some sentences use more than one tense.

1 was – past simple; hadn't remembered – past perfect   2 didn't have, didn't go – past simple   3 wanted, went – past simple   4 was starting – past continuous; tried, didn't work – past simple   5 got, realised – past simple; had left – past perfect

4 Ask students to match the tenses with the correct functions.

1c   2a   3b

5 This exercise could be done in pairs or small groups. Ask students to refer to Exercise 2 if they have problems.

1 suggested   2 was [still] working   3 finished   4 managed   5 had [never] made   6 took

6 Explain to students that these words and phrases can appear at the beginning or middle of a sentence.

1 b   2 a   3 a   4 b

7 Ask students to refer to Exercise 6 to help them complete the task. Go over the answers as a class.

1 Despite   2 even though   3 in spite of   4 although

8 Ask students to underline the words or phrases in the exam task to help them answer the questions.

1F   2T   3F

9 Tell students that there is more than one answer for each gap.

1 even though / although   2 despite / in spite of   3 although / even though

10 Tell students to underline any time linkers and examples of the past simple, past continuous and past perfect in Exercise 9.

1 First, the night before, By the next morning, When   2 past simple: decided, began, enjoyed, was, danced, played, saw, smiled, asked   past continuous: wasn't working   past perfect: had (never) invented, had fixed, had achieved

Exam Practice

Remind students that they must decide which question to write about in Writing Part 2. Encourage them to choose the question that will best show their English writing ability.

Question 2
Sample answer
I prefer learning about what is going on in the world on TV, but only on news channels that I really trust. I don't like getting the news from social media, even though that is what most people seem to do these days.

I believe it is extremely important to keep myself up-to-date with world events. I want to understand what is going on and watching or reading the news has often made me change my own actions. For instance, I saw on the news that Greta Thunberg has inspired millions of children to protect the environment and now I try to do the same too.

Comment
This article is an acceptable length (106 words). The article is well-organised as it focuses on a different content point for each paragraph. It has no spelling or grammar errors and includes a range of tenses and vocabulary.

Question 3
Sample answer
I was so excited when I arrived at the music festival. I had never been to one before and was really happy when my parents bought me tickets! I arrived early because I wanted to stand near the stage. I'm glad I did because I had an incredible view.

When my favourite band was performing, they saw me singing along with their songs and invited me on stage. I couldn't believe it! Although I was really excited, I was nervous too. I'd never stood in front of a huge audience before. Despite being with my favourite band, I didn't know what to say!

Comment
The story has a clear link to the opening sentence and is an appropriate length (103 words). It is consistently written in the first person and shows a range of tenses and vocabulary without any spelling or grammar mistakes.

Test 2 Listening Part 1

Exam task type:
three-option multiple choice with seven picture-based questions

Training focus:
vocabulary related to holidays and entertainment; expressing positive and negative ideas

Training

Students read the bullet points about this part of the test and answer the questions. They then check their answers with a partner. Point out that each dialogue is on a different topic, so if students don't know the answer to one, they should move on to the next when they hear the number. Remind them that they will have time to look at all the pictures before they listen and that they should think about vocabulary they might hear related to the pictures.

- seven short monologues
- You have to choose the best matching picture, according to the question you are being asked.

1 Write *eating in a restaurant* on the board. Ask students to give you examples of what people might talk about when eating in a restaurant (e.g the type of food, the quality of the food, the service, the atmosphere, the price of the meal). Then ask them to look at Exercise 1 and tell you which sentence matches question 1 (g). Students complete the exercise in pairs.

1 g   2 e   3 b   4 c   5 d   6 h   7 f   8 a

Extension

In groups, students could write their own sentences about the different activities and then 'test' another group. They read out their sentences and the other group has to guess which activity they're talking about.

2 Focus students on question 1. Ask students which words in the sentence help them to choose the correct answer: *score* (*final minute, team, won*). Students do the rest of the exercise individually before checking answers with a partner.

1 score   2 cap   3 flight   4 shop   5 meal   6 keyboard   7 voice   8 soundtrack

Extension

Encourage students to record vocabulary in topic areas with possible collocations, e.g.

Sports:
score (verb) – score a goal / a point
score (noun) – The score was two–nil.
Cinema:
soundtrack (noun) – My favourite song was part of the soundtrack for the movie.

3 Ask students to describe what is happening in each of the pictures. Ask questions to elicit some of the vocabulary associated with each activity. *What is necessary for a sailing boat to move? What kind of sport is hockey? Do you play it alone? What do you use to play table tennis? Do you play it alone?* Point out that in this part of the test, students will hear information related to all three pictures. After playing the recording, ask students what they heard that gave them the correct answer (*What I really loved was …*).

A

4 The aim of Exercise 4 is to encourage students to think about how speakers can express negative ideas using negative verb forms, *too / not enough*, negative adjectives, etc. Look at question 1 with the whole class and ask for suggestions for the answers. Students then complete the exercise in pairs. Check answers with the class and explain any words the students are not sure about.

1 b,f   2 c,h   3 a,e   4 d,g

5 Remind students of the pronouns *anyone, anybody, anything, anywhere* (*anywhere* can also be an adverb) and explain that they refer to people, things or places. Students then complete the exercise in pairs. Check answers with the class and explain any words the students are not sure about.

1 none   2 don't   3 anywhere   4 too   5 not   6 nobody
7 enough   8 didn't

6 Ask students to tell you where the phone is in each picture and elicit the vocabulary they might hear. Play the recording, stopping it for students to identify the reasons for selecting or rejecting answers.

B (It's here under your pillow.!)

Exam Practice

Students read the questions carefully, then listen and choose the correct pictures. Play the recording twice. Remind students to check their answers during the second listening, even if they are sure they have the right answer. Discuss the possible responses to the questions.

1 C   2 C   3 A   4 A   5 B   6 A   7 B

Exam task type:
three-option multiple-choice with six questions

Training focus:
identifying how people feel; understanding the speaker's intention

Training

Students read the bullet points about this part of the test and answer the questions. They then check their answers with a partner. Remind them that, as in Part 1, each question is a conversation on a different topic. Tell them that they will hear references to all three options in the questions so they should read the question carefully to decide what information they are listening for.

- *six short dialogues*
- *You have to choose the best option, according to the question you are being asked.*

1 Write the adjectives *excited, exciting, shocked, shocking, confused, confusing, disappointed, disappointing* on the board and ask students to give you examples of when they might use these words.

Students complete Exercise 1 in pairs. Check answers with the class and explain any words that students are not sure about.

1 *sad, shocking* 2 *unreliable* 3 *exciting, fun* 4 *cross*
5 *ashamed, worried*

2 Before listening, check students know the meanings of the adjectives. Play the recording twice. The second time, pause after each question for students to explain their answers.

1 *relieved* 2 *jealous* 3 *disappointed* 4 *exhausted* 5 *annoyed*
6 *nervous* 7 *confused* 8 *proud*

Extension

Students can create their own dialogue in pairs to illustrate one of these feelings. They can perform their dialogue in front of the class who should guess which feeling it might be.

3 Tell students that in Listening Part 2, they are not simply listening for information. They need to interpret the reason why the speakers are giving the information. So they need to understand the intention of the speaker, such as giving advice or apologising. Read out sentence 1 and ask students to identify what the intention is (d – giving advice). Ask students to complete the exercise individually and compare keys with a partner.

1 *d* 2 *g* 3 *b* 4 *a* 5 *e* 6 *f* 7 *c*

Extension

Focus students on the Tip box. Write these sentences on the board: *1 I am ashamed I did it. 2 I don't understand.* Say the word *Sorry?* with rising intonation and ask students to match this with sentence 1 or 2 (2). Then say *Sorry* with falling intonation and ask them to do the same (this matches sentence 1).

In class, make posters with lists of functional expressions that can be used to invite, offer, suggest, etc. As more expressions come up in class, students can add them to the lists.

4 Stop the recording after each question and ask students to decide the answer with a partner. Play the recording again and ask students how they think the speaker feels in each case. You can also discuss the intonation used by the speakers.

1 *a* 2 *d* 3 *b* 4 *g*

5 The aim here is to help students understand that it is not only the words they hear but the way a speaker says them that may help them to get the right answer. Play the recording twice and ask students to explain why they chose the answer they did. Ask students why the boy said *I'm sorry* (he felt sorry for the girl because of her situation, but he wasn't apologising) and what expression he used to give advice (*You should try …*).

A (You should try to make more effort.)

Exam Practice

Ask students to discuss when they usually decide which the correct option is. Tell them they can write on the question paper in the exam, for example using crosses for options that they're fairly sure are wrong to then check in the second listening.

Play the recording twice. Students complete the task. Discuss the possible responses to the questions in the Advice boxes:

9 *What was interesting about the experience for the boy?* (making new friends) *Do they say it was unusual for the train to be delayed?* (No, the trains are often late.) *Who thought the delay was dull?* (the girl)

12 *What stage of the competition did the girl get to?* (the semi-finals) *What did her trainer say?* (She had definitely improved.) *Did she always play perfectly?* (No, she made some silly mistakes.)

Go through the answers and ask students to read the audioscript for each item that they answered incorrectly and work out why they got the question wrong.

8 *B* 9 *A* 10 *C* 11 *A* 12 *B* 13 *A*

Exam task type:
monologue with notes to complete

Training focus:
topic vocabulary; identifying distractors

Training

Students read the bullet points about this part of the test and answer the questions. They then check their answers with a partner. Remind students that this monologue may be information about a person's life and experiences, or it may be information about a specific trip or event, e.g. a course, trip or holiday activity.

● *one long monologue*
● *You have to complete sentences or notes with words or numbers you hear.*

1   This activity focuses on vocabulary for topics that may come in Listening Part 3. Pause the recording after Speaker 1 and ask students for suggestions for the answer and to tell you what words they heard that helped them identify the topic. Repeat for each speaker.

Speaker 1 – a club (members, teams)
Speaker 2 – a trip (bus, set off from school, arrived)
Speaker 3 – a website (upload, posting, social media)
Speaker 4 – a hobby (make models)
Speaker 5 – a competition (prize, winners)

2   This exercise gives students further practice in choosing the correct option from two possibilities. Students complete the exercise individually and then check answers in pairs.

1 80
2 8.00
3 photography
4 6
5 sweatshirt

3   Remind students that they can often predict the kind of answer they might hear if they pay attention to the context and read the question carefully. Look at the first question with the whole class and ask: *What kind of word will you hear? Is it a name, a number, an object, a date?* Elicit suggestions. In pairs, students complete the exercise.

1 c   2 b   3 d   4 a

4   Play the recording and pause after question 1. Ask students which of the three options from Exercise 3 they heard (all of them). Ask questions to check what the correct answer is, e.g. *What do the students do on Friday evening?* (other activities) *What's happening at the pool on Saturday afternoon?* (It's closed). Repeat with the other questions.

1 Sunday morning
2 in the countryside
3 in a car park
4 Tall Trees

Exam Practice

Remind students that they should read the title and the gapped sentences before listening and try to think of possible words that could go in the gaps. Point out the rubric that says *one or two words or a number or a date or a time* and tell students that if they write more than two words, they may be penalised in the test. They should also be aware that although they may not hear the words written in the question, they will hear the exact words to complete a gap.

Students then listen and complete the task. Discuss the possible responses to the Advice box questions:

Gap 14: *How many different ways can you say a date in English, such as 22/6?* Check that students know the different ways of saying dates and also remind them that they can write numbers in figures instead of words.

Gap 17: *What did the students make last year?* (T-shirts) *What will the organisers give everyone this year?* (a backpack)

14 April 21st
15 recycling
16 Improve Earth
17 backpack
18 secretary
19 scarborough

Exam task type:
an interview, with six multiple-choice questions

Training focus:
vocabulary related to technology; ways of talking about future plans

Training

Students read the bullet points about this part of the test and answer the questions. They then check their answers with a partner. Remind them that in this task they will have to listen for different kinds of information for each question, not only details but also the speaker's attitude, feeling, opinion or recommendation.

- an interview
- *Choose the correct option to answer six questions.*

1   The aim of this activity is to review vocabulary related to technology. If there are technological devices in the classroom, ask students to name them and their different components. Students complete the task and compare their answers.

> *1 printer   2 screen   3 keyboard   4 mouse   5 mouse mat*
> *6 microphone   7 headphones*

2   Before playing the recording, ask students to think of possible problems we can have with the devices from Exercise 1. Write useful vocabulary that comes up on the board. Play the recording. When checking the answers, ask students to explain what the problem was in each case.

> *1 mouse   2 microphone   3 keyboard   4 screen*

Extension

Encourage students to create mind maps with useful vocabulary and expressions. Demonstrate this with the topic of technology, grouping words into categories such as *Equipment: laptop, printer* etc.; *People: blogger, programmer* etc.; *Verbs: click, drag, record*, etc.; *Activities: games, social media* etc.

⊙   *B1 Preliminary* often use the present simple instead of the present continuous to refer to the future. Point out that we use the present continuous, often with a future time reference, to refer to future arrangements (*I'm meeting my friend tomorrow*). We can use the present simple for the future if we are talking about timetabled actions (*The train leaves at 4.30*).

3   Explain that in English, different verb forms are used to talk about the future, such as the present continuous and *be going to*, as well as *will* + infinitive. Students need to listen carefully to the context to understand the time the speaker is referring to. Look at question 1 with the whole class and ask students to tell you how they know that it is about the present (it uses the present continuous and doesn't refer to a future time). Students continue in pairs, then check answers as a class.

> *1 present   2 future (next time)   3 future (at 6 o'clock)   4 future (I'm going to)   5 present*

4   Students listen to the recording and answer the question. Ask students to listen again for words or phrases that show when Sam did / does / will do each of the activities in the options.

> *C (would be interesting to do something online, maybe write about my travel experiences and tell people about all the cities I've been to)*

Exam Practice

Ask students to work in pairs and underline the important words in question 20. Compare their ideas as a class. Then ask them to continue with the other questions before they listen.

Remind students that the answers come in the same order as the questions and that the interviewer will introduce each one with a similar question. Students should listen for the information on the first listening and use the second listening to check their answers, focusing on details, attitudes or opinions.

Discuss the possible responses to the Advice box questions:

21   *What did he do when he first started working in the studio?* (He moved stuff around and got things people needed.) *And now?* (He's in charge of recording.) *What word does he use to say something is really interesting?* (amazing) *Does he often meet famous people? (*No, they mostly work with unknown bands.)

24   *What does he say he'd like to try?* (organising concerts) *Does he want to play the drums as a job?* (No, as a hobby.)

> *20 A   21 B   22 C   23 B   24 A   25 C*

Exam task type:
conversation with interlocutor

Training focus:
common questions

Training

Students read the bullet points about this part of the test and answer the questions. They then check their answers with a partner.

- *the interlocutor*
- *questions about yourself, including likes and dislikes, present circumstances, past experiences and plans for the future*

1 Ask students who will be in the room while they are taking the Speaking test (themselves, another candidate (or two), the interlocutor and the assessor). Then ask them to look at the three kinds of people in the test and match the person with their roles.

| 1 b   2 c   3 a |

2 Ask students what topics they will be asked about in Part 1 Phase 2, e.g. their free time, their home, people they know. Write these topics on the board and elicit possible questions for each one. Keep the topic prompts on the board for the extension activity later.

Explain that they are going to hear a student answering some questions and that they should listen and complete the answers. Play the recording. Students then check their answers with a partner. Play the recording again for them to check if necessary.

| 1 *large, gym, library*   2 *best, house, running*   3 *few, well, climbing*
| 4 *hockey, drawing*   5 *studied, pronunciation*   6 *cooking, kitchen, food*
| 7 *remember, party, special* |

3 Ask students to read the answers in Exercise 2 again. They should discuss what questions they think the student was asked and write them down. Compare ideas across the class.

4 Students listen and write the questions. Play the recording, pausing after each question to allow time for students to write it down. Check the answers and play the recording again if necessary.

| 1 *Tell us about your school.*
| 2 *Where do you like to spend time with friends?*
| 3 *Tell us about a member of your family.*
| 4 *What do you do in your free time?*
| 5 *How long have you studied English for?*
| 6 *Which do you prefer, eating at home or eating at a café?*
| 7 *What did you do yesterday after school?* |

 B1 Preliminary candidates often make mistakes with the present perfect. Remind students that we use the past simple for completed past actions (*I studied French for two years* = I don't study French now). We use the present perfect for actions that started in the past and are still continuing (*I've studied French for two years* = I started two years ago and I'm still studying it).

5 Students ask and answer the questions in turn with a partner. Monitor as they are working and encourage them to say as much as possible in answer to each question.

Extension

Ask students to choose one of the topics from the board. They should write three more questions that have not already been mentioned in the exercises so far.

Put the students into groups of three or four. They take turns to ask each other questions. Ask them to listen carefully to each other's replies and then assess who gave the best answers and why. Remind them that it doesn't matter what information they give, but they should try to offer as much detail as they can.

Exam Practice

Students read through the questions in Part 1. Remind them that the questions are always the same, so they can prepare their answers to them and should practise them regularly. Encourage them to use full sentences rather than one-word answers.

Students work in groups of three or four to role-play the Speaking test. One of the students is the interlocutor, one is the assessor, and one (or two) is the candidate. The interlocutor uses the script and the candidate answers the questions. The assessor should listen carefully and make notes about what is good and what could be improved in the candidate's answers. Monitor as they are working and encourage the students to give as much information as they can.

Students then swap roles and repeat the activity until all students have had a turn as the candidate answering the questions.

Now tell students that they are going to listen to other students answering some of Part 1 Phase 2 questions. They should listen and compare their own answers with the responses they hear.

Exam task type:
extended turn: asking about a photograph

Training focus:
describing photographs; saying where things are

Training

Students read the bullet points about this part of the test and answer the questions. They then check their answers with a partner. Elicit the things they should talk about and any phrases they might use to do so. Write their ideas on the board.

- *a photo*
- *one minute*

1   Ask students to look at photograph A (also on page C10 in colour) and the prompts. Elicit two or three example sentences about the photograph, using the prompts. For example, *There are three children in the photograph. They're riding their bikes. There are some big trees.* Students then continue the exercise in pairs, taking turns to say something about the photograph using the prompts.

Monitor and encourage them to use a range of prompts and avoid using the same ones all the time.

Suggested answer:
There are three children in the photograph. They're riding their bikes. They're in the countryside and it looks like they're riding through a field. They're wearing T-shirts, so I think it's quite warm. It might be the evening, because it looks like the sun is quite low, or it's nearly sunset. They look like they're having fun because they're smiling. I can see some big trees in the background, and the children are riding on the grass. There are flowers or something like that in the grass – I'm not sure what they are but they're white and there are lots of them.

2   Ask questions about photograph A to elicit the position of things in it. For example, *Where are the children? Where are the trees? Who is on the right of the photograph? Who is on the left? What is in the background?*

Students look at the position prompts. Read out each one in turn and ask the students to point in the right direction.

Focus students on photograph B (also on page C10 in colour) and the sentences. Ask them to complete the sentences with some of the phrases. They should then check their answers with a partner.

1 In the foreground / At the front, there is a girl who is standing on her hand.
2 There is a school building in the background. There is a school building behind/beyond the dancers.
3 The girls on the left / to the left of the photo are watching the girl at the front.

3   Ask students to look at the details in photograph B. Ask them to work with a partner and take turns to describe other things in the photograph, using the prompts. Monitor as they are working and encourage them to say as much as possible about each of the details in the photograph.

4   Explain to the students that they are going to hear a student describing photograph B. They should listen and decide whether the student says the same things about the photograph that they said, or whether there was any new or different information. Play the recording. Students then compare their ideas.

Hold a class discussion about how well the student performed the task. What was good about it? Was there anything that could be improved?

5   Ask students how they can fill in time if they don't know what to say next. Explain that it's important not to leave long silences if possible. Ask them to listen to the recording again and write down anything that the speaker says or does to fill in the time.

Why is it on the ground?
Well …
What else can I say …?

Extension

Ask students to find a photograph in a magazine or book (or online if resources are available). They should look up any useful words that are needed to describe the photograph and write them down.

They then show their photograph to a partner and ask them to describe it, using any new words if necessary. They should listen carefully to their partner and then provide constructive feedback to each other.

Exam Practice

First, students listen to the recordings of students talking about Photographs A, B and C.

Put students into pairs (or groups of three if necessary) and give each of them one of the photograph A or B (and C if in a group or three).

Photograph A is from page C1, photograph B is from page C2 and photograph C is from page C7.

Allow students about 30 seconds to look at their photograph and then give Student A one minute to talk about their photograph. Stop them at the end of the time limit and repeat for Student B (and again for Student C if necessary). Remind them to give positive feedback and advice for improvement.

Exam task type:
discussion between candidates

Training focus:
giving and asking for opinions

Training

Students read the bullet points about this part of the test and answer the questions. They then check their answers with a partner. Remind students that they need to respond to what their partner says and keep the conversation going. If their partner is quiet, they should encourage them to offer their opinions by asking questions such as *What do you think? Do you agree?*

- *with your partner*
- *give your opinions, agree or disagree with your partner, ask your partner for their opinions*

1   Ask students to look at the words in the box and think about how they can be used to create phrases and questions for giving and asking for opinions. Elicit one or two examples, such as *I don't agree, I'm not sure about that.*

Students work in pairs to write down phrases and questions for giving opinions, asking for opinions, agreeing and disagreeing. Monitor as they are working and check grammar where necessary.

Possible answers:
Do you agree? I agree. I don't agree. Do you agree?
Is … a good idea?
In my opinion … What's your opinion?
I'd prefer (to) …
I'm not sure that …
I think (that) … What do you think?
What about you?
… would be good.

2   Ask students to close their books. Explain that the students will listen to Anh and Mathilde doing Part 3 of the Speaking test. Play the first line of the recording and elicit the scenario (they must decide which thing would be most useful for a walking trip in the mountains).

Play the rest of the recording for the students to listen and write down the things that the students are discussing (a map, a phone, a raincoat, walking boots, a torch).

Students open their books and read through the conversation, predicting the answers. Play the recording again for them to complete the conversation. Ask them to compare the phrases and questions with their ideas in Exercise 1.

1 a great idea   2 Do you agree?   3 In my opinion   4 I'm not so sure
5 a good idea   6 I don't think   7 What about   8 would be
9 I'd prefer to   10 What's your opinion   11 I think so, too   12 I agree

3   Ask students to work with a partner to discuss which four options would be the most useful to take on a long car journey. Remind them that they should encourage each other to speak and respond to what their partner says. They should say what they can, but not speak so much that their partner doesn't get a chance to say anything.

Explain that they should keep the conversation going and try to reach an agreement. They should look at each other during the task, and not the interlocutor. Remind them that it doesn't matter if they don't finish the task in the time given.

Exam Practice

The students read the situation and look at the pictures for Exam Practice Test 2, Speaking Part 3 (see page C12). Students then complete the task. Tell them that they have up to three minutes to complete the task and stop them when time is up. This will give them an idea of how long this part of the test lasts.

Ask them whether they found the task hard and why. What problems did they have? Do they have any feedback for their partner? Discuss as a class how this part of the task could be made easier. For example, they could ask each other questions, they could fill in the time, they could provide plenty of detail about their ideas.

When they have finished discussing the scenario, students listen to the sample conversation and compare it with their own. Ask them whether the candidates they listened to did anything better and why.

Exam task type:
discussion related to Part 3

Training focus:
question forms

Training

Students read the bullet points about this part of the test and answer the questions. They then check their answers with a partner.

- with the interlocutor and your partner
- The interlocutor will ask you questions on a topic related to the pictures in Speaking Part 3.

1   Ask students to close their books. Elicit words that can begin questions (*Who, What, Where, When, Why, Which, How, How long, How often*). Then elicit words connected to health, e.g. *diet, exercise, sleep, keep fit, disease, fresh food*.

Students open their books and write three questions of their own for each topic, using the words on the board. Monitor as they are working and help where necessary.

Possible answers:
Do you have a healthy diet?
Where do you go to eat healthy food?
What food do you think is good for you?
How often do you do exercise?
What kind of exercise do you like doing?
When do you exercise?
Which form of exercise do you enjoy most?
How long do you sleep each night?
How important do you think sleep is?

2   Students work with a partner to ask and answer the questions.

3   Ask *How much should you say when you are answering a question?* (as much as you can, giving reasons for your answers).

Students look at the phrases in the box. Explain that they should ask and answer questions 1–5 with a partner, using some of the phrases to give reasons for their answers. Encourage them to give their partner constructive feedback about how well they answered the questions.

4   Tell students that are going to listen to two students answering some of the questions in Exercise 3. Ask them to read through the dialogue first and predict the missing words. Then play the recording for them to listen and complete the conversation. Ask them to compare their answers with a partner and play the recording again if necessary.

1 because   2 It's a good idea   3 So, personally
4 In my opinion   5 Well   6 I doubt

5   Ask the class whether they thought the girl and boy answered the questions well and to give reasons for their opinions.

Suggested answers:
Yes, they did. They gave detailed answers and offered reasons for their opinions.

Extension

Write some topics on the board, e.g. *the weather*, *food and drink*, *travel*, *study*, *hobbies*. Students each choose one of the topics and write three questions about it. Students then move around the class asking and answering questions, and giving reasons for their answers.

Exam Practice

Remind students that the questions they are asked in Part 4 of the Speaking test are linked to the topic in Part 3 (in this case, learning languages). Elicit the task from Part 3 (choosing the best ways to practise a language). Then ask students to read the questions in Part 4.

Students work in groups of three or four, taking turns to be the interlocutor, assessor and candidates. The interlocutor should ask each student individual questions and also ask them to discuss some of the questions together.

Set a time limit of three minutes. This will help prepare students for the real test. Encourage students to keep talking and use some of the phrases they have learned.

When they have finished, play the recording and ask students to assess the candidates' performance and compare it to their own.

Practice Test Key

Test 3

Reading

Part 1

1 B **2** C **3** A **4** B **5** C

Part 2

6 H **7** C **8** E **9** A **10** D

Part 3

11 C **12** B **13** A **14** D **15** C

Part 4

16 G **17** C **18** E **19** A **20** F

Part 5

21 B **22** D **23** B **24** D **25** A **26** C

Part 6

27 To **28** us **29** a **30** than

31 had **32** which

Writing

Part 1

Question 1
Sample answer

Hi René
That's wonderful news that you're going to the wildlife park! I would love to go with you. I've always wanted to visit the park to see all the rare animals they are helping to protect.

You know how much I love animals so I can't wait to see all of them, but I'm especially interested in tigers. I think they're such beautiful animals!

I think we should ride our bicycles there since it's only 5 km away. The weather's supposed to be really nice on Saturday, so I don't want to go on a hot bus!

See you soon!
Levko

Comment
Levko deals with each of the content points clearly. He uses informal language to reply to René, which is an appropriate tone for an email to a friend. He shows a good control of functional language, verb tenses, and his answer is the correct length (102 words).

Part 2

Question 2
Sample answer
I'm from Malaysia and the Lunar New Year is the biggest celebration of the year! We prepare for this important celebration by cleaning every room in our home really well before the first day of the new lunar year. One tradition I love is receiving red envelopes with money inside them. I get them from my aunties, uncles and grandparents.

I can't imagine not celebrating this important time of year with my family and relatives. Everyone looks forward to having a huge dinner together on New Year's Eve. And we always eat certain dishes so that we have lots of good luck in the new year.

Comment
The writer has written about the two questions and provides reasons for their answers, which is good. They have written an appropriate length (106 words) and have organised their article into two paragraphs. The writer also includes personal examples, which makes their article interesting for the reader.

Question 3
Sample answer
The two friends couldn't believe their luck! They were about to meet their favourite science-fiction author Temi Bell! They had been in a long queue with all her other fans for hours. The friends didn't mind because they could both hand Temi copies of her novel to sign.

Temi smiled at the two young girls and asked them if they liked writing stories too. They couldn't believe Temi was actually speaking to them! They had never thought about writing their own stories before, so the author wrote in each of their books, 'I can't wait to read your sci-fi novels one day!'

Comment
The story is a very good attempt at the required word length (102 words). The story is well-organised in two paragraphs with a clear beginning, middle and end. The writer uses a good range of tenses and adjectives, which helps to make the story interesting.

Listening

Part 1

1 A **2** C **3** C **4** B **5** A **6** C **7** B

Part 2

8 C **9** B **10** B **11** A **12** C **13** A

Part 3

14 park

15 13,765

16 cool

17 fountain

18 tissues

19 biscuits

Part 4

20 A **21** B **22** C **23** C **24** B **25** A

Practice Test Key

Test 4

Reading

Part 1

1 C   **2** B   **3** C   **4** A   **5** C

Part 2

6 E   **7** C   **8** A   **9** F   **10** H

Part 3

11 D   **12** A   **13** B   **14** C   **15** D

Part 4

16 D   **17** C   **18** A   **19** H   **20** F

Part 5

21 A   **22** B   **23** D   **24** A   **25** C   **26** B

Part 6

27 why   **28** used   **29** if   **30** were

31 had / 'd   **32** the / their

Writing

Part 1

Question 1
Sample answer

Dear Mrs Rashid
Thanks for sharing the great news about having a school play this year.
I am sure it will be fantastic! In my opinion, I think the play should
be a musical because there are lots of talented singers and dancers at
our school.

I would love to help to make some of the costumes because I am really
good at sewing things. I even have my own sewing machine that I can use.

I would suggest creating some interesting posts on social media. That
way, lots of people will share them and find out about our play.

Yours sincerely
Daisuke

Comment
Daisuke's reply email is well organised in three main paragraphs
to discuss the four content points. He sounds polite by using
an appropriate tone for the email to his teacher. The message is
semi-formal – Daisuke doesn't use contracted forms – and it is an
appropriate length (103 words).

Part 2

Question 2
Sample answer
I don't mind watching reality shows, but only if they're interesting.
I only enjoy watching ones that are a competition like *The Amazing
Race*. I particularly love this reality show because watching people
racing across different countries without using technology or having

much money is exciting. My dream is to go on this show one day!
I'm only 12, and I've found out loads of helpful things from watching
reality TV. For example, one day, I want to travel around the world.
The Amazing Race is a great way to see how people follow maps and
find places they've never been to before.

Comment
The article is a good example as it answers both questions and
provides reasons for the writer's views. The length is appropriate
(104 words) and is organised in two paragraphs. The writer uses
different phrases to answer the questions, which is good (*helpful* for
useful, *found out* for *learn*).

Question 3
Sample answer
The twins discovered a box of old letters in their grandad's garage. They
opened the lid and looked at the letters to their grandad's mum. They
soon realised these letters were written by their grandad to their great-
grandma! They carefully opened one and read it in silence. Moments
later, they both looked at each other. They had no idea their grandad
had gone away from home to study ballet when he was young! In the
letter was an old black-and-white picture of him jumping through the
air. The twins had so many questions to ask their grandpa, so they ran
to find him.

Comment
This is a good example of a story where the writer has paid close
attention to the use of pronouns needed for some of the key words
in the opening line (*twins/they, grandpa/he/him*). The writer uses a
good range of tenses, and some adjectives and adverbs. The story is
an appropriate length (103 words) and has a clear progression in the
storyline.

Listening

Part 1

1 C   **2** A   **3** A   **4** C   **5** A   **6** B   **7** B

Part 2

8 B   **9** C   **10** A   **11** A   **12** B   **13** B

Part 3

14 underground

15 games area

16 second floor

17 (small) market

18 garden

19 11 pm / 23.00

Part 4

20 B   **21** C   **22** B   **23** C   **24** A   **25** A

Practice Test Key

Test 5

Reading

Part 1

1 C   2 A   3 B   4 B   5 C

Part 2

6 F   7 B   8 E   9 H   10 C

Part 3

11 A   12 D   13 B   14 C   15 D

Part 4

16 B   17 H   18 C   19 F   20 A

Part 5

21 B   22 A   23 D   24 C   25 A   26 D

Part 6

27 which   28 have   29 our   30 as / since / because
31 not   32 was

Writing

Part 1

Question 1
Sample answer

Hello Mark
That's so cool about the school garden! I've always wanted to learn how to grow things. I think we should definitely have lots of strawberries because they're delicious.

I don't believe selling everything is a good idea. We should give the stuff we grow to the school canteen, so they have fresh food to cook with. Then maybe our school lunches will taste a bit better!

I'd love to go to the meeting at noon, but I've got gym before lunch. We always have lots of sports equipment to put away, so I'll be a few minutes late.

Fernanda

Comment
The email is an appropriate informal tone for an email to a friend. Fernanda has discussed the four notes with a good range of vocabulary related to the main topics. The email is the correct length (101 words).

Part 2

Question 2
Sample answer
I love getting together with my friends at my place. I don't know why, but our conversations are more interesting than when we chat online. Perhaps because we can do more than just chat. For instance, we sometimes make biscuits, but we can't do anything like that on a video call.

I know spending loads of time on the internet isn't brilliant. In fact, I should probably spend less time online, but I don't because I rely on it for many reasons. For example, it's helpful for looking things up for homework and learning new things. I've even taught myself how to play the guitar from watching online videos.

Comment
The writer expresses their preferences to each of the questions in a well-structured article in an acceptable word length (109 words). They use different ways of referring to vocabulary in the article, which is good (*face-to-face / at my place, chatting / conversations, online / internet, lots / loads*). The writer also gives examples about their personal experiences to show why they have a particular view.

Question 3
Sample answer
I was walking in the forest when I heard a loud noise. It sounded like a big animal – probably a bear – so I stood still, trying to be as quiet as possible. I heard another noise, so I started running down the path as fast as possible. Suddenly, I saw the cottage where my family was staying for the summer. I yelled for help, and my mum opened the front door. I quickly told her about the bear, but then she began to laugh. I looked behind me and saw that it wasn't actually a bear chasing after me. It was my little brother!

Comment
The writer has produced a good example of a story with a clear beginning, middle and end that logically follows from the first line. The story includes a good range of tenses and adjectives to make the story interesting for the reader. The story is an appropriate length (104 words).

Listening

Part 1

1 A   2 B   3 B   4 A   5 C   6 B   7 C

Part 2

8 A   9 C   10 C   11 B   12 B   13 A

Part 3

14 May   15 birds / a bird   16 boots   17 bowls
18 visitors   19 pawshome

Part 4

20 B   21 C   22 C   23 A   24 B   25 C

Practice Test Key

Test 6

Reading

Part 1

1 A   2 C   3 C   4 A   5 B

Part 2

6 E   7 C   8 F   9 H   10 B

Part 3

11 B   12 C   13 A   14 C   15 D

Part 4

16 C   17 H   18 E   19 F   20 D

Part 5

21 B   22 D   23 A   24 D   25 A   26 C

Part 6

27 will / 'll / would / 'd   28 of   29 so   30 was

31 with / using   32 Why

Writing

Part 1

Question 1
Sample answer

Hey Avery

I'm glad you want to enter the short-film competition – it sounds awesome. We should definitely enter the competition together!

I think everyone we know would want to watch a short film about skateboarding. And we know some amazing skateboarders who do incredible things on their skateboards.

We should meet at least twice a week because it takes a lot of time and effort to make a good film, even if it's only a couple of minutes long.

Wouldn't it be cool to win all that money? I think I'd buy a new skateboard and save the rest. What about you?

Bye
Toni

Comment

The email is the correct register for an email to a friend. Toni deals with each of the notes well and organises this information into paragraphs. There is also an appropriate opening and closing for an informal message, and the email length is good at 104 words.

Part 2

Question 2
Sample answer

The thing I most enjoy doing in my free time is playing video games. Some people don't think that video games are a good way to spend time, but I love them and some can teach me a lot. I particularly like games where I can create or build things, like cities or buildings. I also enjoy games that I can play with other people.

Of course, playing video games isn't the only thing I do. That would be boring. I think it's important to do a range of things, for example going out with friends or exercising. That way, I keep healthy and have fun in different ways!

Comment

A good range of vocabulary has been used throughout the article to communicate the writer's views and opinions about enjoying their free time. The writer has written about the three content points and provides clear examples. The length of the article is appropriate (109 words).

Question 3
Sample answer

I looked at my best friend, and we both started to laugh. Then we started to cheer with everyone else in our classroom now that school was over for the school year. We usually weren't this excited at the end of an English lesson, but today was special. Our summer holidays had begun!

Kaya and I were still laughing when we ran out of the main entrance. We couldn't be happier because we had no more school assignments to worry about for another two months. But first, we needed to do something really important – go home and change out of our school uniforms.

Comment

This is a good example of a story because it is clearly linked to the first line and is well-organised. The story is interesting to read because the reader knows how people feel in the story. There is a good range of tenses and vocabulary, and the story is an appropriate length (103 words).

Listening

Part 1

1 B   2 C   3 A   4 A   5 C   6 C   7 A

Part 2

8 A   9 B   10 A   11 C   12 B   13 B

Part 3

14 Thursdays   15 parks   16 (yellow) jacket   17 seats
18 jump   19 playground

Part 4

20 B   21 B   22 A   23 C   24 A   25 A

Sample Answer Sheet for Reading

25851

CAMBRIDGE
English

Candidate Name	[_____]	**Candidate Number** [ ][ ][ ][ ]
Centre Name	[_____]	**Centre Number** [ ][ ]
Examination Title	[_____]	**Examination Details** [___]
Candidate Signature	[_____]	**Assessment Date** [___]

Supervisor: If the candidate is ABSENT or has WITHDRAWN shade here ○

Preliminary for Schools Reading Candidate Answer Sheet

Instructions
Use a PENCIL (B or HB)
Rub out any answer you want to change with an eraser.

For Parts 1, 2, 3, 4 and 5:
Mark ONE letter for each answer.
For example: If you think A is the right answer to
the question, mark your answer sheet like this:

Turn over for Part 6:
Write your answers clearly in the
spaces next to the numbers
(27 to 32) on Page 2.

Part 1

	A	B	C
1	○	○	○
2	○	○	○
3	○	○	○
4	○	○	○
5	○	○	○

Part 2

	A	B	C	D	E	F	G	H
6	○	○	○	○	○	○	○	○
7	○	○	○	○	○	○	○	○
8	○	○	○	○	○	○	○	○
9	○	○	○	○	○	○	○	○
10	○	○	○	○	○	○	○	○

Part 3

	A	B	C	D
11	○	○	○	○
12	○	○	○	○
13	○	○	○	○
14	○	○	○	○
15	○	○	○	○

Part 4

	A	B	C	D	E	F	G	H
16	○	○	○	○	○	○	○	○
17	○	○	○	○	○	○	○	○
18	○	○	○	○	○	○	○	○
19	○	○	○	○	○	○	○	○
20	○	○	○	○	○	○	○	○

Part 5

	A	B	C	D
21	○	○	○	○
22	○	○	○	○
23	○	○	○	○
24	○	○	○	○
25	○	○	○	○
26	○	○	○	○

Turn over for Part 6 ➡

25851

Sample Answer Sheet for Reading

For Part 6:
Write your answers clearly in the spaces next to the numbers (27 to 32) like this:

 | 0 | E N G L I S H |

Write your answers in CAPITAL LETTERS.

Part 6	Do not write below here
27	27 1 0 O O
28	28 1 0 O O
29	29 1 0 O O
30	30 1 0 O O
31	31 1 0 O O
32	32 1 0 O O

Sample Answer Sheet for Writing

You must write within the grey lines.

Write your answer for Part 1 below. Do not write on the barcodes.

Question 1

This section for use by Examiner only:

C	CA	O	L

Sample Answer Sheet for Writing

You must write within the grey lines.

Answer only one of the two questions for Part 2.
Tick (✓) the box to show which question you have answered.
Write your answer below. Do not write on the barcodes.

Part 2	Question 2		Question 3	

This section for use by Examiner only:

C	CA	O	L

Sample Answer Sheet for Listening

CAMBRIDGE
English

Candidate Name		Candidate Number	

Centre Name		Centre Number	

Examination Title		Examination Details	

Candidate Signature		Assessment Date	

Supervisor: If the candidate is ABSENT or has WITHDRAWN shade here ○

Preliminary for Schools Listening Candidate Answer Sheet

Instructions
Use a PENCIL (B or HB). Rub out any answer you want to change with an eraser.

For Parts 1, 2 and 4:
Mark one letter for each answer. For example: If you think **A** is the right answer to the question, mark your answer sheet like this:

For Part 3:
Write your answers clearly in the spaces next to the numbers (14 to 19) like this:

Write your answers in CAPITAL LETTERS.

Part 1

	A	B	C
1	○	○	○
2	○	○	○
3	○	○	○
4	○	○	○
5	○	○	○
6	○	○	○
7	○	○	○

Part 2

	A	B	C
8	○	○	○
9	○	○	○
10	○	○	○
11	○	○	○
12	○	○	○
13	○	○	○

Part 3

		Do not write below here
14		14 1 0 ○ ○
15		15 1 0 ○ ○
16		16 1 0 ○ ○
17		17 1 0 ○ ○
18		18 1 0 ○ ○
19		19 1 0 ○ ○

Part 4

	A	B	C
20	○	○	○
21	○	○	○
22	○	○	○
23	○	○	○
24	○	○	○
25	○	○	○

Acknowledgements

Our highly experienced team of Trainer writers, exam reviewers, and editors have worked together to bring you Preliminary for Schools Trainer 2. We would like to thank Judy Alden (writer), Carole Bartlett (reviewer), Trish Chapman (editor), Helen Chilton (writer/reviewer), Caroline Cooke (writer), Ruth Cox (editor), Mark Little (reviewer), Imelda Maguire-Karayel (reviewer), Andrew Reid (editor), Melissa Thomson (writer), Bruce Williams (reviewer) for their work on the material.

The authors and publishers acknowledge the following sources of copyright material and are grateful for the permissions granted. While every effort has been made, it has not always been possible to identify the sources of all the material used, or to trace all copyright holders. If any omissions are brought to our notice, we will be happy to include the appropriate acknowledgements on reprinting and in the next update to the digital edition, as applicable.

Key: RT= Reading Test, ST= Speaking Test, WT= Writing Test.

Photography

All the photographs are sourced from Getty Images.

RT: xPACIFICA/Stone; Westend61; SensorSpot/E+; Jose Luis Pelaez Inc/DigitalVision; Bloom Productions/Stone; Dougal Waters/DigitalVision; Serg_Velusceac/iStock/Getty Images Plus; Ulrike Schmitt-Hartmann/DigitalVision; Stuart Westmorland/Corbis Documentary; izusek/E+; Maskot; Carey Kirkella/DigitalVision; brusinski/E+; Boy_Anupong/Moment; Tennessee Witney/iStock/Getty Images Plus; urbazon/iStock/Getty Images Plus; Onne van der Wal/Corbis Documentary; Abstract Aerial Art/DigitalVision; VII-photo/E+; JohnnyGreig/E+; raferto/iStock/Getty Images Plus; Vladimir Godnik/fStop; Jasmin Merdan/Moment; Morsa Images/DigitalVision; Yellowdog Productions/DigitalVision; James Whitaker/DigitalVision; Julia Garan/iStock/Getty Images Plus; Cyndi Monaghan/Moment; Sally Anscombe/DigitalVision; Thinkstock Images/Stockbyte; aldomurillo/E+; Leland Bobbe/DigitalVision; VAWiley/E+; skynesher/E+; Matteo Colombo/DigitalVision; Rogan Macdonald/Image Source; Mike Harrington/Photodisc; Flashpop/Stone; FG Trade/E+; Rebecca Nelson/Photodisc; CEZARY ZAREBSKI PHOTOGRPAHY/Moment; Olivier Matthys/Getty Images News; Anatoliy Cherkasov/NurPhoto; Jordan Siemens/Stone; timnewman/E+; Christopher Hopefitch/DigitalVision; Tetra Images/Tetra images; Sean Justice/The Image Bank; GEN UMEKITA/Moment; boric/iStock/Getty Images Plus; Manoj Shah/Photodisc; Josh Hawley/Moment; zhudifeng/iStock/Getty Images Plus; **ST:** Oleg Breslavtsev/Moment; Imgorthand/E+; Zero Creatives/Image Source; kohei_hara/E+; Doug Menuez/Photodisc; skynesher/E+; Sally Anscombe/DigitalVision; Hill Street Studios/DigitalVision; SolStock/E+; Jim Craigmyle/Stone; Thomas Barwick/DigitalVision; Richard Hutchings/Corbis Documentary; RgStudio/E+; Hero Images Inc/DigitalVision; Peter Cade/Stone; Mayur Kakade/Moment; nickylarson974/iStock/Getty Images Plus; Peter Dazeley/The Image Bank; Jupiterimages/Stockbyte; **WT:** MARHARYTA MARKO/iStock/Getty Images Plus; Hammerchewer (G C Russell)/Moment Open; Jupiterimages/The Image Bank; James O'Neil/The Image Bank; fotograzia/Moment.

Illustration

Q2A Media Services Inc.

Audio

Audio recorded by Third Light Films Ltd.

Audio produced by Leon Chambers.

Audio recorded at The Soundhouse Ltd, London.

Candidate A

Candidate A

Candidate B

Exam Practice Test 2 | Speaking Part 2

Candidate B

Candidate A

Candidate A

Candidate B

Candidate B

Candidate A

Candidate A

Candidate B

Candidate B

Candidate C

Candidate C

Candidate C

Candidate C

Candidate C

Candidate C

Training Test 1 | Speaking Part 2

Training Test 2 | Speaking Part 2

A

B

Exam Practice Test 6